Working with Odoo 11
Third Edition

Configure, manage, and customize your Odoo system

Greg Moss

BIRMINGHAM - MUMBAI

Working with Odoo 11
Third Edition

Copyright © 2018 Packt Publishing

Commissioning Editor: Merint Mathew
Acquisition Editor: Aiswarya Narayanan
Content Development Editor: Nikhil Borkar
Technical Editor: Jijo Maliyekal
Copy Editors: Safis Editing
Project Coordinator: Ulhas Kambali
Proofreader: Safis Editing
Indexer: Mariammal Chettiyar
Graphics: Tania Dutta
Production Coordinator: Deepika Naik

First published: August 2015
Second edition: January 2017
Third edition: March 2018

Production reference: 1270318

Published by Packt Publishing Ltd.
Livery Place
35 Livery Street
Birmingham
B3 2PB, UK.

ISBN 978-1-78847-695-9

www.packtpub.com

`mapt.io`

Mapt is an online digital library that gives you full access to over 5,000 books and videos, as well as industry leading tools to help you plan your personal development and advance your career. For more information, please visit our website.

Why subscribe?

- Spend less time learning and more time coding with practical eBooks and Videos from over 4,000 industry professionals

- Improve your learning with Skill Plans built especially for you

- Get a free eBook or video every month

- Mapt is fully searchable

- Copy and paste, print, and bookmark content

PacktPub.com

Did you know that Packt offers eBook versions of every book published, with PDF and ePub files available? You can upgrade to the eBook version at `www.PacktPub.com` and as a print book customer, you are entitled to a discount on the eBook copy. Get in touch with us at `service@packtpub.com` for more details.

At `www.PacktPub.com`, you can also read a collection of free technical articles, sign up for a range of free newsletters, and receive exclusive discounts and offers on Packt books and eBooks.

Contributors

About the author

Greg Moss has been a business and information systems consultant for over 25 years. Starting in 1988, he began to work extensively in financial and accounting-related applications. He has worked extensively in the healthcare, point of sale, manufacturing, telecommunications, entertainment, and service industries. Greg is a Certified Information Systems Auditor (CISA), Certified Six Sigma Black Belt, and former Chief Information Officer of Crownline Boats, Inc.

I would like to thank my wonderful wife, Kelly, for all her love and support; my brother, Eric, for his kindness, generosity, and for always being there when someone needs him; and my mom, a lifelong school teacher who never hesitated to support me in anything that involved learning or creativity.

Special thanks to Diogo Duarte for his professionalism and outstanding contributions to OdooClass.com.

About the reviewer

With an academic background in engineering and mathematics, **Géry Debongnie** has always been passionate about technology. He is now the frontend framework team leader at Odoo.

He has been involved in the design and architecture of the Odoo web client for several years. He has worked on various projects at Odoo, most of them involving JavaScript.

Packt is searching for authors like you

If you're interested in becoming an author for Packt, please visit `authors.packtpub.com` and apply today. We have worked with thousands of developers and tech professionals, just like you, to help them share their insight with the global tech community. You can make a general application, apply for a specific hot topic that we are recruiting an author for, or submit your own idea.

Table of Contents

Preface

Working with Odoo 11 provides a comprehensive walkthrough for installing, configuring, and implementing Odoo in real-world business environments. This book will assist you in understanding the value of Enterprise Resource Planning (ERP) systems and best practice approaches for getting a system up and running in your organization. For those who are new to ERP systems, this book will serve as an introduction so that you will be better prepared to understand more advanced ERP concepts. If you are already experienced in ERP systems, this book will give you an overview of the primary applications for Odoo and how those applications can be used in a real business environment.

Odoo is a feature-filled business application framework with literally hundreds of applications and modules available. We have done our best to cover the most essential features of the Odoo applications you are most likely to use in your business. Unfortunately, there are just not enough pages to cover more advanced topics.

Who this book is for

This book is for everyone who is interested in implementing an ERP system in a business organization. If you are an IT professional looking to get a functional understanding of Odoo, then this book is for you. This book is also appropriate for business and operations managers who wish to get a comprehensive understanding of Odoo and how it can be used to improve business processes.

What this book covers

Chapter 1, *Setting up Odoo 11*, gets you started right away by showing how you can use Odoo online without any setup. Next, the chapter covers the different installation types and prerequisites for both Windows and Ubuntu. Instructions are provided for finding the right download package and setting up Odoo on your own server. The chapter then goes into the basics of configuring Odoo. At the end is a useful collection of tips on how to troubleshoot your Odoo installation.

Chapter 2, *Installing Your First Application*, takes you through a real-world case study that will be used as an example throughout the book. The chapter continues by showing you how to create a company database and configure the basic company settings required to quickly get your first Odoo system up and running. The first module, Sales Management, will be installed, and you'll walk through the steps to enter a customer and a product into the database.

Chapter 3, *Exploring CRM in Odoo 11*, starts with a basic overview of CRM systems and their importance in today's modern business environment. We cover the installation of the CRM module; a lead is entered for our example company. We demonstrate CRM workflow by turning the lead into a customer. Next, a quote is generated for our newly acquired customer and a call is scheduled for follow-up using Odoo's meeting functionality. We also cover the Open Chatter feature, which is used throughout Odoo to provide notes and messages associated with Odoo documents.

Chapter 4, *Purchasing with Odoo*, shows us how to install the Purchasing module, set up suppliers, and begin purchasing and receiving products in Odoo. Later in the chapter, we learn how to tie purchasing into sales orders to automatically generate draft purchase orders based on our business requirements.

Chapter 5, *Making Goods with Manufacturing Resource Planning*, begins to explore some of the primary functionalities of ERP systems for manufacturing operations. You will learn how to set up your manufacturing orders and define bills of materials to specify the raw materials that will go into your final products. Manufacturing operations can then be extended with routing and work centers to provide you with more control over tracking time and resources.

Chapter 6, *Configuring Accounting and Finance Options*, discusses the Accounts Receivable and Accounts Payable basic functions. Then, you're introduced to the chart of accounts and will discover how to set up fiscal periods. This chapter also includes basic accounting reports and how to close a period.

Chapter 7, *Administering an Odoo Installation*, begins by discussing overall considerations for implementing Odoo in a business environment. These include advice on server configurations, documenting your processes, and the importance of considering business continuity. The chapter then goes into how to manage users and groups and set up security roles to manage access to various applications within Odoo. Finally, we look at how to implement internationalization for multiple languages and currencies.

Chapter 8, *Implementing the Human Resources Application*, begins by installing the basic HR modules and going over the employee directory. Other topics in the chapter include time sheets, recruitment, and leave management. At the end of the chapter, you'll see how to create online interviews and hire employees using the tools in Odoo.

Chapter 9, *Understanding Project Management*, covers the features of the Project Management module in Odoo. You'll create a project, see how to enter tasks, and tie a project to a specific customer. Next, team members are assigned to the project, and you'll configure task stages. You'll then go over real-world examples of using the Project Management module to more easily manage complex orders and customer needs. Finally, you'll see how Project Management can be used along with analytic accounting to provide better reporting.

Chapter 10, *Creating Advanced Searches and Dashboards*, demonstrates how to utilize advanced search features and configure custom dashboards in Odoo. By the end of the chapter, the reader will be able to create and save custom searches to reuse later and add search results to dashboards.

Chapter 11, *Building a Website with Odoo*, explores Odoo's powerful new website building platform. At the beginning of the chapter, you'll look at what a CMS (Content Management System) is and some of the other popular website building platforms. You'll follow along with Odoo's website building tutorial and then look at the features that can be used to promote your website right from within Odoo.

i, *Implementing E-Commerce with Odoo*, builds on the previous website chapter by adding a fully functional online shopping cart to the website. You'll see how to publish products to the website and the various options for changing their appearance. Midway through the chapter, you'll see product variants that add more flexibility to how you manage your products within Odoo. Finally, the chapter concludes by examining how to set up a payment processor to take payment online through PayPal.

Chapter 13, *Customizing Odoo for Your Business*, explains how to enter Developer Mode for making a variety of custom changes to Odoo. You will walk through the steps to add fields to the sales order form and then include the fields in tree views for sorting and reporting. From here, you will get into advanced configuration topics to better customize Odoo for your specific business requirements.

Chapter 14, *Modifying Documents and Reports*, goes over the basic reporting mechanisms available in Odoo and weighs the advantages and disadvantages of the various options. The chapter then demonstrates how to install the OpenOffice reporting module and make changes to a report.

`Chapter 15`, *Discovering Custom Odoo Modules*, introduces the process of developing custom solutions in Odoo. You'll build on what you have learned by customizing Odoo and create a module that will persist the custom fields and views within your module. Next, you'll build on the workflow modifications you made in the chapter and upgrade your module to approve art designs for our real-world example.

`Chapter 16`, *Comparing Community and Enterprise Edition*, goes through the recent Odoo 11 features with respect to the community and enterprise editions.

To get the most out of this book

You should have Odoo version 11 installed on your system. To get the most out of this book, you should also have an understanding of basic business operations. For example, you should know the purpose of a sales order and a purchase order. You should also have basic computer skills such as understanding filesystems and installing software. For more advanced customization topics in the book, you should have a basic knowledge of databases and programming concepts.

Download the color images

We also provide a PDF file that has color images of the screenshots/diagrams used in this book. You can download it here: `http://www.packtpub.com/sites/default/files/downloads/WorkingwithOdoo11ThirdEdition_ColorImages.pdf`.

Conventions used

There are a number of text conventions used throughout this book.

`CodeInText`: Indicates code words in text, database table names, folder names, filenames, file extensions, pathnames, dummy URLs, user input, and Twitter handles. Here is an example: "Limit those customers to just the names that include `camp`."

A block of code is set as follows:

```
<span t-if="o.state not in ['draft','sent']">Sales Order # </span>
<span t-if="o.state in ['draft','sent']">Quotation #:</span>
```

Any command-line input or output is written as follows:

```
$ mkdir css
$ cd css
```

Bold: Indicates a new term, an important word, or words that you see onscreen. For example, words in menus or dialog boxes appear in the text like this. Here is an example: "This brings up all the **QWeb views** associated with the report."

Warnings or important notes appear like this.

Tips and tricks appear like this.

Get in touch

Feedback from our readers is always welcome.

General feedback: Email `feedback@packtpub.com` and mention the book title in the subject of your message. If you have questions about any aspect of this book, please email us at `questions@packtpub.com`.

Errata: Although we have taken every care to ensure the accuracy of our content, mistakes do happen. If you have found a mistake in this book, we would be grateful if you would report this to us. Please visit www.packtpub.com/submit-errata, selecting your book, clicking on the Errata Submission Form link, and entering the details.

Piracy: If you come across any illegal copies of our works in any form on the Internet, we would be grateful if you would provide us with the location address or website name. Please contact us at copyright@packtpub.com with a link to the material.

If you are interested in becoming an author: If there is a topic that you have expertise in and you are interested in either writing or contributing to a book, please visit authors.packtpub.com.

Reviews

Please leave a review. Once you have read and used this book, why not leave a review on the site that you purchased it from? Potential readers can then see and use your unbiased opinion to make purchase decisions, we at Packt can understand what you think about our products, and our authors can see your feedback on their book. Thank you!

For more information about Packt, please visit packtpub.com.

Setting Up Odoo 11

1

Odoo is a powerful set of open source business applications built on the OpenObject framework. When you first install Odoo, the only functionality you will have is limited messaging options between users. From there, Odoo allows you to install the modules you need, as you need them. This flexibility makes Odoo much more accessible than many business software solutions.

In this chapter, we will get started working with Odoo by covering the installation and the basics of setting up an Odoo database.

The topics we will cover include:

- Exploring Odoo Online
- Setting up a trial company
- Installing Odoo on Windows and Ubuntu
- Troubleshooting and configuring your installation

What's new in Odoo 11?

While much of the process is the same as previous versions of Odoo, there have been some pricing changes in Odoo 11. No longer are there two free users and you pay for additional users. There is still one free application that you can install for an unlimited number of users, but as soon as you have more than one application, then you must pay $25 for each user, including the first.

In Odoo 11, the online installation documentation continues to improve and there are now options for Docker installations. In addition, Odoo 11 uses Python 3 instead of Python 2.7. This will not change the steps you take in installing Odoo but will change the specific libraries that will be installed.

Community and Enterprise Editions of Odoo

Beginning with Odoo 9, Odoo SA started releasing two versions of Odoo: a **Community Edition** and an **Enterprise Edition**. The Community Edition is free, open source, and primarily supported by the Odoo community. Odoo Enterprise, while also open source, requires a license based on the number of users. More recently, Odoo pricing for the Enterprise version varies depending on region.

Odoo Enterprise offers an alternative (arguably better) user interface. Additionally, there is better functionality in some applications as well as support by SA, and perhaps most critical of all, migration to the new releases of Odoo. More information on the differences between Odoo Community Edition and Odoo Enterprise Edition is available in `Chapter 16`, *Comparing Community and Enterprise Edition*.

This book primarily targets the Community Edition of Odoo.

Getting started with Odoo Online

Not long ago, nearly all companies kept their primary information systems inhouse. This approach not only requires a lot of capital expense in purchasing servers and software licenses, but also creates a lot of responsibility and risk in backing up data and ensuring business continuity. Today, more and more companies are choosing to host their business applications in online networks commonly called the **cloud**. Odoo allows you the flexibility of both options—either hosting on your own hardware, or utilizing Odoo's online software services.

Taking advantage of Odoo Online Instant Access

The best thing about accessing Odoo Online is that you can jump in and start using the software right away. You don't have to decide what operating system to use, and you don't have to install any software at all. Just enter the URL into your web browser and you are ready to get started.

Another added benefit of taking this approach is you will verify that your web browser is up to date and compatible with the latest version of Odoo. So, even if you intend to install Odoo on your own hardware, it is still worth taking a minute to test out the online trial version of Odoo. Expect to put a great deal of time into determining which Odoo applications are right for your company.

Taking a few hours to use the Odoo Online version is time well spent, and you can put off installing Odoo until you are more certain it is the right software for your business.

Use the Odoo trial edition to verify browser compatibility with any older machines.

Odoo browser requirements

Odoo is designed to run on a variety of modern web browsers. Supported browsers include:

- Google Chrome (recommended)
- Firefox
- Internet Explorer
- Safari

Macintosh users will need to make sure they are running **Mac OS X** or above. Users running older Macintosh systems are currently having difficulties running Odoo version 7. Also, in my experience, Google Chrome tends to offer the best experience in working with Odoo. Firefox is also often recommended by others in the Odoo community.

Odoo mobile phone and tablet support

Beginning with Odoo 8, Odoo has included native support for mobile phones and tablets. This has been further improved in Odoo 10. Menus are designed to flow and format properly. The new website application even includes a preview within the portal administration to emulate how the site would appear on a mobile phone. While you still suffer many of the limitations that come with a small screen size, the applications are functional and make it even easier for developers to create mobile Odoo applications.

Odoo's mobile application support covers both the Android and Apple **iOS** platforms. Make sure, however, that for any processes you intend to implement for your business, you test all processes thoroughly for both desktop and any mobile solutions. The smaller screen sizes might make some data unreadable or very awkward to work with.

Accessing the Odoo free online trial

Accessing the online trial version of Odoo Online could not be simpler. Just open up your browser and navigate to `https://www.odoo.com/trial`.

Please be aware that Odoo Online's trial is the Enterprise Edition of Odoo. While very similar to the Community Edition, the interface will be slightly different.

You will then be prompted to choose one of Odoo's primary business applications, as shown in the following screenshot:

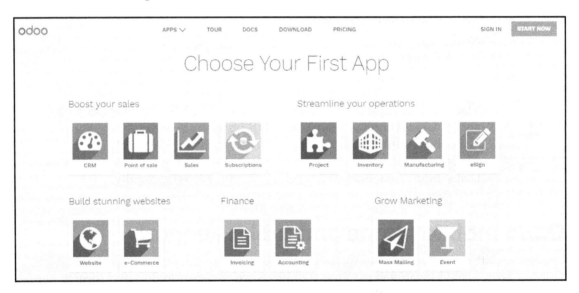

Don't worry, because you can add more applications later.

Clicking on the appropriate button for the application immediately begins installing your own unique Odoo instance.

For our example, let's go ahead and install the CRM application by clicking on the **CRM** button, which looks like the following:

Next, you will be taken to a simple sign-up page as follows:

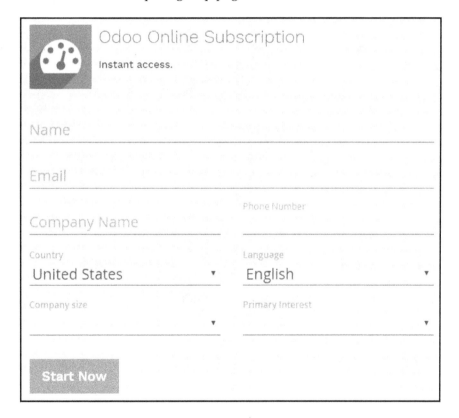

After filling out the form, simply click **Start Now**.

Be patient, as it can take 30 seconds or longer for the servers to build the database and bring up the starting page. When the installation is complete, Odoo automatically signs you in so you can begin trying out the software. The goal of this approach is to get users to start using the software right away, and avoid having to fill out lengthy forms or create logins and passwords to begin using the software. It really is just one click and you have your own version of Odoo to evaluate.

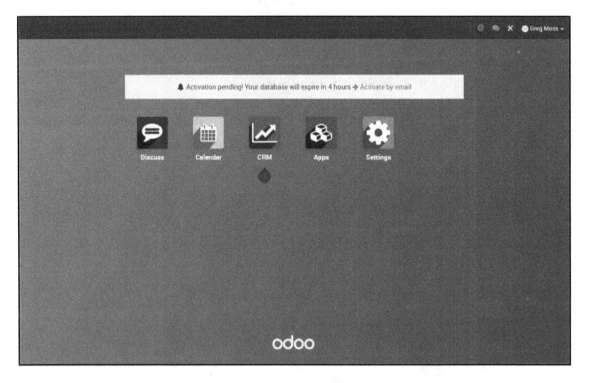

The screen now contains the Odoo dashboard for the Enterprise Edition. Please be aware that this will look a lot different than the Community Edition of Odoo, even though they are very similar in terms of functionality.

We will discuss the CRM application in detail in Chapter 3, *Exploring CRM in Odoo 11*.

Take a few minutes to look around in Odoo to get familiar with the interface. You don't have to worry about breaking anything or doing anything wrong. If you run into problems or get confused, just close your web browser and try again.

 This is a demonstration and will only last for one four-hour session. If you close your browser, you will lose your setup and have to start over again.

Continuing to use the trial version of Odoo

At the very top of the Odoo application, just under the address bar in the browser, you will see a message that informs you of how much longer your trial version of Odoo will run before you need to register. Also, remember that it is possible to lose this instance of Odoo before the time runs out, as seen here:

 Activation pending! Your database will expire in about 4 hours ➜ Activate by email

Clicking on the **Activate by email** link will send a message to the email address that you provided, containing a link to activate your Odoo database. Currently, you may use Odoo for free as long as you only install one application.

 Odoo SA has experimented quite a bit with different trial terms, so do not be surprised if the trial options are slightly different by the time you are reading this.

Subscribing to Odoo

You can use one Odoo application for free without subscribing. If you wish to install more applications (as you likely will), you must subscribe to Odoo in order to keep using their Enterprise cloud-hosted version of the software.

For each user, the current pricing is $25 per-month at the time of writing. Each application you use will also incur a monthly cost, which varies by application.

Below is the **Odoo Online Pricing** calculator for February 2018 in the United States with one user and three applications.

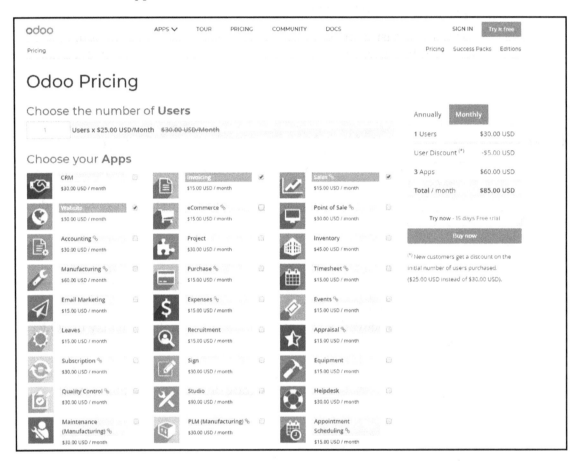

You can locate the **Odoo Online Pricing** page at `https://www.odoo.com/pricing-online`.

Odoo Online is priced for employees that use the applications. You are not charged for customers or suppliers that access Odoo through the web portal.

Depending on your requirements, an Odoo subscription might be a good decision. Installing and maintaining an Odoo installation takes a degree of expertise and has risks for production systems. You must maintain adequate disaster recovery procedures in case of server crashes or hard drive failures. There are also complexities in applying bug fixes and migrating to newer versions of Odoo. This book will help you with many of these tasks. It can be quite convenient to have an Odoo subscription so that you can focus on the functional, rather than the technical, aspects of working with Odoo.

Using Odoo without subscription fees

If you choose not to pay the subscription fee, do not fear! The remainder of this chapter will assist you with installing Odoo on your own hardware.

Getting to know the Odoo architecture

Setting up and managing an Odoo installation will require a basic understanding of the components that make up Odoo. Every business system has a set of technologies and underlying software platforms that are required for the system to function. Fortunately, unless you plan to customize Odoo, you only need to understand the very basics of the Odoo architecture to complete a successful installation.

In this book, we provide a basic overview of the Odoo architecture. If you wish to get more detailed documentation on the Odoo architecture, and technical documentation, visit
`https://www.odoo.com/documentation/11.0/`.

Introducing the PostgreSQL database

Like most ERP systems, Odoo has specific database requirements: in this case, PostgreSQL. PostgreSQL is an open source, cross-platform **Object Relational Database Management System (ORDMS)**. While not popular on the scale of Microsoft SQL Server or **MySQL**, **PostgreSQL** is an enterprise-class database server with many advanced features. In fact, PostgreSQL stacks up very well against far more expensive databases such as Microsoft SQL Server and Oracle Database.

PostgreSQL runs on every major operating system. For most Odoo installations, Ubuntu is the operating system of choice. However, PostgreSQL will also run quite well under other versions of Linux, Microsoft Windows, and even **Mac OS X**.

You can learn more about PostgreSQL at `http://www.postgresql.org/`.

Writing code with Python

The primary programming language of Odoo is Python. Like the other technologies underlying Odoo, the Python language is open source and runs on all the major contemporary operating systems. It is an extremely popular programming language, which makes it very easy to find resources to help you get started.

You can learn more about the Python programming language at `http://python.org/`.

Following the Model-View-Controller design

Odoo is built upon a **Model-View-Controller** (**MVC**) architecture. One of the primary goals of this architecture is to separate the visual display of the information from the business rules and management of the underlying data. For example, if you need to change the way data is organized in the model, it is desirable not to have to make dramatic changes to how you view data. This is true for maintaining flexibility in viewing data. Today, it is common to have many different client applications sharing the same underlying data.

Designing models

The model is essentially the data that makes up your Odoo installation, which is stored in the PostgreSQL database. Odoo is unique in that database structures are typically defined by the Odoo modules at the time they are installed. The Odoo framework takes the model definitions and automatically creates the necessary table structures inside of the PostgreSQL database. Furthermore, a web interface in Odoo allows administrators to easily extend the Odoo data model in a variety of ways without having to modify the Odoo source code.

Rendering views

Each view in Odoo is defined in XML documents. The Odoo framework is responsible for rendering these view files in a web browser. Alternative views can be built to render Odoo functionality upon other platforms such as mobile devices.

Authoring controllers

The controller component of the architecture is where the business logic and workflow rules of the Odoo application are applied. The controller components in Odoo are written in Python code and stored as objects in Odoo modules.

Choosing your installation operating system

In this section, we will discuss some of the advantages and disadvantages of choosing Ubuntu or Windows for your first Odoo installation.

Choosing a Microsoft Windows Odoo installation

For the most part, Ubuntu has been the platform of choice for most Odoo installations. However, there are some reasons why you might choose to run Odoo under a Windows installation.

Some of you, after buying this book, might have already jumped ahead and installed Odoo on your Microsoft Windows computer. So, for you go-getters, that working installation of Odoo might function just fine for researching and testing its features. Often the Windows all-in-one installer provides a simple method to get Odoo up and running in a snap on your hardware. Basically, you do not have to install a new operating system.

Learning Ubuntu is not required

If you are familiar with Windows and have no Ubuntu experience, you might get going a little faster by sticking with a Windows installation for your first setup. Downloading and installing modules and making changes to configuration files will be much easier if you are familiar with the operating system.

Introducing Ubuntu

While Microsoft Windows does not really need an introduction, it is probably worth giving a brief introduction to Ubuntu. In short, Ubuntu (pronounced oo-boon-too) is a very popular open source operating system based on the Linux **kernel**. It has enjoyed increasing popularity because it is easy to install and very stable. Ubuntu can be installed either as a server operating system without a graphical interface, or as a desktop operating system with a graphical interface that closely resembles Windows.

You can learn more about the Ubuntu operating system, and why it is so popular, at `http://www.ubuntu.com/`.

Choosing an Ubuntu Odoo installation

It is generally accepted that Ubuntu is the recommended operating system for running a production installation of Odoo. There are several reasons why this is true:

- **Ubuntu is the primary target platform**: While Odoo is released for Windows and still well supported, the Ubuntu installation continues to be favored. The development team for Odoo works primarily with Ubuntu for bug fixes and platform releases. It can be expected that, for the most part, Odoo development will be optimized around Ubuntu, not Windows or Mac.
- **Ubuntu is open source**: Installing Odoo on any Windows operating system is going to require a license from Microsoft. While using Odoo on your Windows PC or Mac is a viable and perhaps desirable solution for testing and development, it is unlikely you will want to run Odoo on a Windows desktop system for any production environment. Why? Well, this requires Windows Server, which has much higher license costs than desktop editions. With an Ubuntu installation, you get an entirely open source and virtually cost-free solution.
- **Ubuntu has additional scalability options**: It is possible to configure a more scalable solution under Ubuntu than what you can currently configure under Microsoft Windows Server.
- **Ubuntu has strong community support for Odoo**: The fact is that a vast majority of the production installations of Odoo are running under Ubuntu. When you run into trouble or management issues with your Odoo installation, you may find it easier to get assistance if you are running an Ubuntu installation.

Choosing another OS option for Odoo

Although this book will focus on Window and Ubuntu installations, you do have several other options. In the past, Odoo has been deployed under a variety of Linux distributions and even the Mac OS. There are also many community members actively developing client frontends for mobile platforms such as Google's Android OS.

Understanding Odoo releases

When deploying an Odoo system, it is important to understand the various Odoo versions as well as the release and upgrade policies. There is currently one major release for versions 9.0, 10.0, and 11.0, as well as a master branch that is the latest development version, which will become Odoo Version 12.0. The stable versions are the standard support versions of Odoo, and typically the ones you should choose to install for most situations. The master version is the development version and will often contain bugs and unfinished features. This is primarily downloaded by developers and those who wish to get a look at the latest features.

Upgrading Odoo

The goal of the Odoo development team is to release two stable version upgrades each year. Odoo further labels some stable versions as **Long-Term Support** (**LTS**) versions. These releases are supported by Odoo for those that have an Odoo Enterprise support contract. For any production environment, it is smart to choose an LTS version. Most importantly, installing an LTS release of Odoo will make bug fixes and patches much easier to implement.

At the time of writing, the most recent stable LTS version is version 11.0.

Installing Odoo on Windows OS

We begin our installation by locating the packages that are currently available to install. You can find the current list at `http://nightly.odoo.com/`:

Odoo Nightly builds

Builds

Every night, a new set of packages is generated for the branches listed below. This set consists of **deb** and **rpm** packages for Debian and RedHat distributions, an **exe** package for Windows and a **source** package.

11 (stable) - Community Edition
Odoo 11 was released in October 2017 and is supported until Odoo 14 - the recommended version.

10 (stable) - Community Edition
Odoo 10 was released in October 2016 and is supported until Odoo 13.

9 (stable) - Community Edition
Odoo 9 was released in October 2015 and is supported until Odoo 12.

master (dev) - Community Edition
This branch contains experimental features - for testing only.

Check out our installation and deployment guides.

The preceding screenshot is the **Odoo Nightly builds** page, which is the jumping-off point for downloading the source files for installation.

The examples and case studies in this book use Odoo 11.0. This means you should select the 11.0 (stable) version of Odoo to download. You can navigate directly to the Odoo 11.0 downloads here: `http://nightly.odoo.com/11.0/nightly/`.

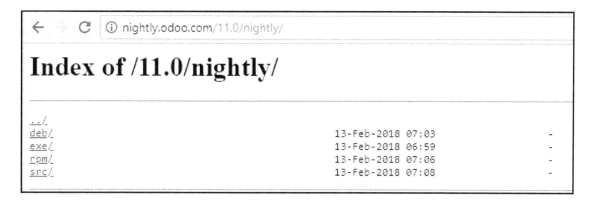

 It is entirely possible that Odoo will change the URL as new versions are released. To best follow the examples in this book, download an 11.x installation of Odoo.

Windows installations use the EXE packages. Click on the **exe/** directory to get the list of downloads that are available.

Naturally, the specific download packages are going to change on a nightly basis.

The latest version of the stable LTS release will contain the most current Odoo build, with bug fixes included, and will appear at the bottom of the list. By the way, the upload dates you'll see are in **Coordinated Universal Time (UTC)**, and therefore might be many hours ahead of your time zone, especially if you live in the Western Hemisphere.

Click the latest EXE file to download the latest build to your computer.

Performing an all-in-one Odoo installation on Windows

Installing Odoo using the all-in-one package is very simple. After the package has finished downloading, double-click on the .exe file to begin the installation wizard.

The first screen will prompt you to select the language for your installation.

After you have selected the language and clicked on **OK**, the wizard will continue with the installation. From here, everything will continue like a normal Windows installation.

I highly recommend that you choose **Custom install**, so you can select the directory for installation. The default directory name contains the lengthy build number, making it rather difficult to work with in the command prompt.

Configuring PostgresSQL on Windows

During the install, you will be asked to provide information for the PostgreSQL connection.

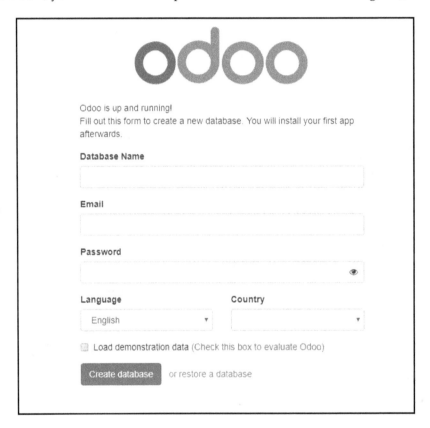

It is recommended that you change the username and password for security purposes. The default username/password is shown in the preceding screenshot. These values will be written into the Odoo configuration file. The username and password provided will be the administration credentials for the PostgreSQL database, so be sure to remember them.

After the wizard is complete, if you leave **Start Odoo** checked and then click on **Finish**, Odoo should open up in your default browser.

If Odoo fails to launch, you can look at the *Troubleshooting and Odoo management tips* section later in this chapter for solutions to some of the problems commonly encountered during installation.

Installing Odoo on Ubuntu

This book will walk you through the installation procedure for Odoo on Ubuntu using the latest all-in-one nightly package. Depending on your Ubuntu installation and how you want to work with Odoo, there are alternative installation methods.

At the time of writing, Odoo is most commonly installed on Ubuntu version 16.04.

Modifying the sources.list file

Installing Odoo in Ubuntu is easy when you use the Debian repository. In order to perform these operations, you may have to be the root user. If you have an account that has the permissions to do so, you can temporarily switch to the root user by opening a Terminal window, and entering the following:

```
sudo -s
```

For better security and to guarantee you are installing the correct package, Odoo now signs their distributions. The following command adds the correct key to your Ubuntu installation so that it will recognize the Odoo package:

```
wget -O - https://nightly.odoo.com/odoo.key | apt-key add -
```

Next, we want to add the distribution to the /etc/apt/sources.list file with the following command:

```
echo "deb http://nightly.odoo.com/11.0/nightly/deb/ ./" >>
/etc/apt/sources.list.d/odoo.list
```

This installs the package.

You can start the installation process by entering these commands into a Terminal window:

```
sudo apt-get update
sudo apt-get install odoo
```

The Odoo packages will first be downloaded and then installed. This is an all-in-one installation and should set up all the necessary packages, PostgreSQL, and library dependencies required to run Odoo.

By default, the deb installation will place the source in the following directory:

```
/usr/lib/python3/dist-packages/odoo
```

Testing your Odoo installation

Point your browser to http://localhost:8069 and you should see the Odoo database creation page appear.

Troubleshooting and Odoo management tips

As far as ERP installations go, Odoo is typically very easy to install. Unfortunately, it is possible for an installation to fail for a variety of reasons. In this next section, we will discuss some of the most common installation issues, and provide some troubleshooting tips for diagnosing problems with an Odoo installation.

Checking your browser destination

If you have followed the default installation, then your Odoo installation should be accessing Odoo at http://localhost:8069.

Make sure the URL is exactly as you see it above. If you did change the port number during installation, make sure you change the port in the URL.

Verifying that the Odoo service is running

If you are unable to pull up Odoo in the browser, it might be good to verify that the Odoo services are running.

Checking for the Odoo services running in Windows

Pull up the task manager and go to the **Services** tab, then look for **odoo-server-11.0**. The status should be running, as shown in the following screenshot:

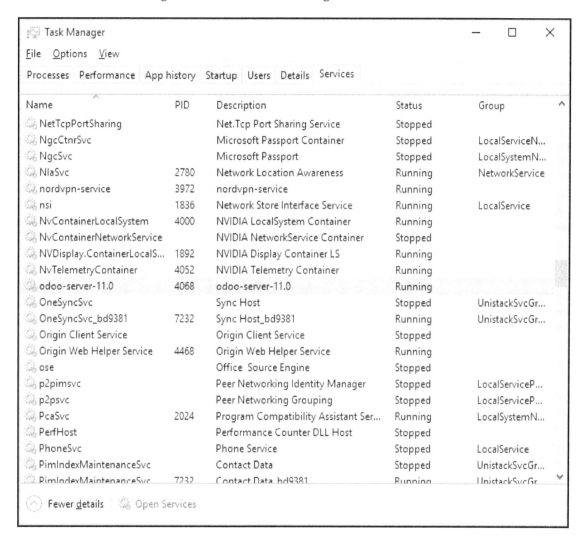

Here is an example of the **odoo-server-11.0** service successfully running on Windows.

Additional Odoo troubleshooting steps for Windows can be found at
`https://doc.Odoo.com/install/windows/server/complementary_install_information/`.

Checking for Odoo services running in Ubuntu

In Ubuntu, you can locate the Odoo service by running the following command in a
Terminal window:

```
ps aux | grep Odoo
```

You will then see the Odoo service listed if it is running:

```
root@ubuntu:~# ps aux | grep odoo
odoo        14341  1.0 11.1 925300 111756 ?        Sl   11:40   0:02 /usr/bin/python /usr/bin/o
doo --config /etc/odoo/odoo.conf --logfile /var/log/odoo/odoo-server.log
postgres  14489  0.0  1.1 308992 11016 ?        Ss   11:42   0:00 postgres: odoo postgres [l
ocal] idle
root        14539  0.0  0.1  21292  1008 pts/17   S+   11:45   0:00 grep --color=auto odoo
root@ubuntu:~# ▮
```

Starting and stopping Odoo services in Ubuntu

When managing an Odoo server, one of the most common tasks you will find yourself
performing is starting and stopping the Odoo service. Odoo allows you to start and stop the
service with a command switch.

To start the service, use:

```
sudo /etc/init.d/odoo start
```

To stop the service, use:

```
sudo /etc/init.d/odoo stop
```

Finding the primary Odoo log file

Odoo writes many messages, warnings, and error messages to a log. Often when
troubleshooting problems, this log file is valuable in determining what action you should
take. In a default installation, the log file is located at `/var/log/odoo/odoo-server.log`.

The log is especially valuable for locating problems you may have when installing new modules.

Modifying the Odoo configuration file

The Odoo framework allows you to specify a configuration file for your installation. By default, this file is located at `/etc/odoo/odoo.conf`.

Using this file, you can change many of the attributes of Odoo.

Changing port numbers

By default, Odoo runs on port 8069. For many installations, the default port will work fine. There are situations, however, where it can be useful to change this default port. One common scenario would be the need to run more than one version of Odoo. Multiple installations cannot run on port 8069, so you will need to modify the port. Sometimes, there are security reasons behind changing ports as many hackers are aware of the default ports people use.

Fortunately, changing the default port number is easy.

Simply specify the following:

```
Port=[port]
```

For example, `Port=8059` will change the default port for the web client to port 8059.

Accessing the database management tools

Odoo offers database management tools that can be accessed easily through your web browser. This makes it easy to create, back up, and even delete databases all through a web interface. While there are sometimes links available on the login page that will take you to these tools, it is possible that when installing some applications, such as the website builder, you will not find a link easily.

To access the database management tools, use the following path:

```
[ServerAddress]:[port]/web/database/manager
```

Changing the admin password

As mentioned earlier, by default, Odoo sets the password for its operations to `admin`. To secure your server, it is necessary to change this password in your configuration file:

```
Admin_password=[your password]
```

Also, be careful not to start up your Odoo server from the command line without specifying an alternative password or the path to the configuration file. If you do, you leave the instance open with the default password.

Finding additional resources on installing Odoo

Installing and configuring Odoo can quickly become a very complex task that is outside the scope of this book.

Summary

In this chapter, we saw how easy it was to get started using Odoo Online. We discussed how to set up a trial company, and the basics for creating a database and installing your first module. If you choose not to use the online services, you likely found the topics on installing Odoo on Windows or Ubuntu helpful. Finally, we discussed various methods of troubleshooting and configuring Odoo.

In the next chapter, we will begin to jump into our first real business applications in Odoo. You will get introduced to our real-world case study, and set up the basic configuration for the company. We will walk you through setting up your first product and, finally, creating and printing your first sales order.

Installing Your First Application 2

We have learned about the various applications that Odoo has to offer and how you can install Odoo on your own system. Before the release of Odoo 8, most users were focused on ERP and finance-related applications. Now, Odoo 11 has added several important applications that allow companies to use Odoo in much greater scope than ever before. For example, the website builder can be installed to quickly launch a simple website for your business, a task that typically would have been accomplished with a content management system such as WordPress.

Despite all the increasing options available in Odoo, the overall process is the same. We begin by looking at the overall business requirements and decide on the first set of applications that we wish to implement. After understanding our basic objectives, we will create an Odoo database and configure the required company information.

Next, we begin exploring the Odoo interface for creating and viewing information. We will see just how easy Odoo is to use by completing an entire sales order workflow. We will finish up the chapter by reviewing some of the more advanced sales order configuration options.

Topics that we will cover include:

- Adding a password-protected database to our installation
- Installing and configuring the Sales Management module
- Using interface features to view, edit, and find information
- Entering a new customer
- Adding our first product to sell
- Writing an order and confirming it for invoicing

What's new in Odoo 11?

For the most part the Odoo 11 upgrade was focused primarily on improving Odoo's underlying architecture. Instead of using Python 2.7, Odoo now uses Python 3.5. The improved design in Odoo 11 allows many operations to run up to 3x faster. This means that there are not all that many differences between Odoo 10 and Odoo 11 from a functional standpoint. Still there are a few welcome improvements that make the user experience more enjoyable.

Odoo 11 now features a new activities system that is integrated with Odoo's applications, VoIP, calendar and notes. Clicking on a small icon on the menu bar will display the current activities. Here is an example of what a **Lead/Opportunity** activity looks like in Odoo 11.

In Sales Management and CRM, Odoo 11 provides small interface enhancements, improving the user experience.

Gathering requirements

Setting up an Odoo system is no easy task. Many companies get into trouble believing that they can just install the software and throw in some data. Inevitably, the scope of the project grows and what was supposed to be a simple system ends up a confusing mess. Fortunately, Odoo's modular design allows you to take a systematic approach to implementing Odoo for your business.

Implementing Odoo using a modular approach

The bare-bones installation of Odoo simply provides you with a limited messaging system. To manage your Odoo implementation, you must begin by planning the modules with which you will work first. Odoo allows you to install just what you need now, and then install additional Odoo modules as you better define your requirements. It can be valuable to take this approach when you are considering how you will implement Odoo for your own business.

 Don't try and install all the modules and get everything running all at once. Instead, break down the implementation into smaller phases.

Introducing Silkworm – our real-world case study

To best understand how to work with Odoo, we will build our exercises around a real-world case study. Silkworm is a mid-sized screen printer that manufactures and sells T-shirts, as well as a variety of printing projects. Using Odoo's modular design, we will begin by implementing the **Sales Order** module to set up the selling of basic products. In this specific case, we will be selling T-shirts. As we proceed through this book, we will continue to expand the system by installing additional modules.

Creating a new database in Odoo

If you have installed Odoo on your own server, you will need to first create a database. As you add additional applications to Odoo, the necessary tables and fields will be added to the database you specify.

 Odoo Online
If you are using Odoo Online, you will not have access to create a new database, and instead will use Odoo's one-click application installer to manage your Odoo installation.

If you have just installed a fresh copy of Odoo, you will be prompted automatically to create a new Odoo database.

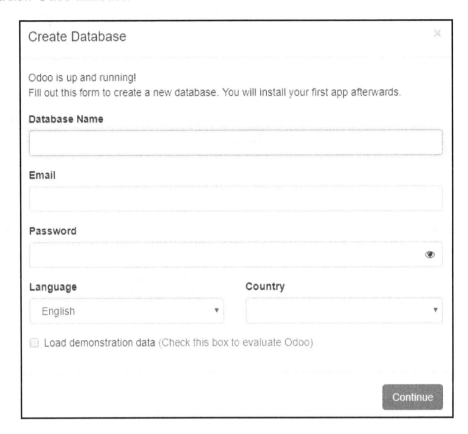

Create Database form

In the preceding screenshot, you can see the Odoo **Create Database** form.

Odoo provides basic instructions for creating your database. Let us quickly review the fields and how they are used.

Selecting a database name

When selecting a database name, choose a name that describes the system and that will make clear the purpose of the database. There are a few rules for creating an Odoo database:

- Your database name cannot contain spaces and must start with a number or letter
- Also, you will need to avoid commas, periods, and quotes
- Underscores and hyphens are allowed if they are not the first character in the name

It can also be a good idea to specify in the name whether the database is for development, testing, or production purposes.

For the purposes of our real-world case study, we will use the database name as SILKWORM-DEV.

We have chosen the -DEV suffix, as we consider this a development database that will not be used for production or even for testing.

 Take the time to consider what you will name your databases. It can be useful to have standard prefixes or suffixes depending on the purpose of your database. For example, you may use -PROD for your production database, or -TEST for the database that you are using for testing.

Loading demonstration data

Notice the **Check this box to evaluate Odoo** box. If you mark this checkbox when you create a database, Odoo will preload your tables with a host of sample data for each module that is installed. This may include fake customers, suppliers, sales orders, invoices, inbox messages, stock moves, and products. The purpose of the demonstration data is to allow you to run modules through their paces without having to key in a ton of test data.

You should only use the demonstration data for trying out Odoo. You should never load demonstration data if you plan to use the database for a production environment.

For the purposes of our real-world case study in this book, do not load demonstration data.

Specifying our default language

Odoo offers a variety of language translation features with support for more than twenty languages. All of the examples in this book will use the *English (US) language* option. Be aware that, depending on the language you select in Odoo, you may need to have that language also installed in your base operating system.

Choosing an email and password

Unlike previous versions of Odoo in which the database was created with an administrator account named admin, Odoo 11 uses the email address you provide as your administrator account. This is also known as the superuser account.

The password you choose during the creation of the database will be the password for this admin account.

 Choose any password you wish and click on **Create Database** to create the SILKWORM-DEV database.

Managing databases in Odoo

The database management interface allows you to perform basic database management tasks such as backing up or restoring a database. Often, with Odoo, it is possible to manage your databases without ever having to go directly into the Postgres database server. It is also possible to set up multiple databases under the same installation of Odoo. For instance, you may want in the future to install another database that does load demonstration data, and may be used to install modules simply for testing purposes.

You can access the database management interface directly by going to the /web/database/manager path.

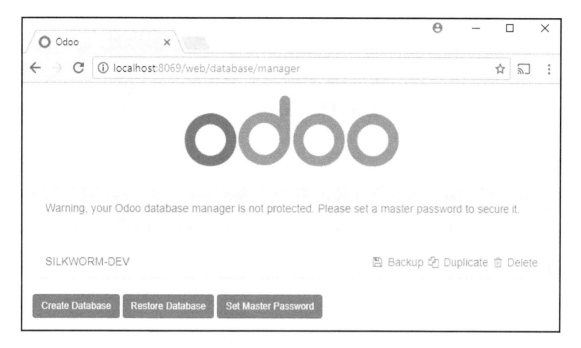

In the simple interface, you can create, backup, duplicate, delete, and restore databases.

Securing the Odoo database manager

In addition, you can set a master password for the Odoo database manager. Simply click the **Set Master Password** button and you can specify a password. Unlike setting a password for the SILKWORM-DEV database we created in the previous step, this password is to prevent access to the database manager.

This is a very important step in securing an Odoo installation and you should take the warning seriously. If you do not set this password, then anyone can perform all these operations.

Installing the Sales Management module

After clicking on **Create Database**, there may be a slight delay, depending on your system, before you are shown a page that lists the available applications.

This screen lets you select from a list of the most common Odoo modules to install.

There is very little you can do with just an Odoo database with no modules installed. Now, we will install the **Sales Management** application so we can begin setting up our business selling T-shirts.

Click on the **Install** button to install the **Sales Management** module.

While modules are being installed and during other long operations, you will often see a **Loading...** icon at the top center of your screen. Unlike previous versions of Odoo, which that prompted for accounting and other setup information, Odoo now completes the installation unattended.

Getting to know the basic Odoo interface

After the installation of the sales order application, Odoo 11 takes you to the **Discuss** menu, where your inbox and other communication activities are located. You will also notice that Odoo provides small purple tear drops that provide helpful tips. These will show up in most Odoo applications you install.

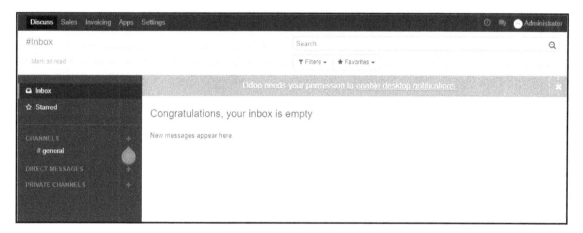

As you can see, the application menus are across the top of the interface. Click the **Sales** menu to bring up the **Sales** application. This takes you directly to the **Sales** dashboard. As we have just installed the application, there is very little to see in the dashboard, but we can see the available menu options along the left edge of the interface.

The menus along the top allow you to change between the major applications and settings within Odoo, while the menus down the left side outline your available options in the current application. In the following screenshot, we are in the main **Sales** menu:

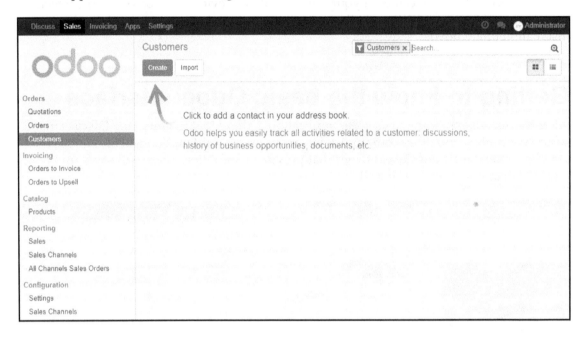

The first menu item in the **Sales** application that we are brought to by default is **Quotations**. As we have not entered any quotations yet Odoo is providing us with some helpful instructions on how to create a quotation. For now, let's look at one of the main set of records that we will be using in many Odoo applications, **Customers**. Click the **Customers** menu on the left.

Let's take a moment to look at the screen elements that will appear consistently throughout Odoo. In the top left of the main form, you can clearly see that we are in the **Customers** section.

Using the Search box

In the top right corner of our form, we have a search box:

The search box allows you to quickly search for records in the Odoo application. If you are in the **Customers** section, naturally the search will be looking for customer records. Likewise, if you are looking at the **Product** view, the search box will allow you to search product records that you have entered into the system.

Picking different views

Odoo also offers a standard interface to switch between *Kanban view* and *List* view. In some forms you will have additional options such as the *graph view*. You can see icon selections under the search box in the right corner of the form:

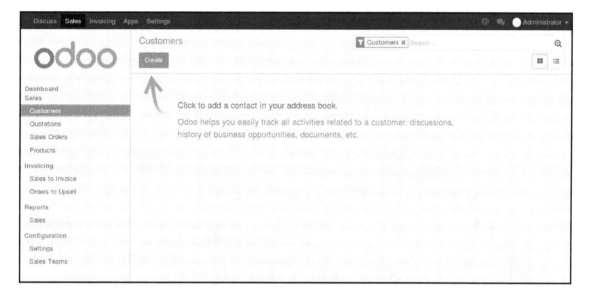

The currently selected view is highlighted in dark. If you move the mouse over the icon, you will get a tooltip that shows you the description of the view. As we have no records in our system currently, let us add a record so we can further explore the Odoo interface.

Creating your first customer

Helpful instructions prompt you to begin entering your first customer into Odoo by clicking the **Create** button.

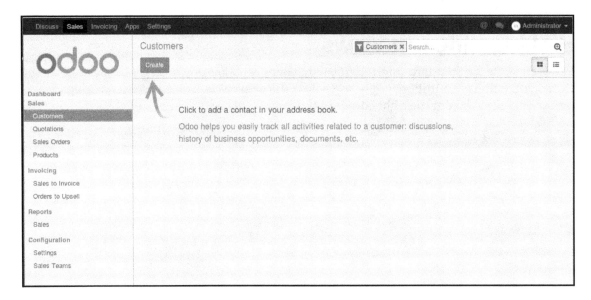

This is the Odoo **Customers** form. Clicking **Create** will generate a customer record.

Silkworm sells T-shirts to both businesses and retail customers. For this example, we will use a fictional customer named Mike Smith who wishes to purchase several T-shirts. Odoo offers flexibility in collecting customer information, and by default most fields are not required. If you see a field that is purple, that is a required field. In Odoo 10, the only required field for the customer is the name.

The rest of the fields are optional. Later, we will learn how you can configure Odoo to make additional fields required.

In this example, we have filled out some of the basic fields for our fictional customer, Mike Smith:

Basic fields for our fictional customer

Is this customer a company?

At the very top of the form is a radio selection option to inform Odoo if this customer is an individual or a company. For our example, we are using a walk-in retail customer. If you were doing a business-to-business type operation, then often your customers would select the **Company** option.

In previous versions of Odoo, you were not allowed to have multiple contacts if you had the **Individual** option selected. In Odoo 11, you can create contacts for individuals as well as companies.

Entering data into Odoo forms

Odoo utilizes a consistent interface to enter data throughout the application. Once you have learned how to enter data into one form, you should have no problem entering data into other forms in Odoo.

Required fields will always be in purple. If you see a purple field, you must fill in that data or you will not be able to save the record. You can move between fields by using your mouse or the *Tab* key. *Shift+Tab* will take you back to the previous field. Unlike some systems, you cannot move between fields in Odoo by using the arrow keys.

In many forms, you will have to select lists that allow you to choose from a list to populate the field. You can use your keyboard to type and limit the items that are displayed in a select list. By using the *Tab* key on your keyboard to find the appropriate item in the list, it is possible to enter data into a form with limited use of the mouse.

 While not the case in the latest build of Odoo 11 we used for this book, in many builds of Odoo it is necessary to first go down and choose the country before the states list can be populated. If you try to enter the state first, the list will be empty if there is no country selected.

Many selection lists have two options at the bottom that will allow you to use additional search options, or to create an item that is not in the list.

Additional search options

In this example, we see a list of states, with the option for additional searching or to create a new state that is not in the list.

Language: Odoo has the ability to work with customers in a variety of languages. For our example, we will leave this as English. If, however, you were working with a company that preferred their documents in other languages, you could specify that language and Odoo will manage the required translation.

Use the **Internal Notes** area to enter any additional notes that you wish to keep on the customer.

Editing customer Sales & Purchases

The bottom area of the customer screen is divided into a series of tabs or pages that assist in organizing customer information. In the **Sales & Purchases** page, we can assign such options as a salesperson and other sales-related options.

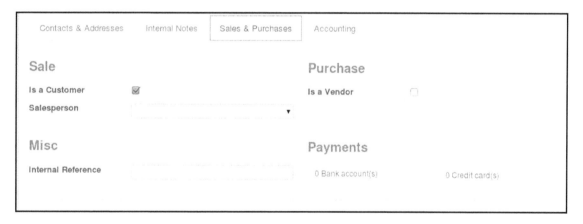

Sales & Purchases page

The available options in the customer **Sales & Purchases** page are:

- **Is a Customer**: This is the customer checkbox known in Odoo as a **Boolean** field. It can be marked checked or unchecked. Odoo has a unique method of storing data related to people in the system. All individuals are stored in the same table (res_partner) regardless if they are a customer or supplier. The customer flag tells Odoo that this is in fact a customer record. This field must be checked for Odoo to recognize Mike Smith as a customer.

- **Salesperson**: The salesperson field allows you to select who the direct salesperson will be for this customer. While the field is not required, it is often populated if you are integrating your sales management system with the **Customer Relationship Management** (**CRM**) module. We will use this field in the chapter on CRM; for now, we can leave the field blank.

- **Internal Reference**: Often when implementing Odoo, a company already has an existing customer numbering system in place. The reference field is the perfect field to populate with an existing customer number. Otherwise, this field can be left blank or used for another purpose. For our example, we are going to leave this field blank.

- **Is a Vendor**: Because Odoo stores customer and vendor data in the same table, it is possible to be both a customer and a supplier. In this example, we will keep `Mike Smith` as a customer only.

 Odoo uses a common database to store customer and supplier records. This makes it easier to manage data as customers, and suppliers are designated by simple checkboxes in the **Sales & Purchases** page on the customer screen.

Editing customer invoicing

In previous versions of Odoo, the invoicing (formally named Accounting) page was quite intimidating to new users. Thankfully, in Odoo 11, the invoicing page is much simpler and allows you to specify terms and fiscal information.

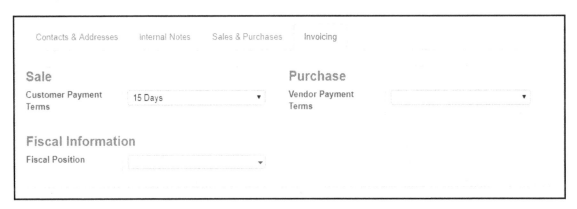

Customer invoicing page

Here are the available options in the customer invoicing page:

- **Customer Payment Term**: It is common in many businesses for different customers to have different payment terms. Perhaps, for a lifelong customer, you would extend 30- or even 60-day net terms for them to pay their invoice. For a new customer, you may require immediate payment. Additional terms can be configured in Odoo depending on your needs. The default payment terms included are:
  - **Immediate Payment**
  - **15 Days**
  - **30 Net Days**

  For our example, we will set the payment **Customer Payment Terms** to **15 Days**.

- **Vendor Payment Term**: Much like the **Customer Payment Term**, this field will determine the payment terms for the supplier. Because a partner can be both a customer and supplier, we have separate terms for each.
- **Fiscal Position**: The **Fiscal Position** field is sometimes also known as the tax status, and is in some systems represented simply as taxable. Odoo 9 now provides a robust fiscal position framework that allows you to set up rules for your customers and vendors for almost any scenario. Fortunately, for simple installations you can avoid this field entirely.

Remember to click on the **Save** button to add your new customer record to the database.

If you are unable to save your customer record because it is missing required fields, it is likely you did not pick a country when you created your Odoo database. You can fix this clicking **install more packages** under **Install More Packages** in the **Settings** option under invoicing.

Entering a product in Odoo

Now that we have a customer, it is time we enter some products to sell to our new customer. For our example, we are going to enter a medium, white-cotton T-shirt. Click on the **Products** item in the menu on the left:

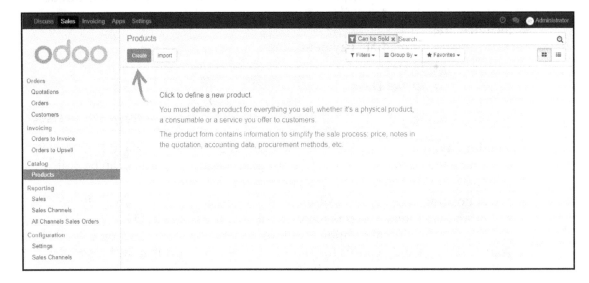

Products item

Creating products in Odoo

Create a new product by clicking the **Create** button.

The following screenshot is of the **General Information** page of the **Products** form, which you use to enter a product record into Odoo:

General Information page of the Products form

Product Name

The **Product Name** is what will display on the sales orders, invoices, and in all other screens that refer to this specific product. For our example, we are selling a `Medium White T-Shirt`.

Can be Sold

Much like the customer active flag, you can remove products from showing up in product lists by unchecking **Can be Sold**. For our example, we want to sell this T-shirt to `Mike Smith`, so we will leave the option checked.

Can be Purchased

Even though we have not yet installed the purchasing system, Odoo 10 lets you specify if a product can be purchased. We will accept the default that we, in addition to selling this T-shirt, can purchase them as well. This will play an important function when we get to the chapter that discusses the Odoo purchasing application.

Product Type

Product type is the first option in the **Information** page on the product screen. There are two available product types:

- **Consumable**
- **Service**

Service product types will not create procurements in purchase orders. **Consumables** are products that you actually sell, and can be configured to generate purchase orders. For our example, we will set the product type to **Consumable**.

Internal Reference

For the most part, Odoo utilizes the **Product Name** field and the description when displaying product information. It is very common that a company may have a coding system for its products. The **Internal Reference** field is useful to enter an alternative product code or number for the product. In this example, we will leave the **Internal Reference** field blank.

Sale Price

This field sets the sales price of the item as it will appear on the sales order. For our example, we are setting the **Sales Price** of the T-shirt to $16.50.

Cost Price

This field sets the item cost, which can be utilized for simple profit margin calculations. Here will set a cost of $7.25 for the T-shirt.

Nothing in the Sales page

Installing the **Sales** application creates a **Sales** page in the **Products** form. By default, however, this page is completely empty. As we install more applications and change configuration settings, this page will be populated with appropriate information. This is a common occurrence in Odoo. As you configure your applications, make sure you check back in forms as you will likely have additional options.

Entering a product's invoicing page

By default, Odoo has set up a tax of 15% for both customer taxes and vendor taxes. However, there will be times when you have a product that has a specific tax. In the United States, one example is that cigarettes often have a more substantial tax than other items, such as food. Odoo allows you to specify additional tax options for a given product in the invoicing page. Taxes can be specified for both the customer and the supplier separately.

The following screenshot shows the invoicing page in the **Products** form:

Invoicing page

You will also notice that Odoo allows you to have multiple taxes for the same product. This allows you to have a base tax applying to all products, and then simply add an additional tax, or even a tax credit, depending on that specific product.

The invoicing policy

By default, Odoo configures invoicing so that the line items of the invoice will be created based on the ordered quantities from the sales order. This means that even if none of the items have shipped, the customer will still be invoiced. Alternatively, you can change the invoicing policy so that the customer is invoiced on delivered items. If you have items on a sales order that have not shipped yet, the customer will not be invoiced for those items.

Saving the product record

Clicking the **Save** button stores the product record in Odoo. If you click on **Discard**, you will be warned that you will lose your changes.

Setting company information

We have entered both a customer and a product. However, before we create a sales order, we still have some work to do in setting up our company. Currently, Odoo does not even know the name of our company and has, by default, used Your Company as the name.

We can locate the company information by choosing **Settings** from the top menu and then clicking the **Set Up** button from the dashboard.

After you click the button, you will get taken to the company information form. The following screenshot is a company record filled in with the data for our sample case study:

Company record

Here, we have supplied the company name along with the address, email, phone, website, and company slogan. It is also possible to click the photo icon at the top left to assign a logo to the company.

Saving company information

Click **Save** to update the company information. We are now ready to enter our first sales order.

Entering your first sales order

Now for the moment we have all been waiting for. We finally get to sell our products by entering a sales order. To get to the **Sales Order** screen, click **Sales** in the top menu, and then choose **Orders** from the sub-menu on the left.

The following screenshot shows existing sales orders and allows users to create a new sales order:

Create a new sales order

Click on the **Create** button to create a new sales order. Every brand-new sales order begins as a quotation and stays in that state until you confirm the sale. Only after confirming the quotation will your sale be referred to as a sales order.

The following screenshot is a new sales order form with the cursor set on the **Customer** field:

Sales order form

Selecting the customer

When you create a new quotation sales order, you are prompted to first select the customer from the drop-down. As you add customers, you will have the option to search and locate customers for the sales order. For now, we will be selecting the customer we entered earlier in the chapter: **Mike Smith**.

Unlike previous versions of Odoo, you can now begin entering line items before you have specified the customer for the sales order.

Expiration Date

By default, there is no expiration date for the quote. However, if you would like to specify a date in which the quote will no longer be valid, you can specify it here:

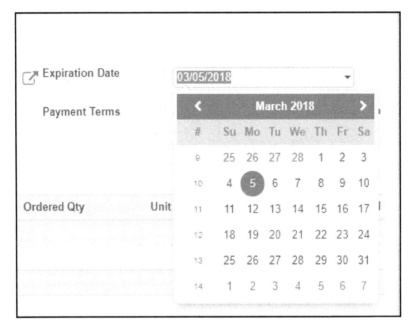

Expiration date for the quote

Payment terms

Odoo will automatically bring in payment terms for the customer you select. On the sales order, you have the option to override a customer's payment terms for the specific sales order.

Entering line items on a quotation sales order

Now we are ready to begin specifying the product we wish to sell. Click **Add an item** in the line item area to add a line to the grid. The first field will be **Product**. Select **Medium White T-shirt** from the list box. Your **Line Item** fields should populate and look like this:

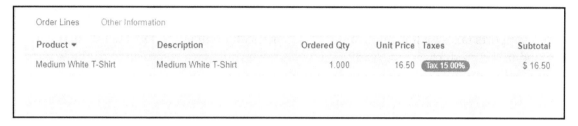

Order Lines	Other Information					
Product ▾	Description		Ordered Qty	Unit Price	Taxes	Subtotal
Medium White T-Shirt	Medium White T-Shirt		1.000	16.50	Tax 15.00%	$ 16.50

Line Item fields

Product field

Each line item starts out by selecting the product. You can add products on the fly by choosing **Create and Edit...** from the bottom of the list. Once there are more products in the list, you can also bring up a product search window using the **Search more...** option. After you select the **Product** field, Odoo retrieves the tax and pricing information from the server to display in the line item.

In Odoo 11, the total is automatically updated as you add new line items. Still, Odoo provides an update link next to Total on the form. You should consider hitting this if you have any doubt as to the accuracy of the total.

Description

Odoo will pull the description from the product record to populate the **Description** field on the line item. It is possible to override the description on the quotation sales order. For this example, we will leave the description as-is.

Ordered quantity

The product quantity will be 1 by default. Naturally, you will change this field to the quantity of products you have sold. We will just leave the quantity as 1 for this example.

Taxes

Odoo supports taxes by line item, and will automatically pull in the 15% tax rate that we defined in the product record. Additional taxes can be added or removed from the line item. For this example, we will leave the tax at 15%.

Unit price

Odoo pulls the sale price from the product record to populate the unit price in the line item. It is possible to override the price in the line item. For this example, we will leave the **Unit Price** at $16.50.

Be careful about changing prices in Odoo line items. It is possible that, if you click back on the **Product** field or tab through other fields in a line item, the **Unit Price** will flip back the price in product record. If you are changing prices in the line items, make sure you double-check your unit prices before you confirm your sales order.

Saving a sales order as a quotation

Click **Save** to save the quotation. The form will refresh, displaying the full customer address as well as updating the tax and final total of the quotation sales order.

The following screenshot shows our first quotation in Odoo:

Our first quotation in Odoo

Understanding the sales order workflow

Although we started out entering a sales order, the current state of this order is a **Quotation**. Odoo 11 displays the current state of transactions in the top right corner of the form.

Current state of transactions

This indicator makes it very easy to see the current stage of a transaction throughout the Odoo workflow. In this example, we can see that this is currently a **Quotation**. We can also see that the quotation will typically need to be sent before the sales order can finally be considered done.

The available actions you can take on this quotation are displayed in the top-left corner of the form.

The following screenshot shows available actions for an Odoo quotation:

Available actions for an Odoo quotation

Confirm Sale

The **Confirm Sale** button will convert the quotation into a sales order and push the transaction further down the sales workflow.

Print

Even in the digital age, it is still very common to need a printed copy of a quotation or sales order. Clicking the **Print** button will generate a PDF document containing your quotation.

Send by Email

Clicking the **Send by Email** button will send a copy of the quotation to the email address in the customer's file. Setting up your email configuration will be a topic for another chapter.

Cancel

Clicking the **Cancel** button will prompt you to cancel this quotation. The quotation is not deleted and can still be viewed. Cancelling the quotation ends the sales order workflow, and the quotation will only be kept in the system for archive purposes.

Click on the **Confirm Sale** button to convert this quotation into a sales order. You will see the status change for the sales order from **Quotation** to **Sales Order**.

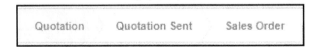

Invoicing the sale

Depending on the workflow of the business, a lot of different things can happen after you have confirmed a sales order. In manufacturing companies, you may need to both purchase products and create a manufacturing order to produce the final product before you invoice the customer. In our example, we are going to go ahead and invoice the customer for the T-shirt they have ordered. Click the **Create Invoice** button to generate an invoice for the sales order.

An Odoo **Invoice Order** wizard pops up to walk you through the invoice creation process.

The following screenshot shows the **Invoice Order** wizard:

Invoice Order wizard

What do you want to invoice?

Odoo provides a variety of options for invoicing the entire sales order, or instead invoicing based on other methods. The available choices are:

- **Invoiceable lines/Invoiceable lines (deduct down payments)**: Choose this option if you both want to invoice the lines and deduct any down payments you have received. This is the default option. Using **Invoiceable lines** without deducting down payments will simply ignore any of those payments when producing the invoice.

- **Down payment (percentage)**: You will be prompted to enter the percentage amount of the down payment.
- **Down payment (fixed amount)**: You will be prompted to enter a fixed amount for the down payment.

Creating the invoice

For our example, we will be using the default option. As we have no down payments, Odoo will process the sales order as if you had chosen the first option, **Invoiceable lines**. Click **Create Invoices** to generate the invoice. Initially, the invoice is created in a **Draft** state. Clicking **Validate** will confirm the invoice and post the transaction.

If you have followed along and everything worked as it should, then you will see an invoice similar to the following one:

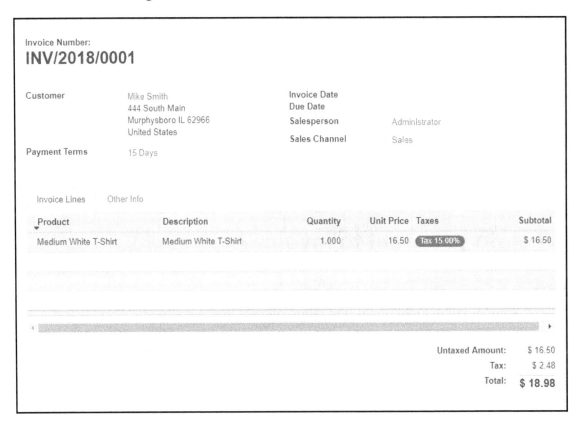

Invoice

At this time, it is worth noting Odoo's use of an interface feature called *breadcrumb*. These links, which appear on form views just below the topmost menu, allow you to traverse from your invoice back to the relevant sales order from which it is derived.

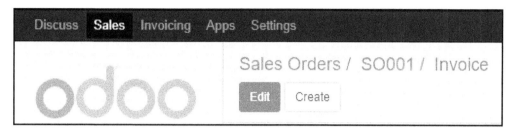

Using these links is the preferred method for backtracking to prior screens, as opposed to using your browser's Back button.

Summary

In this chapter, we started by creating an Odoo database. We then installed the **Sales Order Management** module and created our first customer. With our customer created, we turned our attention to setting up a product in Odoo and entering our basic company information. Next, we created a quotation and followed the workflow all the way through to confirming the sales order and generating an invoice.

In the next chapter, we'll look at our sales strategy and what we want to achieve via CRM software.

Exploring CRM in Odoo 11 3

Until recently, most business and financial systems had product-focused designs while records and fields maintained basic customer information, processes, and reporting typically revolved around product-related transactions. In the past, businesses were centered on specific products, but now the focus has shifted to center the business on the customer. The **Customer Relationship Management (CRM)** system provides the tools and reporting necessary to manage customer information and interactions.

In this chapter, we will cover the following:

- Looking at what it takes to implement a CRM system as part of an overall business strategy
- Installing the CRM application and setup salespersons that can be assigned to our customers
- Learning how to create and manage leads
- Creating opportunities and scheduling events in Odoo
- Discovering the Odoo Open Chatter feature
- Managing multiple sales teams

Using CRM as a business strategy

Before jumping into the specific CRM features of Odoo, it is valuable to briefly discuss the importance of a comprehensive approach to implementing a CRM system in your business. The fact is that successfully implementing a CRM system requires much more planning than just installing software and asking employees to fill in the data. CRM software systems are only a technical tool in assisting your sales and marketing department in acquiring and keeping customers. Certainly the software will play an important role, but to obtain real benefits from a CRM system you must do the hard research to understand your customer and exactly how you wish to shape their customer experience.

It is critical that the sales people share account knowledge and completely understand the features and capabilities of the system. They often have existing tools that they have relied on for many years. Without clear objectives and goals for the entire sales team, it is likely that they will not use the tool. A plan must be implemented to spend time training and encouraging the sharing of knowledge to successfully implement a CRM system.

Managing the customer experience

Today, customers face a wide range of choices when it comes to purchasing products and services. At the most fundamental level, customers often build great loyalty to brands with which they have a positive customer experience. Companies such as Apple and Harley Davidson are successful largely because of fierce brand loyalty based on positive customer experiences. Making the most of a CRM system requires you to put yourself in the role of your customer and developing a consistent strategy to improve their overall customer experience.

Treating your customer like a real person

As computers became more common, it wasn't long until people began to feel as if they were treated like a number by many companies. In many ways, CRM systems turn the tables around. Instead of treating customers like cattle, a smart account manager using a CRM system can greatly personalize the customer experience. You treat your customer like an individual, and they will reward you with their loyalty.

Because you are looking to create a very personalized customer experience, it is important to thoroughly look at your customer's interactions with the company when designing your own CRM system. A company who sells high-end security systems to government institutions will need to provide drastically different customer experiences than a company that is marketing a pool maintenance service.

Using your mission statements and company goals to drive the design of your CRM system

A good CRM system will build around the core goals and mission of your company. If your company does not have customer-focused goals or mission statements, then you should address that before beginning to design a CRM system. Most critically, there needs to be focus on concerns and interactions that have a direct impact on customer experience. A good CRM system will not just manage the sales process, but the entire customer experience and interactions before and after the sale.

Real-world case study – improving customer experience

Now we will take a detailed real-world look at how a CRM system can be implemented to improve customer experience. We begin by looking at the company slogan:

"We make great first impressions last."

Here, we have a slogan that most certainly speaks to the value of customer experience. To make that great first impression and keep it, there are several critical service expectations:

- Orders must be accurate and easy for customers to place
- Orders must be delivered on time
- Quality must be excellent

While listing these customer service goals may seem obvious, explicitly naming your objectives is important when building a CRM system. There is a natural tendency when building a CRM system to focus almost exclusively on customer acquisition and pre-sale activities. We must take care to remember that a CRM system must also support processes that manage the entire customer experience.

These are the kinds of scenarios that you want to consider when building your own CRM system:

- How are problem orders handled?
- How is the customer contacted if there is a product back order?
- If the customer calls, can the service representative easily provide delivery tracking information?

Installing the CRM application

If you have not installed the CRM module, log in as the administrator and then click on the **Apps** menu. In a few seconds, the list of available apps will appear. The CRM will likely be in the top-left corner:

Apps menu

Click on **Install** to set up the CRM application.

Your first look at the CRM Dashboard

Like with the installation of the **Sales** application, Odoo takes you to the Discuss menu. Click on **Sales** to see the new changes after installing the CRM application. New to Odoo 10 is an improved CRM Dashboard that provides you a friendly welcome message when you first install the application. You can use the dashboard to get an overview of your sales pipelines and get easy access to the most common actions within CRM.

Assigning the sales representative or account manager

In Odoo 10, like in most CRM systems, the sales representative or account manager plays an important role. Typically, this is the person that will ultimately be responsible for the customer account and a satisfactory customer experience.

While most often a company will use real people as their salespeople, it is certainly possible to instead have a salesperson record refer to a group, or even a sub-contracted support service.

We will begin by creating a salesperson that will handle standard customer accounts. Note that a sales representative is also a user in the Odoo system.

Create a new salesperson by going to the **Settings** menu, selecting **Users**, and then clicking the **Create** button. The new user form will appear. We have filled in the form with values for a fictional salesperson, Terry Zeigler.

The following is a screenshot of the user's **Access Rights** tab:

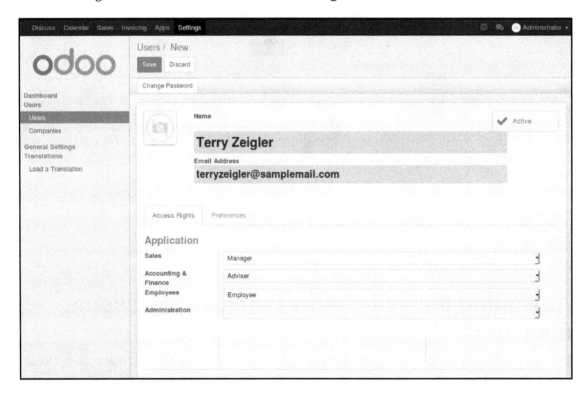

Specifying the name of the user

You specify the username just like you assigned the name of your customer in the preceding chapter. Unlike some systems that provide separate first name and last name fields, with Odoo you specify the full name within a single field.

Email address

Beginning in Odoo 9, the user and login form prompts for email as opposed to username. This practice has continued in Odoo version 10 as well. It is still possible to use a user name instead of email address, but given the strong encouragement to use email address in Odoo 9 and Odoo 10, it is possible that in future versions of Odoo the requirement to provide an email address may be more strictly enforced.

Access Rights

The **Access Rights** tab lets you control which applications the user will be able to access. By default, Odoo will specify Mr.Ziegler as an employee so we will accept that default.

Depending on the applications you may have already installed or dependencies Odoo may add in various releases, it is possible that you will have other Access Rights listed.

Sales application settings

When setting up your sales people in Odoo 10, you have three different options on how much access an individual user has to the sales system:

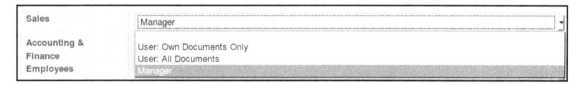

User: Own Documents Only

This is the most restrictive access to the sales application. A user with this access level is only allowed to see the documents they have entered themselves or which have been assigned to them. They will not be able to see Leads assigned to other salespeople in the sales application.

User: All Documents

With this setting, the user will have access to all documents within the sales application.

Manager

The **Manager** setting is the highest access level in the Odoo sales system. With this access level, the user can see all Leads as well as access the configuration options of the sales application. The **Manager** setting also allows the user to access statistical reports.

We will leave the **Access Rights** options unchecked. These are used when working with multiple companies or with multiple currencies.

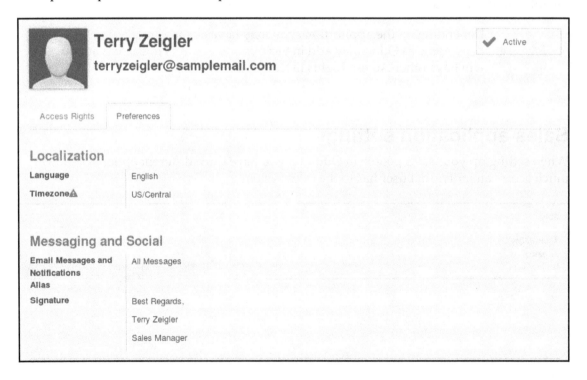

The **Preferences** tab consists of the following options:

Language and Timezone

Odoo allows you to select the language for each user. Currently, Odoo supports more than 20 language translations. Specifying the **Timezone** field allows Odoo to coordinate the display of date and time on messages.

 Leaving **Timezone** blank for a user will sometimes lead to unpredictable behavior in the Odoo software. Make sure you specify a timezone when creating a user record. Better yet, check the customization chapter on how you can make timezone a required field!

Email Messages and Notifications

In Odoo 7, messaging became a central component of the Odoo system. In version 10, support has been improved and it is now even easier to communicate important sales information between colleagues. Therefore, determining the appropriate handling of email, and circumstances in which a user will receive email, is very important. The **Email Messages and Notifications** option lets you determine when you will receive email messages from notifications that come to your Odoo inbox.

For our example, we have chosen **All Messages**. This is now the new default setting in Odoo 10. However, since we have not yet configured an email server, or if you have not configured an email server yourself, no emails will be sent or received at this stage.

Let's review the user options that will be available in communicating by email.

Never: Selecting **Never** suppresses all email messaging for the user. Naturally, this is the setting you will wish to use if you do not have an email server configured. This is also a useful option for users that simply want to use the built-in inbox inside Odoo to retrieve their messages.

All Messages (discussions, emails, followed system notifications): This option sends an email notification for any action that would create an entry in your Odoo inbox. Unlike the other options, this action can include system notifications or other automated communications.

Signature

The **Signature** section allows you to customize the signature that will automatically be appended to Odoo-generated messages and emails.

Manually setting the user password

You may have noticed that there is no visible password field in the user record. That is because the default method is to email the user an account verification they can use to set their password. However, if you do not have an email server configured, there is an alternative method for setting the user password.

After saving the user record, use the **Change Password** button at the top of the form.

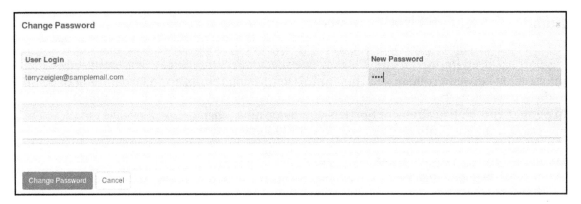

A form will then appear allowing you to set the password for the user.

Now in Odoo 10, there is a far more visible button available at the top left of the form. Just click the **Change Password** button.

Assigning a salesperson to a customer

Now that we have set up our salesperson, it is time to assign the salesperson their first customer. Previously, no salesperson had been assigned to our one and only customer, **Mike Smith**. So let's go to the **Sales** menu and then click on **Mike Smith** to pull up his customer record and assign him **Terry Ziegler** as his salesperson. The following screenshot is of the customer screen opened to assign a salesperson:

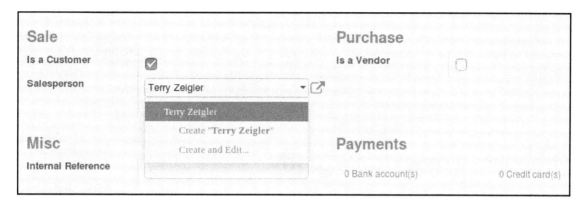

Here, we have set the sales person to **Terry Zeigler**. By assigning your customers a salesperson, you can then better organize your customers for reports and additional statistical analysis.

Understanding Your Pipeline

Prior to Odoo 10, the CRM application primarily was a simple collection of Leads and opportunities. While Odoo still uses both Leads and opportunities as part of the CRM application, the concept of a Pipeline now takes center stage. You use the Pipeline to organize your opportunities by what stage they are within your sales process. Click on **Your Pipeline** in the **Sales** menu to see the overall layout of the **Pipeline** screen:

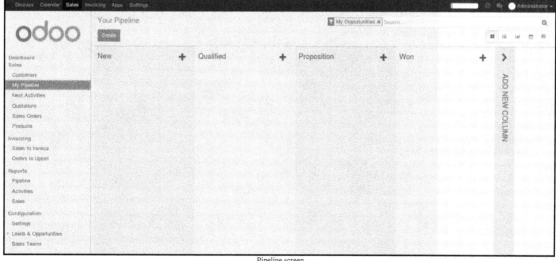

Pipeline screen

In the preceding **Pipeline** forms, one of the first things to notice is that there are default filters applied to the view. Up in the search box, you will see that there is a filter to limit the records in this view to the **Direct Sales** team as well as a **My Opportunities** filter. This effectively limits the records so you only see your opportunities from your primary sales team. Removing the **My Opportunities** filter will allow you to see opportunities from other salespeople in your organization.

Creating a new opportunity

In Odoo 10, a potential sale is defined by creating a new opportunity. An opportunity allows you to begin collecting information about the scope and potential outcomes for a sale. These opportunities can be created from new Leads, or an opportunity can originate from an existing customer.

For our real-world example, let's assume that `Mike Smith` has called and was so happy with his first order that he now wants to discuss using `Silkworm` for his local sports team. After a short conversation we decide to create an opportunity by clicking the **Create** button.

You can also use the + buttons within any of the pipeline stages to create an opportunity that is set to that stage in the pipeline.

In Odoo 10, the CRM application greatly simplified the form for entering a new opportunity. Instead of bringing up the entire opportunity form with all the fields you get a simple form that collects only the most important information. The following screenshot is of a new opportunity form:

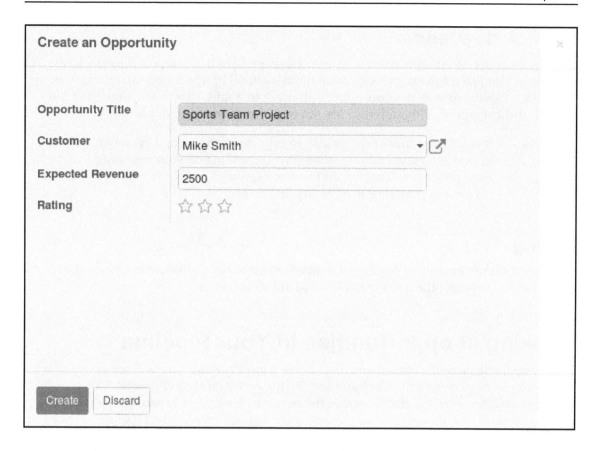

Opportunity Title

The title of your opportunity can be anything you wish. It is naturally important to choose a subject that makes it easy to identify the opportunity in a list. This is the only field required to create an opportunity in Odoo 10.

Customer

This field is automatically populated if you create an opportunity from the customer form. You can, however, assign a different customer if you like. This is not a required field, so if you have an opportunity that you do not wish to associate with a customer, that is perfectly fine. For example, you may leave this field blank if you are attending a trade show and expect to have revenue, but do not yet have any specific customers to attribute to the opportunity.

Expected revenue

Here, you specify the amount of revenue you can expect from the opportunity if you are successful. Inside the full opportunity form there is a field in which you can specify the percentage likelihood that an opportunity will result in a sale. These values are useful in many statistical reports, although they are not required to create an opportunity.

 Increasingly, more reports look to expected revenue and percentage of opportunity completions. Therefore, depending on your reporting requirements you may wish to encourage sales people to set target goals for each opportunity to better track conversion.

Rating

Some opportunities are more important than others. You can choose none, one, two, or three stars to designate the relative importance of this opportunity.

Looking at opportunities in Your Pipeline

When you navigate to the Sales menu and choose **Your Pipeline**, you will see your opportunities displayed in the **Kanban** view. Here, we see our brand new $2,500 opportunity along with the customer and the next action we need to take and when we need to take it. The following is a screenshot of the Kanban view of the pipeline:

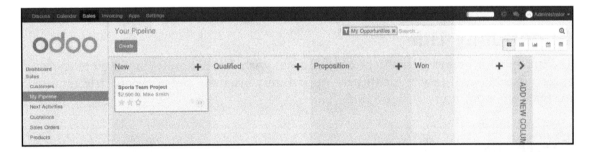

Clicking the small arrow on the Kanban card will bring up a small menu allowing you to perform actions related to the opportunity.

Let's edit the opportunity by double-clicking on it and choosing the Edit button:

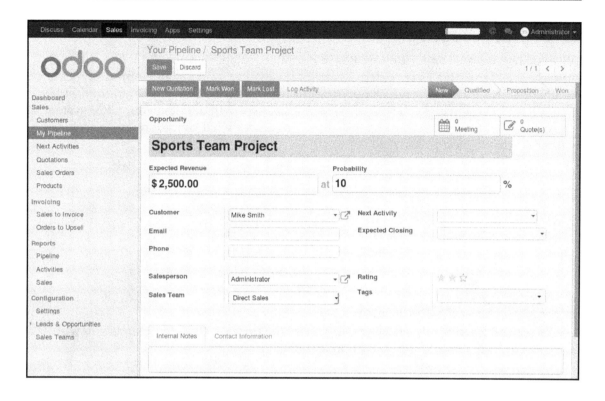

Next Activity

Previously in Odoo 9, you really only tracked one action at a time. Now in Odoo 10, Odoo will automatically keep a historical log of the activities you take on a given opportunity. The **Next Activity** field allows you to specify what type of activity you need to do next on your opportunity. Currently, you are allowed to specify the activity as either a **Call**, **Email**, or **Task** that you need to perform. You can then specify the date of the task along with an optional note providing more details on the task.

Once you complete the task, you can use the **Done** link at the bottom of the **Next Activity** area to finish and set another activity to continue handling the opportunity. You can use the **Cancel** link to clear the activity.

Expected Closing

When managing your opportunities, it is important to establish a goal for when you wish to close the sale. Providing an expected closing date is handy for managing opportunities and running reports, identifying which opportunities are due to be closed. The priority setting ranges from lowest to highest, with three settings between. In defining your CRM system, you should identify business rules for determining under what conditions an opportunity will receive the highest priority.

Tags

Odoo also allows you to assign multiple tags to an opportunity. For example, you could choose trade show and sports as tags to designate an opportunity that is sports-related and will take place at a trade show.

Email and Phone

The **Email** and **Phone** fields allow you to specify the primary contact methods you will likely use to communicate with your opportunity.

Internal Notes

The **Internal Notes** area is where you provide all the details on the opportunity. For our example, we kept the notes brief, but when you are working with real opportunities, make sure you take advantage of the internal notes area to document anything that will help you in closing the sale.

The Contact Information page

When you create an opportunity from either a customer or a lead, the information is automatically brought over into the **Lead** page tab in the **Opportunity**. The following screenshot is of the **Lead** tab of **Opportunity form**:

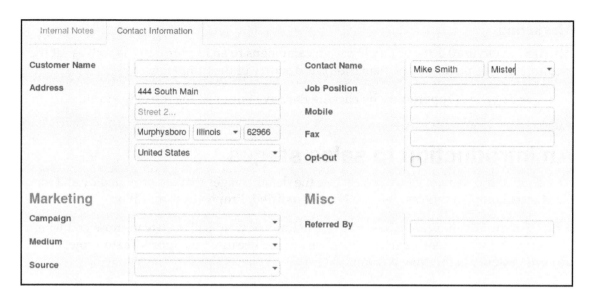

Address and Contact Information

The top half of the **Contact Information** page contains the standard address and other contact information. This information is automatically populated if you choose a customer, but can be overwritten for the opportunity if you desire. The **Function** field could be used to provide a bit of detail on the event that triggered the opportunity.

Odoo does not provide separate fields for first and last names, like many other accounting systems. Consider this as you plan how to organize customers in your system.

Mailings

The **Opt-Out** checkbox prevents the lead or customer associated with this opportunity from receiving mass mailings.

Marketing

Also new in Odoo 10 is the ability to assign campaigns to an opportunity, as well as set the medium (that is, phone, email, television), and source of the campaign.

- Save the **Opportunity** by clicking the **Save** button at the top of the form.

An introduction to sales stages

At the top of the Kanban view, you can see the default stages that are provided by an Odoo CRM installation. In this case, we see **New**, **Qualified**, **Proposition**, and **Won**.

As an opportunity moves between stages, the Kanban view will update to show you where each opportunity currently stands. Here, we can see because this **Sports Team Project** has just been entered in the **New** column.

Viewing the details of an opportunity

If you click the three lines at the top right of the **Sports Team Project** opportunity in the Kanban view, which appears when you hover the mouse over it, you will see a pop-up menu with your available options. The following screenshot shows the available actions on an opportunity:

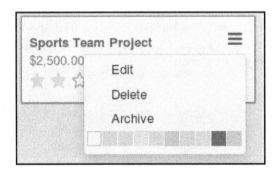

Actions you can take on an opportunity

Selecting the **Edit** option takes you to the opportunity record and into edit mode for you to change any of the information. In addition, you can delete the record or archive the record so it will no longer appear in your pipeline by default.

The color palette at the bottom lets you color code your opportunities in the Kanban view. The small stars on the opportunity card allow you to highlight opportunities for special consideration. You can also easily drag and drop the opportunity into other columns as you work through the various stages of the sale.

Using Odoo's OpenChatter feature

One of the biggest enhancements brought about in Odoo 7 and expanded on in later versions of Odoo was the new **OpenChatter** feature that provides social networking style communication to business documents and transactions.

As we work our brand new opportunity, we will utilize the **OpenChatter** feature to demonstrate how to communicate details between team members and generate log entries to document our progress.

The best thing about the **OpenChatter** feature is that it is available for nearly all business documents in Odoo. It also allows you to see a running set of logs of the transactions or operations that have affected the document. This means everything that applies here to the CRM application can also be used to communicate in sales and purchasing, or in communicating about a specific customer or vendor.

Changing the status of an opportunity

For our example, let's assume that we have prepared our proposal and made the presentation. Bring up the opportunity by using the right-click **Menu** in the Kanban view or going into the list view and clicking the opportunity in the list.

It is time to update the status of our opportunity by clicking the **Proposition** arrow at the top of the form:

Notice that you do not have to edit the record to change the status of the opportunity. At the bottom of the opportunity, you will now see a logged note generated by Odoo that documents the changing of the opportunity from a new opportunity to a proposition. The following screenshot is of **OpenChatter** displaying a changed stage for the opportunity:

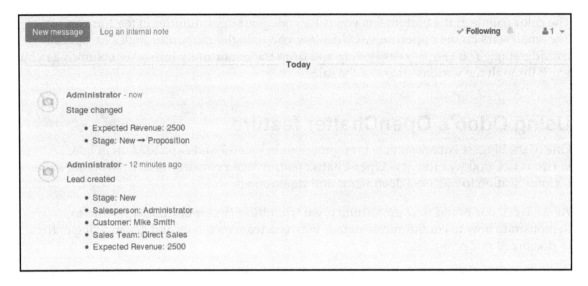

Notice how Odoo is logging the events automatically as they take place.

Managing the opportunity

With the proposal presented, let's take down some details from what we have learned that may help us later when we come back to this opportunity. One method of collecting this information could be to add the details to the **Internal Notes** field in the opportunity form. There is value, however, in using the **OpenChatter** feature in Odoo to document our new details.

Most importantly, using **OpenChatter** to log notes gives you a running transcript with date and time stamps automatically generated. With the **Generic Notes** field, it can be very difficult to manage multiple entries. Another major advantage is that the **OpenChatter** feature can automatically send messages to team members' inboxes updating them on progress. let's see it in action!

Click the **Log an Internal note** link to attach a note to our opportunity. The following screenshot is for creating a note:

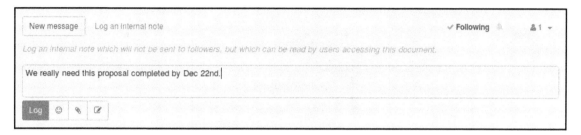

The activity option is unique to the CRM application and will not appear in most documents. You can use the small icons at the bottom to add a smiley, attach a document, or open up a full featured editor if you are creating a long note.

 The full featured editor also allows you to save templates of messages/notes you may use frequently. Depending on your specific business requirements, this could be a great time saver.

When you create a note, it is attached to the business document, but no message will be sent to followers. You can even attach a document to the note by using the **Attach a File** feature. After clicking the **Log** button, the note is saved and becomes part of the OpenChatter log for that document.

Following a business document

Odoo brings social networking concepts into your business communication. Fundamental to this implementation is that you can get automatic updates on a business document by following the document. Then, whenever there is a note, action, or a message created that is related to a document you follow, you will receive a message in your Odoo inbox. In the bottom right-hand corner of the form, you are presented with the options for when you are notified and for adding or removing followers from the document. The following screenshot is of the OpenChatter follow options:

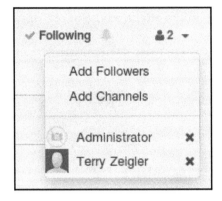

In this case, we can see that both **Terry Zeigler** and **Administrator** are set as followers for this opportunity. The **Following** checkbox at the top indicates that I am following this document. Using the **Add Followers** link you can add additional users to follow the document.

The items followers are notified are viewed by clicking the arrow to the right of the following button. This brings up a list of the actions that will generate notifications to followers:

The checkbox next to **Discussions** indicates that I should be notified of any discussions related to this document. However, I would not be notified, for example, if the stage changed.

When you send a message, by default the customer will become a follower of the document. Then, whenever the status of the document changes, the customer will receive an email. Test out all your processes before integrating with an email server.

Modifying the stages of the sale

We have seen that Odoo provides a default set of sales stages. Many times, however, you will want to customize the stages to best deliver an outstanding customer experience. Moving an opportunity through stages should trigger actions that create a relationship with the customer and demonstrate your understanding of their needs. A customer in the qualification stage of a sale will have much different needs and much different expectations than a customer that is in the negotiation phase.

For our case study, there are sometimes printing jobs that are technically complex to accomplish. With different jerseys for a variety of teams, the final details need to go through a final technical review and approval process before the order can be entered and verified.

From a business perspective, the goal is not just to document the stage of the sales cycle; the primary goal is to use this information to drive customer interactions and improve the overall customer experience.

To add a stage to the sales process, bring up **Your Pipeline** and then click on the **ADD NEW COLUMN** area in the right of the form to bring up a little popup to enter the name for the new stage:

Your Pipeline

After you have added the column to the sales process, you can use your mouse to drag and drop the columns into the order that you wish them to appear. We are now ready to begin the technical approval stage for this opportunity.

Drag and drop the **Sports Team Project** opportunity over to the **Technical Approval** column in the Kanban view. The following screenshot is of the opportunities Kanban view after adding the technical approval stage:

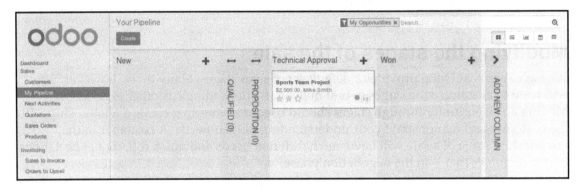

Technical Approval column

We now see the **Technical Approval** column in our Kanban view and have moved over the opportunity. You will also notice that any time you change the stage of an opportunity that there will be an entry that will be created in the **OpenChatter** section at the bottom of the form. In addition to the ability to drag and drop an opportunity into a new stage, you can also change the stage of an opportunity by going into the form view.

Closing the sale

After a lot of hard work, we have finally won the opportunity, and it is time to turn this opportunity into a quotation. At this point, Odoo makes it easy to take that opportunity and turn it into an actual quotation.

Open up the opportunity and click the **New Quotation** tab at the top of the opportunity form:

Unlike Odoo 8, which prompts for more information, in Odoo 10 you get taken to a new quote with the customer information already filled in:

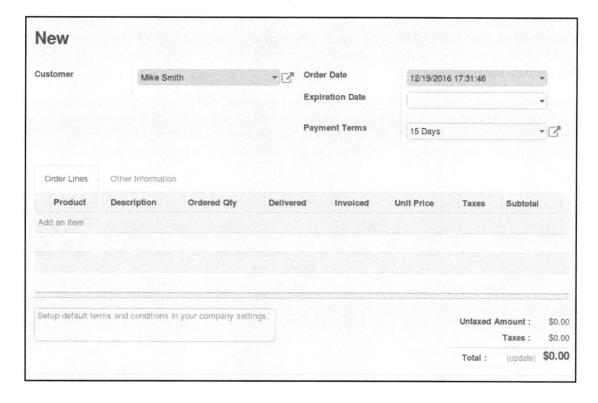

Your opportunity converted to a quotation

The workflow in Odoo handles moving over all the required information from your opportunity to your quotation document. At this point, you are ready to begin adding line items and creating a quotation just like we did in `Chapter 2`, *Installing Your First Application*.

Please note that just because you create a new quotation from an opportunity, Odoo still leaves the opportunity open. Therefore, you must go back into **Your Pipeline** and mark the opportunity as won if you are truly done with the opportunity.

Leads and opportunities

Odoo provides two primary documents for managing interactions with your customers or potential customers. You can think of Leads as less critical, and perhaps less likely to turn into a real sales situation, than an opportunity. A good example of Leads would be that you get a few dozen business cards from people you met at a conference. You could add each of them as a Lead for further follow up. An example of an opportunity would be if you met someone at a conference and had a detailed conversation on how your company provides appropriate services.

Many people get confused between when to use Leads and when to use opportunities. The best way to remember is that Leads are intangible and are essentially potential contacts. Opportunities should be more clearly defined, have some sort of expected income of successful, and provide significant project details and scope compared to a simple lead.

Turning on Leads in Odoo 11

When you first install the Odoo CRM application, Leads are turned off by default. You can enable Leads by first choosing **Settings** under the **Configuration** section in the **Sales** menu. In the settings form under the Leads, you can turn on Leads by selecting the second option and then clicking **Apply**:

Once you have applied the changes to the settings, Odoo will refresh and add a **Leads** option to your sales menu.

Creating Leads in Odoo

Many a times, it can take quite a bit of work to uncover an opportunity. In Odoo, you create Leads when you need a qualification step before creating an opportunity or a customer. For example, you may receive a business card or an unqualified lead from your website. Another common situation is that Leads are purchased perhaps from a mailing list and then imported into Odoo.

Let's create a new lead for a potential customer we met at a local event.

Under the **Sales** menu, click **Leads** and then the **Create** button to open a new lead. The following screenshot is of the form used for creating a new lead:

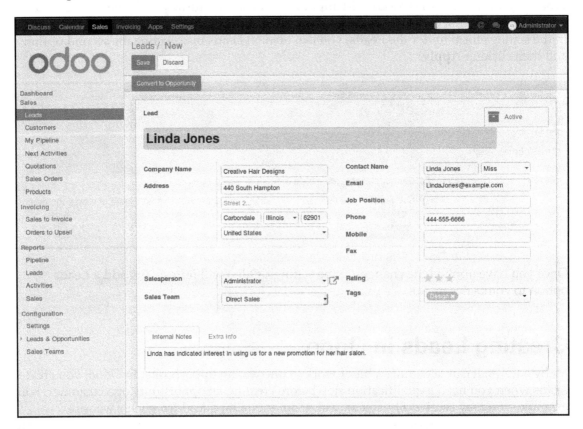

As you will see, the form is very similar to the standard customer screen. There is a good reason for this, as Odoo uses a standard structure to hold address information for Leads, customers, suppliers, and users/employees. In our example, we have filled out the basic contact and address information, as well as assigned our sales representative to this Lead.

Converting a Lead into an opportunity

Leads will stay Leads indefinitely until you take some action to either turn them into opportunities or mark them as lost/dead. You will notice at the top left of your form there is a button labeled **Convert to Opportunity**. At any point, you can convert a lead into an opportunity simply by clicking this button:

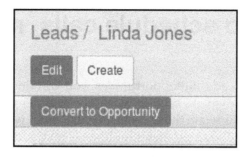

Once you click **Convert to Opportunity**, you will get presented with an Odoo wizard that will allow you to choose how you wish to handle converting the lead into an opportunity:

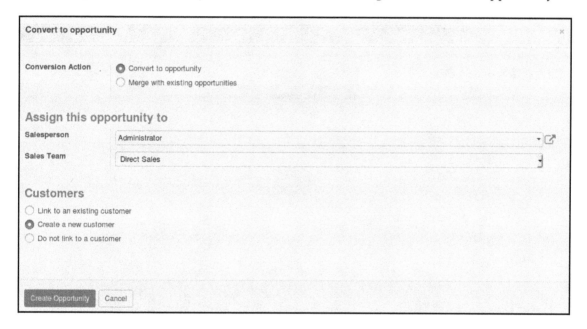

Each of the options presented are pretty well self-explanatory. The conversion action determines whether you will create a new opportunity or merge this lead with an existing opportunity. You get the option of assigning the opportunity to a specific sales person.

Finally, you get to tell Odoo if you wish to create a new customer for this opportunity or if instead you wish to assign this opportunity to an existing customer.

Using Odoo to schedule calls, meetings, and events

Often when working with Leads and opportunities, you will find it beneficial to schedule meetings and calls. Odoo provides a built-in meeting scheduler that you can use specifically to manage your schedule and relate those events to customers within Odoo. Odoo considers it so useful that they have a dedicated menu for it! Let's take a look at how we can schedule an event in Odoo. Meeting scheduling is handled in the messaging menu of Odoo. Begin by choosing **Calendar** from the main menu.

Odoo will then display your personal calendar:

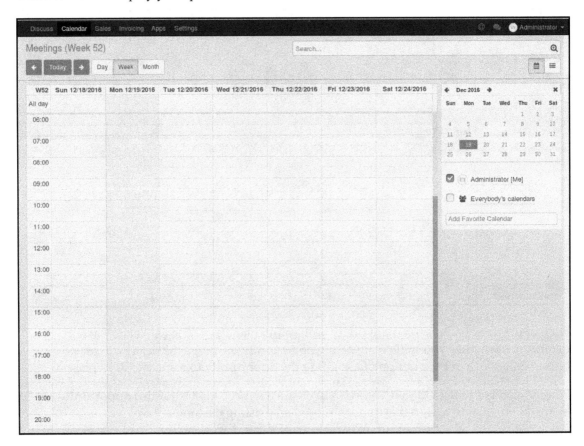

Odoo will bring up the current week. Arrows at the top left of the form allow you to quickly navigate to the previous and next month, respectively. To the right of the title is the option to look at the calendar by week or by day. This can be particularly valuable to see more information when you have many meetings scheduled.

On the far right, you have a small calendar for the next month. This small calendar is interactive and you can use it to quickly jump to that month and even a specific day.

Scheduling an event

Scheduling an event is very easy. Simply click on the day you wish to schedule an event. You will then be prompted to give a name to the event and to either create or edit the event.

After entering the event summary, you will have two options. You can directly create the event, or you can choose **Edit** to provide additional details about the event.

Depending on how you want to organize and manage your meetings, it may work for you just fine to create the event; provided the event summary is enough information for you to take the action you require. Typically, however, it will be a better practice to edit this event and provide some more details.

Click **Edit** to create an event and automatically bring it up for editing:

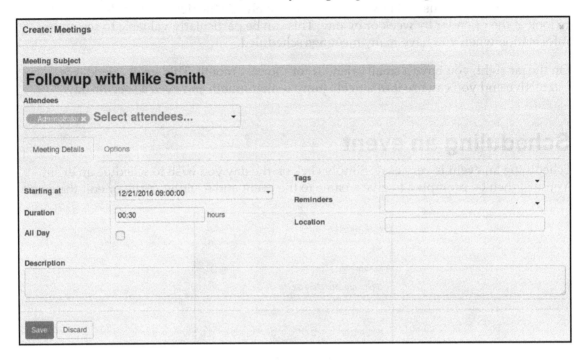

Odoo will automatically bring over the event summary that you filled in after clicking on the day. Notice, however, that instead of **Event Summary** the title is now **Meeting Subject**. Perhaps Odoo will modify this in the future for greater consistency.

Adding attendees to your meeting

By default, you are the only person attending this meeting. When you are meeting with a client, customer, or vendor, it is largely up to you if you wish to add the attendee here in the list. For our purpose, we will add Mike Smith to the list of attendees. Odoo will automatically search in real time as you type out the name.

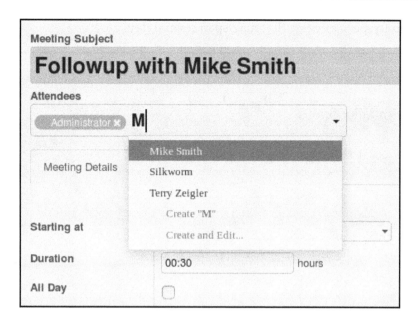

Odoo will then add the attendee to the attendees list. For internal communications, this can be used to make sure all of the necessary team members are notified of the meeting if they are also using the Odoo schedules.

Odoo will provide you a warning if you add an attendee that does not have an email address. In this case, Odoo will still add the attendee, but naturally any automated notifications cannot be delivered to the attendee.

Specifying meeting details

Odoo's meeting scheduler offers quite a few different options that assist you in customizing the meeting. One of the first things to notice is that by default, Odoo schedules a meeting for the full day. If your meeting does not have a specific time, you can check the **All Day** option. After you have checked the option, the **Duration** field disappears and is replaced with an **Ending at** field to specify the ending day for the event.

This allows you to specify events that may span several days.

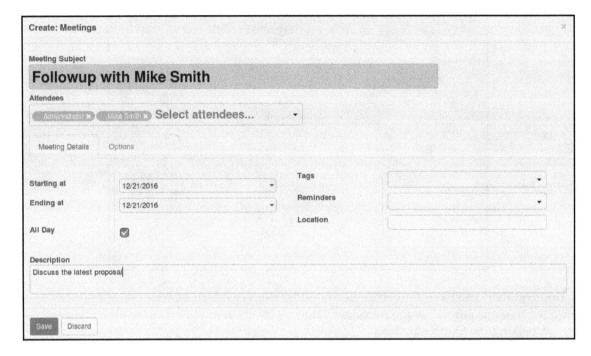

Specifying tags for your meeting

Odoo provides a set of default meeting tags that quickly tell you the overall scope of the meeting. You can specify multiple tags as well as create new tags to organize your meeting schedules.

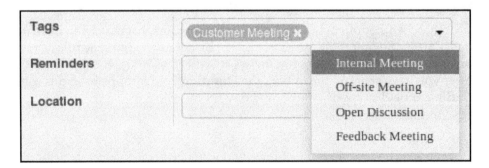

Setting up reminders for your meeting

Often, you will want to have a reminder or a little bit of notice before your meeting. Setting reminders can help prevent you from missing an important meeting. Odoo offers two kinds of basic reminders, notifications and email reminders.

Notifications will prompt you visually on screen in the top right corner of your window when the time before the meeting is reached. Email reminders will send you an email.

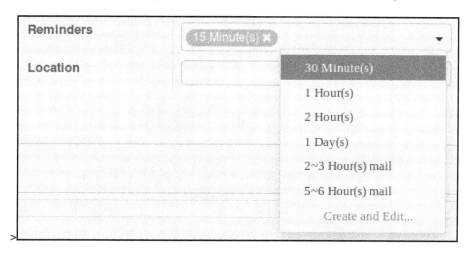

In addition to tags and reminders, you also have the option to specify the location of the meeting. This location is a simple text field and is just some extra information that you can use to keep your team members informed.

Specifying additional meeting options

Under the options page, Odoo allows you to specify several additional options for meetings. One of the most powerful features is the ability to configure recurring meetings. When you select the recurring option, additional options will become available in which you can select the interval.

Depending on the interval you select, the form will refresh with the appropriate options for that interval. In the following screenshot, we have selected a weekly interval. Odoo then allows us to select which day(s) of the week the meeting will repeat.

In addition to selecting the specific days, you can also specify how long until the recurring meeting will end. The preceding example demonstrates how you can specify a meeting to end based on the number of repetitions. If you choose, you can select an end date to stop the recurring meeting.

Summary

In this chapter, we started by discussing the role of a CRM system in a modern day business. We installed the CRM module, created salespeople, and proceeded to develop a system to manage the sales process. In our example, we walked an opportunity through the various stages in the sales process. Finally, we saw how to modify stages in the sales cycle and turn the opportunity directly into a quotation.

In the next chapter, we will turn our attention to purchasing products and setting up the MRP application to handle production operations.

Purchasing with Odoo 4

In this chapter, we start getting into what could be considered the core functionality of most ERP systems. We will begin by setting up a vendor and then purchasing raw material components. After the products arrive, we will receive the products into inventory and pay the invoice to complete the purchasing cycle.

Topics we will cover in this chapter include:

- Examining a typical purchasing process for a business
- Setting up your vendors and warehouse locations
- Entering a quote and turning it into a purchase order
- Receiving products from your vendors
- Paying invoices

What's new in Odoo 11

Aside from a small number of small interface changes, the Purchase Management application in Odoo 11 is very similar to Odoo 10. One of the major changes is that Odoo now manages procurements by creating messages in Odoo 11's new activities button on the menu bar.

Understanding the overall purchasing process

Let's begin by taking a 30,000-foot view of the purchasing process. Putting together a purchasing system requires several steps, and initially it can be confusing for people new to ERP systems. But when you break the steps down and look at them individually, the process becomes much easier to understand.

Setting up a vendor

When you set up a vendor, you are determining the individuals or companies that are providing you with products. Sometimes, vendors are also referred to as suppliers. In Odoo, it is perfectly possible to create a product and sell it without implementing a purchasing system. However, to begin using your system for purchasing, you will need to configure the vendors.

The steps you take to set up a vendor are much the same as setting up a customer. In fact, now is as good a time as any to tell you that Odoo maintains core customer, employee, and vendor records all in the same model (or table), named `res.partner`. Odoo distinguishes between customers, vendors, and those who are both, with the use of the **Is a Customer** and **Is a Vendor** checkboxes.

Setting up warehouse locations

Once you have decided to start using Odoo to purchase your products, you will need to set up locations to receive them. In a simple small business, you may only have one location, but other companies may have literally hundreds of warehouse locations. In Odoo, each location can maintain its own address, and it is possible to create nested sub-locations for better management and reporting of inventory.

Generating quotations and purchase orders

To acquire the raw product, you will need to create **Request for Quotations** and/or **Purchase Orders** to send to your vendors. In purchasing, these are the documents you create that tell the vendors which products you require, the quantity in which you require them, and what you expect to pay for those products. Often, this process is referred to as **procurement**. Depending on the industry and the specific location of the company, it is possible that there might be a variety of methods to manage quotations and approvals when purchasing products.

Receiving the product

In a simple purchasing workflow, once your purchase order has been received by the vendor, you will be waiting for them to fulfill the order. At some point, you will receive the product. Depending on your industry, this could be the same day or can even stretch to months. When the delivery is complete, you receive the products and they will move into the location you select. Now that the product has been received, you are ready to create a manufacture order. But first, let's pay the vendor for what we ordered.

Settling the invoice

Once you have received the product, it is just a matter of time before you must pay for it. Invoicing can happen at the time you order the product, before the product is shipped to you, or after you have received the product. Regardless of when you get an invoice, you can be sure that if you are receiving products, you will eventually be invoiced for them.

When an invoice is received, it is essential to compare it to the purchase order for accuracy. Any discrepancies between the purchase order and invoice must be resolved before the invoice is paid. Essentially, this is your way of ensuring that you are only paying for the products you have authorized for purchase. Finally, it is good practice to match the receiving or delivery order to the purchase order and invoice as well. This *three-way match* ensures that you get exactly what you ordered, and that the invoice reflects exactly what you are required to pay.

Installing the purchasing application

Odoo is a modular set of applications in which you only install the applications you need. Therefore, we must install the **Purchase Management** application to continue. By this point, you should be familiar with the process of installing a new application to Odoo. The following is a screenshot of the **Purchase Management** application in the **Apps** list:

When you install the purchasing application, you will get two new menus:

- Purchases
- Inventory

It is possible that these menus may already exist, or that purchasing may already be installed if you have installed another module, such as eCommerce, that requires **Purchase Management** as a dependency.

The **Purchases** menu is where you can create quotations and purchase orders for the products you purchase from your vendors. In the **Inventory** menu, you can manage physical inventories. If you take a few moments to look through the menus, you will notice you can access some of the same features from both menus. For example, you can get to the **Products** view from either menu.

Setting up your first vendor

To begin setting up your first vendor, you should select **Purchase | Vendors** and click on **Create**:

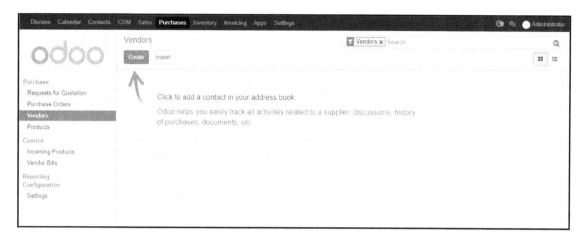

This is the **Vendors** listing, but as it is empty, you will see instructions on how you can add a new vendor. Odoo also lists a few of the features that you can expect from vendor management, such as tracking discussions, purchase history, and documents associated with a vendor.

After clicking **Create**, Odoo will bring up the vendor form for you to fill out:

This form is very much like the customer form because it is based on the same basic structure. In fact, it is perfectly acceptable for a customer to also be a vendor. When you create a new vendor record, a vendor checkbox is automatically marked for you under the **Sales & Purchases** page on the form. Sometimes, this can get a little confusing for people new to Odoo. This chapter will start to make the relationships between companies, contacts, customers, and vendors in Odoo clearer.

Designating vendor as Individual or Company

Much like when you set up a customer, the **Individual** and **Company** options at the very top of the form are where you inform Odoo of the relationship you have with this vendor. Typically, you will be purchasing products from a company.

For our example, we will choose the **Company** option.

Once you've filled in the vendor name, address, and other contact information, as well as the required accounting information, click **Save** at the top of the form.

Configuring your product for procurement

When we set up our first product, we were only concerned with selling the product to a customer. We essentially named the product and set the price at which we wish to sell it. To purchase the product from our vendor, we must provide a little more information. To do this, we will edit the product and change the information under the **Inventory** tab.

Go to **Purchase** | **Products**, then click on the option for `Medium White T-Shirt` to bring up the product form. Then, click **Edit** to enter edit mode.

The following is a screenshot of the **Inventory** section of the product form:

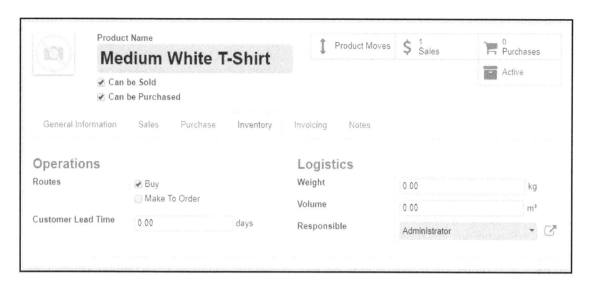

At the top of the form, check **Can be Purchased** so that the purchasing system knows to include this product in the list of products when you make a purchase order.

Supply chain information

By default, Odoo sets up two of the most common routes. These routes are **Buy** and **Make to Order**. For purchasing, we must check the **Buy** checkbox so that Odoo can properly route the products we purchase from our vendor to our internal warehouse location.

Using buy routes

When you configure a buy route, you can purchase products in one of two ways. One of the ways to purchase this product would be to create a purchase order and add the product to the purchase order manually. This is the typical manual purchasing system, where a purchase agent perhaps uses other events outside Odoo or examines reports in Odoo to create purchase orders.

In addition to creating manual purchase orders, you can also create re-ordering rules that will automatically create draft purchase orders when the stock of the product dips below a set minimum. This method works well on products that are ordered frequently, and frees your purchasing managers from having to manually create purchase orders for some or even most of your inventory.

Using Make to Order

When you configure a make to order route, you are telling Odoo that you wish for draft purchase orders to be created when a sales order includes that specific product, regardless of the stock you have on hand. For example, even if you had 2,000 of a product in stock and a customer orders 10 of that product, Odoo will create a draft purchase order for 10 units if you have the **Make To Order** route checked.

Often, a business would use the make to order option when they do not need to keep stock of a product, and instead will either manufacture or purchase the product for reselling once a sales order is confirmed. It is certainly possible to use a combination of buy and make to order with re-ordering limits to set up a system in that you always keep a minimum quantity in stock, but a draft purchase order is created for sales orders which include that product. Remember, draft orders can always be canceled, so depending on the processes in your purchasing department, it may be desirable for them to get make to order purchase drafts even if they wish to maintain their own minimum and maximum limits within Odoo.

Purchasing information

In addition to the changes under the **Procurement** tab, there are also a few changes we need to make under the **General Information** page on the product form:

Product type

When you configure purchasing, you will want to pay special attention to product type. For this example, we have chosen **Stockable Product** because we wish to manage the inventory of the product and perhaps sell directly to the customer. Alternatively, you can choose a consumable product type. This would be a good choice for products you don't wish to manage in inventory and just plan to purchase and use, such as office supplies or coffee filters for the break room.

Setting the cost price of the product

Often, you will wish to assign a cost to the product. This will be the cost that will appear on your purchase quotations, though it can be overwritten at any time to reflect a vendor's new pricing. If your vendor happens to give you a one-time discount, you will want to reflect that change on the actual purchase order, rather than here in the base product record. For our example, we have set the cost price of the shirt to 7.25.

Assigning vendors to the product

You can use the **Purchase** tab to bring up the list of vendors for the product. It is very common that a company may have multiple vendors that offer the same product.

Click on **Add an Item** in the vendor grid to add the vendor to the product:

Establishing the vendor

You have the choice in the drop-down list to search for vendors, as well as to create and edit a new vendor on the fly. To the far right of the drop-down, you can use the small icon to edit the current vendor. In the pop-down, we have selected **T-Shirt Supply Co**. as the company to provide our blank `Medium White T-shirts`.

Designating the vendor product name and product code

Because a vendor may use different product codes or product names than your company does to describe a given product, here you have the option to specify how the vendor identifies the product. This information will be displayed on the purchase quotations and purchase orders you create to make sure you get the right product from the vendor.

Setting minimum quantity

Vendors will often have a minimum order quantity for a product. Sometimes, vendors may actually sell you a lower quantity, but the cost per unit is dramatically higher. Setting a minimum quantity in this form allows you to prevent those problems by forcing purchase quantities to be at least the minimum quantity value. For our example, we will set the minimum quantity to `12`.

Calculating delivery time

Depending on the vendor, a product may take more or less time to obtain. Often, this can make a difference when you are putting together a time-sensitive purchase quotation. A product may be cheaper, but if the delay is too long and puts the delivery time in jeopardy, you may need to buy the product at a higher price from another vendor who can deliver the product faster. Setting the delivery time in days for the vendor to deliver the product provides your purchasing agents with the information they require to make decisions based on price and availability. For our example, we have set the delivery time to `4 days`.

Setting price and validity

Now, in Odoo 11 you can also specify the price for the item from that specific vendor. This simplifies managing your vendor pricing. When you select the given item for a specific vendor, you will get the price you have specified here. Optionally, you can specify validity dates, so that you can proactively manage products when suppliers bring on new products or perhaps discontinue a product.

Creating your first purchase quotation

Now that we have our vendor entered and the product associated with the vendor, we are ready to create our first **Request for Quotation** (**RFQ**). This is typically the document you will create when requesting pricing from a vendor (sometimes called a supplier) prior to actually ordering the product. For our example, we are going to create a request for quotation for one dozen Medium White T-Shirts.

Go to **Purchase** | **Requests for Quotation** and click on **Create** to make a new RFQ:

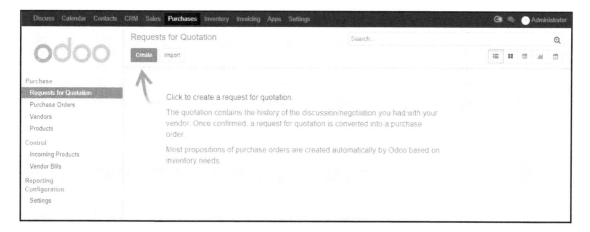

After you click on **Create**, the RFQ will appear for you to enter the required information:

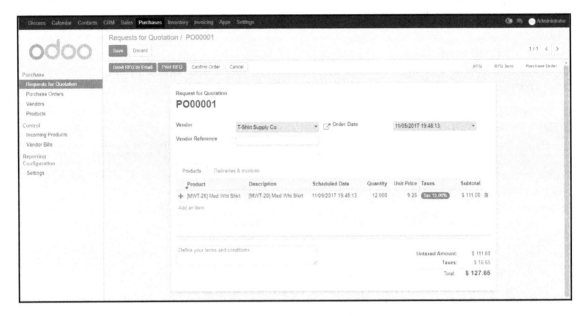

RFQ

When you first create the request for quotation, the order date will be automatically populated with the current date. You can then select the vendor you wish for the RFQ, as well as include an optional vendor reference and source document. An example of a source document would be a sales order number that triggered the purchase order process.

Adding products to your request for quotation

After you click **Add an Item**, you can select the product from the drop-down list on the far left. The description will automatically be filled in. The scheduled date will be determined based on the delivery delay from the vendor. We also find the minimum order quantity from the vendor has been pulled to the RFQ. Finally, the unit cost is populated from the vendor unit cost we specified.

Printing RFQs and updating status

For now, we will skip the **Deliveries & Invoices** and go right to printing our RFQ. By default, Odoo will print to a PDF file. This file can easily be attached to emails. Once you have configured an email server, you can configure Odoo to automatically send the purchase order by email.

Confirming a purchase order

Once you have a final quotation, you are ready to confirm the purchase order. It is very important to understand that once you have confirmed, it becomes a purchase order and it can no longer be modified. Once you are sure you wish to finalize the purchase order, click the **Confirm Order** button. Any modifications that need to be made at this stage would require you to duplicate and cancel the original order. This is necessary so that Odoo can maintain an audit trail.

 If you happen to receive an error message reading **No Expense Account** when you attempt to confirm the order, check your settings for your chart of accounts. You must have an expense account designated for the products contained on the PO.

The following screenshot shows an example of a confirmed purchase order:

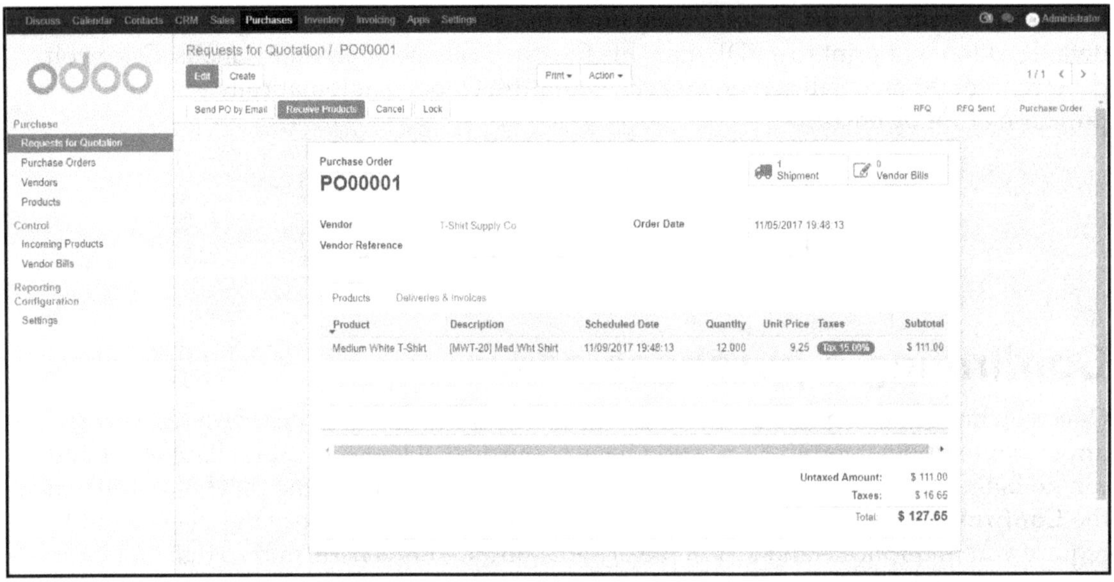

A confirmed purchase order

Once you have confirmed, the form will refresh to show the new status of the purchase order. At this point, you are waiting on the vendor to deliver the products and send you an invoice. The status is updated to **Purchase Order** and is now just one step from the **Done** condition.

After clicking **Confirm**, you will notice in the upper-right corner that we can see there is one incoming shipment. Each of these is an active button that you can click to see the corresponding shipments or invoices associated with this purchase order.

Receiving products

If everything goes as planned, the products we have ordered will be arriving within four days or less. Once the products have arrived, we must receive our products into inventory.

Click **Receive Products** to bring up the **Receiving** form:

Inventory / Silkworm: Receipts / WH/IN/00001

| Edit | Create | | Print ▾ | Action ▾ | | | | | 1 / 1 | ‹ | › |

| Validate | Print | Cancel | Unlock | | | | Draft | Waiting | Ready | Done |

WH/IN/00001

| Partner | T-Shirt Supply Co | Scheduled Date | 11/09/2017 19:48:13 |
| | | Source Document | PO00001 |

Operations Additional Info

| Product | Initial Demand | Done |
| Medium White T-Shirt | 12.000 | 0.000 |

Getting ready to receive

At this point, we have not actually received the product yet. This is just showing us the details on the product that we are ready to receive. The **WH/IN/00001** is sequentially assigned for each transaction.

> Please be aware that it is possible the transaction name **WH/IN/000001** may be different in your installation, as Odoo changes the sequences that are defined in a default installation from time to time. These names can be user-configured by going to **Settings | Sequences & Identifiers | Sequences**. You could even change the default prefix from **PO** to whatever you desire, as long as it does not conflict with the prefix of another module.

The **WH** in the name is short for warehouse and the **IN** is short for incoming goods. When we are receiving products into inventory, we are creating an inventory transaction. You can see the associated purchase order under the **Source Document** field on the right side of the form. We can also see the actual time the order was received compared to the scheduled time of the order. In this case, we can see we received the order in plenty of time.

Receiving our goods

By editing the transfer and changing the value in the **Done** column, you can specify an alternate quantity if what you have received does not match the quantity on the purchase order. For this example, we will assume that the entire product arrived as expected.

When you click the **Validate** button near the top of the form, you will get a confirmation to receive the quantity that was on the purchase order:

Once you click **Apply**, the quantity in the **Done** column matches the **To do** quantity; the product is now in inventory. Since all of the products on this purchase order have been received, the purchase order status at the top right is set to **Done**. Finally, you will notice the **Reverse** button that is available for instances in which you need to manage product returns:

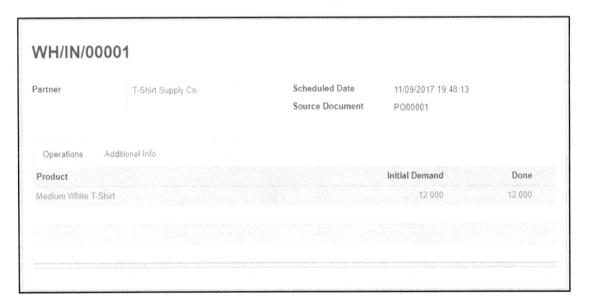

If you would like to verify that your goods have been received into inventory, look up the `Medium White T-Shirt` under **Products** and click on the **Inventory** tab. You should notice its quantity on hand increased by 12 units. Odoo automatically adjusts stock levels as products are received into your company's inventory. Likewise, stock levels are decremented if products are returned to their vendor.

Handling Back Orders

Sometimes for various reasons you will not receive all the product you have ordered. For the products that have not arrived it is common to designate them as being on back order. You will be prompted to create a back order whenever you enter less into the Done column than the Initial Demand column.

Below you can see the form that lets you decide how to handle receipts that do match the initial quantity you ordered.

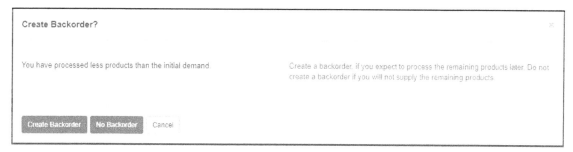

Clicking Create Back Order will create another receiving ticket with the remaining quantity. If however you wish not to expect the missing quantity you can click No Back Order and instead the remaining products will be canceled.

After a back order is created you can see it referenced within the list view so you know always how the back order is tied to the original order. In the example below we can tell that the receipt reference WH/IN/00003 was created because we didn't receive all the items in receipt WH/IN/00002. We can also see that both receiving tickets, which are recorded as Transfers within Odoo, are from purchase order PO00002

Insert image_ B08599_04_26.png

Also, you can continue to create additional back orders from back orders. For example, if all of the remaining items don't come in for a back order you can just receive less items and another back order will be created.

Paying vendor bills

Once you have received your product, sooner or later you should receive a bill. This is often called a supplier or vendor invoice. It is of course possible to receive a bill before you receive products. Each business will have to decide the exact workflow for when they pay bills, and under what conditions.

To create a vendor bill, go to the **Invoicing** menu and select **Purchases | Documents | Vendor Bills**:

Vendor bill

Click **Create** to bring up the **Vendor Bills** form.

In the workflow, the user should now have received the vendor bill either electronically, by mail, or in another form that they need to pay. Use the **Vendor** drop-down menu to select the vendor.

Next, use the **Add Purchase Order** drop-down menu to select the purchase order **PO00001 : $ 100.05** as the one we wish to pay:

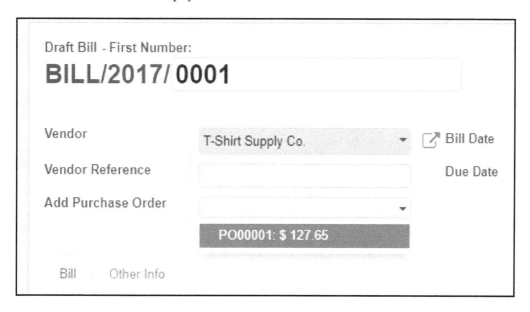

At this point, you will see all the necessary information from the purchase order, including the product, description amount, and tax:

From here, you can click **Validate** to create the bill. This will then leave the bill in an open status until you register a payment or ask for a refund.

So, let's pay this bill. Click on **Register Payment**:

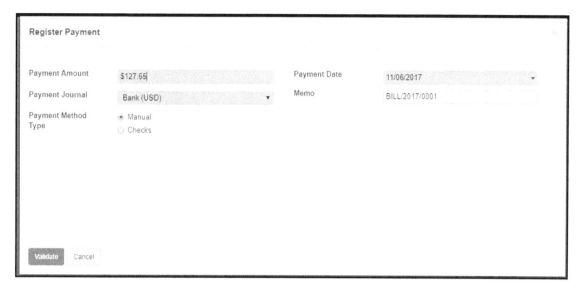

Most of the information will automatically be filled out, including **Payment Date** and **Payment Amount**. You can change these if necessary. The one piece of information you must provide is the **Payment Method**. For our example, we have chosen **Bank (USD)**.

The **Memo** can be used to create whatever note you wish to document this payment. For example, you can use the **Memo** field to specify the check number you use to pay your vendor.

 When implementing a purchase order system, it is critical to train users thoroughly on how transactions are tied together. While many forms allow you to click on a link to view a related record, fields like **Payment Ref** store the reference to the other document just as text. Train and encourage users to quickly use copy-and-paste rather than re-entering data into search fields.

Odoo will allow you to configure multiple payment methods. For now, choose **Bank** and click **Validate** to complete the transaction.

You have now completed the entire purchasing cycle from purchasing, to receiving, to finally paying for the product:

In the prior screenshot, you can see the final paid invoice for our purchased products. Notice at the bottom right of the form it shows that we have a balance of zero. Now, we can also see a summary of the payment by hovering over the little information icon above the amount due.

Handling Complex Units of Measure

By default, all the products you enter in to Odoo use the same unit of measure, units. Often however you will find a need to purchase and sell products in alternate unit of measure. Silkworm has some products they purchase which come in cases. For example, they may need to purchase cases of coffee mugs they will sell as individual units in their retail stores. Let's see how we can configure Odoo to handle complex units of measures.

You turn on complex unit of measures by going to the Sales menu, then under Configuration choosing Settings.

Settings

On the far right you have the option Units of Measure. Check this option to allow multiple units of measure in Odoo. Click Save to confirm the change.

Looking at the defined Unit of Measures

Odoo provides you many pre-defined units of measure that are some of the most common. Click Units of Measure to see a list of the units of measure you can use for your products.

For our real-world example, let's assume we are going to purchase in Dozen(s). This means that if we purchase one unit of a product that has a unit of measure of Dozen(s) that you will receive 12 individual units. If you purchase 2 Dozen(S) then you will receive 24 individual units. You can then choose to sell the product either by Dozen(s) or by individual units.

Examining a specific Unit of Measure

Let's examine the unit of measure configuration for Dozen(s) by clicking it.

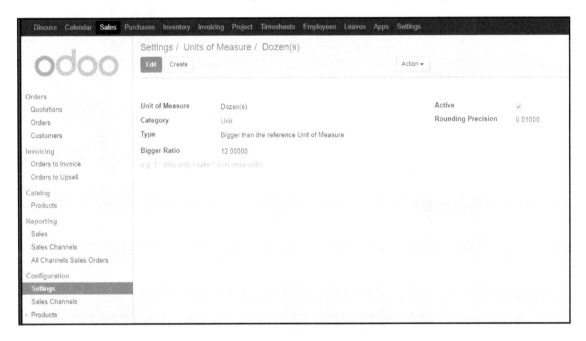

At the top we can see the name of our Unit of Measure, Dozen(s). Odoo performs the calculations that are based on a reference Unit of Measure. In this case, the reference unit of is Unit. The Type is used to specify if the Unit of Measure is smaller or bigger than the reference. Because Dozen(s) is the larger unit, we choose Bigger than the reference Unit of Measure for our calculations. The Bigger Ratio is then specified as 12 because there are 12 to a dozen.

Examine existing Unit of Measures and their relationships to help you better understand how to create your own custom configurations.

Configuring the Product to purchase in Dozen(s)

Click Products under Catalog and Create a new product.

Create a new product

Here you can see that we have setup a product Coffee Mugs. Most important in this example is that we have left Unit of Measure as Unit(s) but have changed our Purchase Unit of Measure to Dozen(s).

With this configuration when you issue a purchase order you specify what you order by dozen(s). When you sell the product, you specify the quantity in individual units.

Understanding costing methods and inventory valuation

When you purchase and sell products there are various methods in which you can track your costs and the overall value of your inventory. By default, Odoo uses the standard cost of your product that you specify for all calculations. With this method, if you change the cost in the product record you can re-run your reports and see the change reflected.

Many times, however you want the ability to track your product purchases and sales more accurately using a removal strategy. Typically, this is either FIFO (First in First Out) or LIFO (Last in Last Out). In FIFO operations the first product you purchase is the first product you sell. This affects your costing and inventory valuation because you may have purchased products at different prices and you may have also sold products at different prices.

A full explanation of inventory valuation and costing is beyond the scope of this book.

Setting up costing in Odoo

In Odoo, removal strategies and costing methods are specified at the product category level. This means that you could have one set of products that use standard costing while another uses a FIFO strategy. Let's see how to setup a FIFO strategy for our coffee mugs.

Go to the Inventory menu then under Configuration choose Products->Product Categories.

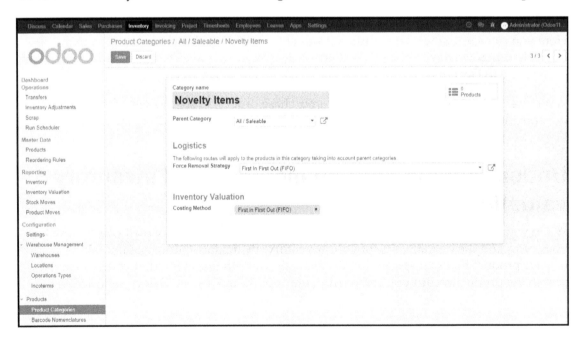

Product Categories

Here we see that we have setup a category Novelty Items that has the Parent Category of All / Saleable. Under Logistics we have chosen the First in First Out option. Finally, under Inventory Valuation we have chosen First in First Out (FIFO) for our Costing Method.

After clicking Save you can then assign the Coffee Mugs product to the Novelty Items category.

If you watched carefully, you will notice that an Inventory Valuation option appears once you assign Coffee Mugs to the Novelty Items category. Now it will be up to you to take the time experimenting with various removal strategies and costing methods. Create purchase order and sales orders and see how they affect your inventory valuation and other reports.

Odoo offers a nice little resource for seeing the various costing strategies and how they affect various report calculations. It can be found here: `https://www.odoo.com/documentation/functional/valuation.html`

Summary

In this chapter, we installed the purchasing application and set up a vendor to purchase products. Next, we successfully purchased products and received those products into inventory. After our products were received into inventory, we proceeded to pay the invoice to complete the payment cycle.

In the next chapter, we will take the raw materials we have just received into inventory and use them to manufacture and deliver a finished product. We will create manufacturing orders to define the steps of the production process and allocate the required resources. Coordinating all of your resources, including machinery and manpower, can be a daunting and time-consuming task, but we are learning how Odoo makes this significantly more manageable.

Making Goods with Manufacturing Resource Planning

5

In this chapter, we will cover how you can use Odoo to manage the process of manufacturing products. Once you have received the required raw products in your inventory, you can begin manufacturing the end product. Part of the functionality of an ERP system is to assist you in scheduling these orders, based on available resources. One of the resources is, of course, the raw product. Other resources could include available labor or the availability of a particular machine. Essentially, the goal is to schedule the manufacturing order at a time when all the resources are available and produce the product for on-time delivery.

In this chapter, we will cover the following topics:

- Setting up the manufacturing process
- Defining our bill of materials
- Manufacturing our final product
- Analyzing the inventory report

What's new in Odoo 11?

Like many of the other applications, Odoo 11's manufacturing application is more streamlined and easier to use when it is first installed. More complex operations such as work orders and routings are hidden until you turn them on.

Creating manufacturing orders

Manufacturing orders define the product you wish to build, the resources required, and when you wish to produce the product. The resources often include raw products or ingredients that are created by a bill of materials. A bill of materials is essentially a list of products and the quantity required to produce the final product.

Producing the product

When it is time to produce the product, you then inform Odoo of each of the products produced, and your manufacturing order changes to a status of **Complete**. In a typical workflow, your raw materials are moved out of the inventory, and your finished product is added into your inventory.

Delivering the order

After a product has been produced and has been put into the inventory, it can be packaged and delivered to the customer. Depending on the specific manufacturing environment, a product may not even sit in a physical inventory location at all, and instead may be shipped almost immediately to the customer. Meanwhile, in another industry, you may have a product that is produced and then sits in a warehouse for months before delivery. Of course, it is always possible that something gets produced and gets left in dead stock. In this case, you would never have a delivery order and instead use a process to determine how to manage that dead inventory.

Defining the workflow for your business

Much like configuring the CRM application, often the most complex part of setting up a purchasing and manufacturing system is not the ERP software itself. Instead, the real challenge is to understand the business requirements and how the current processes can best be implemented. If you have never set up a purchasing and manufacturing system before, it is highly recommended that you supplement your knowledge with additional source material on the subject.

A real-world example of producing a custom printed T-shirt

In Odoo, you manufacture products by creating manufacturing orders. For our example, we will be printing T-shirts that have a custom-designed logo. The basic manufacturing process itself involves using a screen to apply ink to each of the T-shirts. For now, we don't need to know all the details of this process to begin using Odoo to help schedule and track the manufacturing of the product.

The basic steps in the process are simple:

1. Define a bill of materials that determine what items are needed to produce the final product
2. Use a manufacturing order to print a design on the blank T-shirts
3. Deliver the printed T-shirts to a customer

Installing Manufacturing Resource Planning

We must now install the **Manufacturing Resource Planning** (MRP) application so that we can begin configuring our T-shirt production. By now, you should have begun to understand the modular nature of Odoo. Install the MRP applications just like you did with the other Odoo applications:

Choose **Apps** and install the MRP application:

Clicking the **Install** button installs the MRP application.

Creating your first manufacturing order

The flexibility of Odoo provides a variety of approaches that you can take in setting up your system. Manufacturing can also become a complex topic and is one of the more challenging aspects of setting up any ERP system. For our first manufacturing order, we will ignore many advanced options.

 Keep it simple at first. There are many options and it will take time to understand them all. If you are new to manufacturing systems, it will take you longer to implement Odoo, and you should consider hiring professional consultants to assist you.

To create your first manufacturing order, go to the **Manufacturing** menu, choose **Manufacturing Orders**, and then click **Create**:

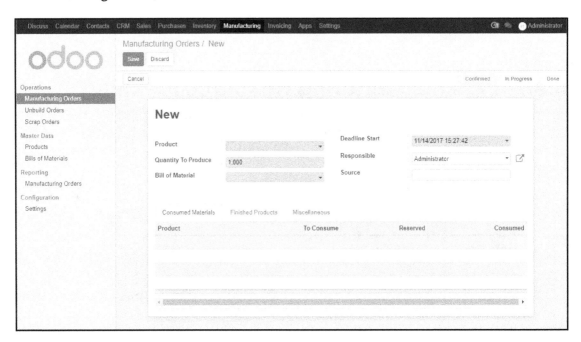

This is the manufacturing order as it appears just after you have hit **Create**.

Take a minute to look through the various tabs and get an idea of the information that is collected for a manufacturing order. Don't worry if you don't understand all the options yet. We will begin with a simple product and look at some of the most important aspects of creating a manufacturing order. Later, we will explore some of the more complex manufacturing scenarios.

What product are we going to manufacture?

The only product we have entered into Odoo so far is the medium white T-shirt, which is blank. Nothing is printed on the T-shirt when it is received from the supplier. Now, we want to create a manufacturing order that will produce a new product in which we print on the T-shirt a design of the customer's choice.

For our operations, we can still use the medium white T-shirt. But now, instead of selling the blank T-shirt directly to our customer, it will be used as a raw material for our manufacturing order.

Let's first configure the final product that is to be created during the manufacturing process, that is, the complete T-shirt with the final design that will ship to the customer. For our example, it will be a `Class of 2017 T-shirt`.

Odoo allows you the ability in most forms, where it is appropriate, to create a product on the-fly. Let's create a product by clicking the drop-down arrow in the **Product** tab, and choosing **Create and Edit...**:

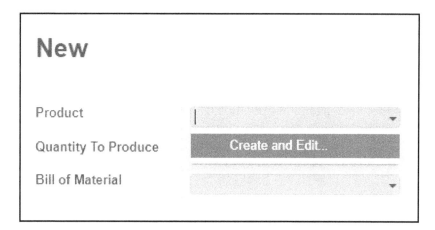

Using the quick **Create and Edit...**, you can add your finished products directly when creating a manufacturing order. In some workflows, where you may use a separate system for handling sales orders, this option can be a fast way to create the required finished products to push into the inventory.

Next, you will fill out the product form with the fields required for a finished product:

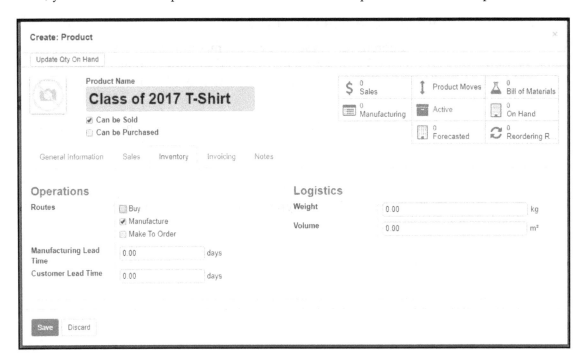

The **General Information** and **Inventory** tabs should look familiar by now. Starting in Odoo 9, Odoo provided routes that allowed a lot of flexibility in defining complex workflows and supply management operations. Fortunately, the more common routes are already configured, and we can check **Manufacture** to let Odoo manufacturing know that this product is part of the manufacturing workflow. Only products that have the supply method of **Manufacture** can be selected as a product on a manufacture order.

Please also notice at the top of the form that the **Can be Purchased** box is unchecked. This will keep this product from appearing in the product list on a purchase order. Since we cannot purchase this product directly from a supplier, we don't want it appearing in our product list when working within purchasing.

Building your Bill of Materials

A **Bill of Materials** (**BOM**), is essentially a list of products that are required to produce another product. You can think of it like the list of ingredients for a recipe. Odoo needs to know what materials are required for us to produce this `Class of 2017 T-shirt` product.

In complex products, a bill of materials can be nested. For example, it may take many products to make a sub-product, and then several sub-products to make a final product.

 Don't let nested BOMs intimidate you. Once you understand how a simple BOM is processed, you will more easily see how you can group parts together. Think about grouping more complex BOMs by assembly and workcenters. This makes it easier to see your inventory in real time, as BOMs can be processed at each stage of your operations, properly using up materials and creating finished sub-assemblies.

For our first BOM example, we will be keeping it simple. We are just going to require the white T-shirt. The rest of the operation, printing the actual T-shirt, will be incorporated into the manufacturing order. In other words, if there are enough white T-shirts, this manufacturing order can be processed, and we can produce the final product. For now, the inks and screens will not be managed in the manufacturing process. This is an example of starting simple and adding more complexity as we build up the system.

A smart button at the top right of the form shows you a count of BOMs attached to this product:

Clicking this button will bring up the bill of materials listing for that product:

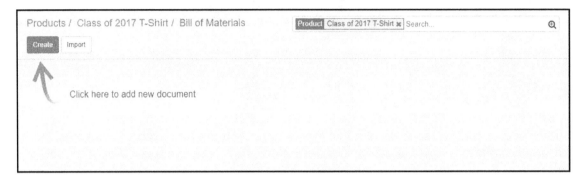

Naturally this is a blank list, as we have not yet defined any bill of materials for this product. Notice in the top-right corner the product filter that is restricting this list view to only display the **Bill of Materials** that are for the Class of 2017 T-shirt.

Clicking **Create** will now bring up a blank **Bill of Materials** form with the Class of 2017 T-shirt automatically pre-populated as the finished product to build:

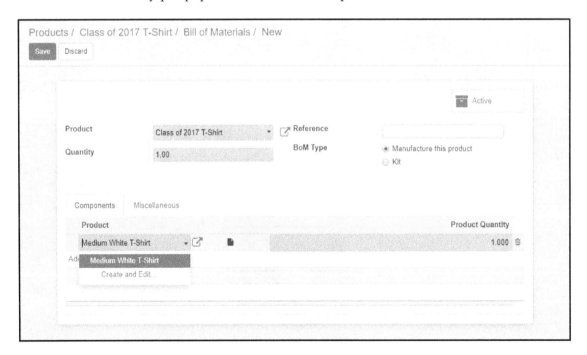

Many of the fields will be automatically filled out as Odoo knows we are creating a bill of materials for our `Class of 2017 T-Shirt` product. In this example, we have added the **Medium White T-Shirt** to the bill of materials. When we manufacture one `Class of 2017 T-Shirt`, we will require one medium white T-shirt.

Many times, if not most of the time, a bill of materials will contain multiple items. Regardless of the number of items in the bill of materials, the way they are processed is the same.

 It is possible that your manufacturing order or bill of materials screen may look slightly different than the ones you see here. One reason is that, depending on the modules that are installed and what options are selected, the forms may have different content. Another common reason is that Odoo is currently getting frequent updates that can change the appearance of a given form.

Confirming production

Once you click **Confirm Production**, you are ready to manufacture the product. Odoo will provide reasonable defaults, which you can override as required. When production is confirmed, that does not mean that production has taken place. Confirming production has only informed the system that production is ready to proceed. You can tell we are ready to begin manufacturing because the **Produce** button is available.

Here is what our `Class of 2017 T-Shirt` **Manufacturing Order** looks like now:

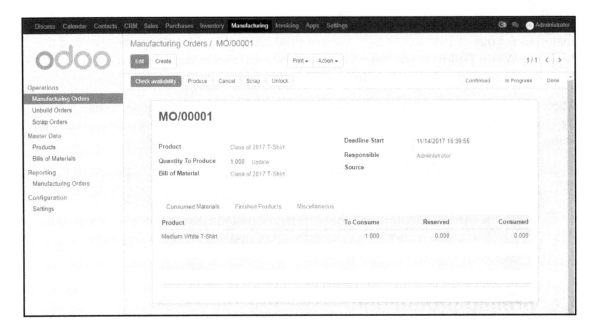

This is the manufacturing form showing the products waiting to be consumed to produce the order. In this case, it is our **Medium White T-Shirt**. You will also notice that this item is in red, and at the top of the form you can see the warning **Raw materials not available!** This informs us that we must check the availability of our raw goods before we can begin manufacturing this product.

Checking availability

Odoo manufacturing links into the inventory automatically and it will use available stock to complete the order. As we have already purchased **Medium White T-Shirts** in the previous chapter, clicking the **Check Availability** button will hide the button and remove the red highlight on the **Medium White T-Shirt**, as well as remove the material warning message.

Please be aware that at this stage, if you don't have an available quantity, Odoo will continue to display the **Check Availability** button and the warning message until the product is acquired and put into the inventory. Each time you click **Check Availability**, Odoo will look in the inventory to see whether we have the necessary products to complete the manufacturing order. Alternatively, you can click **Produce** to identify to Odoo manufacturing that you are ready to produce this product, even if the inventory within the system does not meet the necessary requirements. Note that doing this will give you negative inventory quantities in your warehouse.

After the raw product has been acquired and we are ready to produce our final product, the form will be updated and the state changed:

Here, we can see in the grid the quantity of **Medium White T-Shirt** available, the amount we will consume in the manufacturing order, and finally the total that will be consumed once the order is complete.

Producing the product

After you click the **Produce** button, you will be prompted to confirm that the product has been produced:

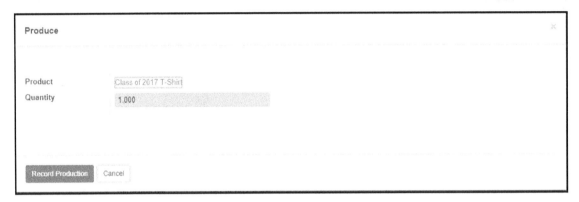

In Odoo 11, the production wizard has been simplified to ask only for the quantity of finished goods you wish to produce. For our example, we will leave the quantity set to one unit.

Click the **Record Production** button to produce the product:

The product has then been produced and is ready to be posted into the inventory. If, at this stage, you go and look at the product record, you will not see any **Class of 2017 T-Shirt** on hand. At this stage, you can click the **Mark as Done** button and Odoo will both post the inventory and mark the manufacturing order as done. Alternatively, you could click the **Post Inventory** button to add the **Class of 2017 T-Shirt** to the inventory, and then use a separate step to click the **Mark as Done** button to move the order to the **Done** state.

Congratulations, you have just used Odoo to manufacture your first product!

Analyzing stock valuation

In our example, we have taken a raw material and increased its value by producing a finished product. One of the easiest ways to see the effect of our manufacturing order is to look at the inventory valuation report, which can be found at **Inventory | Inventory Valuation**.

Here, you will see that we now have one **Class of 2017 T-Shirt** and eleven medium white T-shirts. The inventory is accurately reflecting the purchases made by us, as well as the products consumed and produced by our manufacturing order.

Unlike previous versions of Odoo, in the Odoo 11 community edition, the valuation does not let you drill down into details from the report.

Managing production by work orders

This first manufacturing order was very simple, and our bill of materials only contained one product. In many companies, the manufacturing operations are more complex. For example, in some instances, depending on the attributes of the product, the manufacturing could involve different work centers or alternative steps to produce the final product. By default, Odoo's manufacturing application takes a more simplified approach.

In Odoo 11, you must first turn on developer mode by going to **Settings** and then clicking the **Active the Developer Mode** link on the far right. Now, you can go to the user that needs to manage the work orders and select the appropriate option:

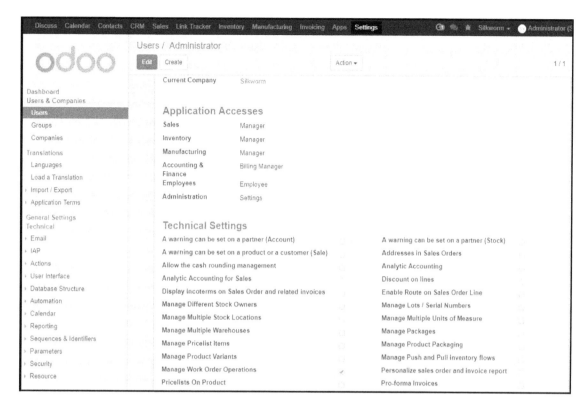

After you apply the changes, the menus will refresh, and new options will be added to the manufacturing application.

Sometimes when adding new functionality to Odoo, such as applications or modifying settings, it can be helpful to do a *Shift*+refresh in your browser to make sure Odoo is refreshed with the latest options.

Creating a work center

In our previous simplified manufacturing order, we specified the raw product required in a bill of materials, and then turned that into a finished product. Now, we will expand this example to specify the human labor that goes into printing our **Class of 2017 T-Shirt**. In Odoo, we define the parameters in a work center.

For our example, we will create a work center, `Printing`, that is responsible for taking the blank T-shirt and applying the design to create the final product. We begin by going to the manufacturing application, and under the **Master Data** menu, choosing the **Work Centers** option. Then, we click **Create** to set up a new work center record:

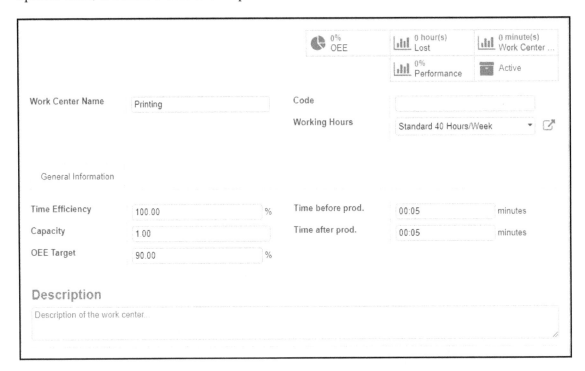

In our example, we have named the work center **Printing**. In a full implementation, it would be common to have different work centers based around the work performed. There is also an optional field for **Code**. This could be a short description that you use internally to designate a work center. **Working Hours** by default is set to **Standard 40 Hours/Week**.

Setting General Information

When defining a work center, it is possible to define **General Information** that will allow you to estimate the cost and time required to produce your products. In our example, we are going to configure this work center so that we can estimate the time required to produce a T-shirt.

Time Efficiency

Time Efficiency is a metric of how efficient this work center is at completing tasks. Often, the **Time Efficiency** is most valuable in allowing you to tweak your work center capacity without modifying requirements on the manufacturing order. If, for example, you have an efficiency factor of `200.00` (or `200` percent), then the work center will complete twice as many tasks. For our example, we are leaving the efficiency factor as the default of `1.00`, or `100%`.

Capacity

Capacity allows you to determine how many tasks the work center can do in parallel. For example, if you had a work center that could be configured with three workers and all three workers can complete a cycle at the same time, you could set the capacity per cycle to three. When a manufacturing order is then routed to the work center, the work center can complete three tasks at the same time. For our example, we will assume one worker, and therefore one capacity per cycle.

OEE target

In Odoo 11, the manufacturing application now places far more emphasis on tracking and reporting. A metric central to the information provided is **Overall Equipment Effectiveness** (**OEE**). This is essentially a calculation that determines what percentage of your manufacturing time is used in actual production. The closer this is to 100%, the more efficient use you are making of your resources. By setting a work center goal, you can determine how well your work center is meeting expectations.

Time before and after production

Many work center operations will have time required for setup and teardown times outside of the time consumed by actually producing the product. This is certainly true for our example. It takes time for someone to prepare a printing press with inks before the first T-shirt can be printed. For our example, we have estimated five minutes of setup time. Likewise, when we are done producing the last product in our work order, it takes time to clean up and prepare for the next job. In this example, we have estimated five minutes of time at the end of production for cleanup operations.

Creating routing orders

After defining a work center, you need to define a way to specify under which conditions you should use the work center. This is accomplished by defining routings. For our example, we are going to keep it simple and use routing to send our manufacture order to the printing work center for the finished product to be produced. In a real-world example, the job may use routings to go through many work center operations before the final product is produced.

To create a routing order, go to the **Manufacturing** application and choose **Routings** under the **Master Data** submenu. Click **Create** to bring up the new routing form:

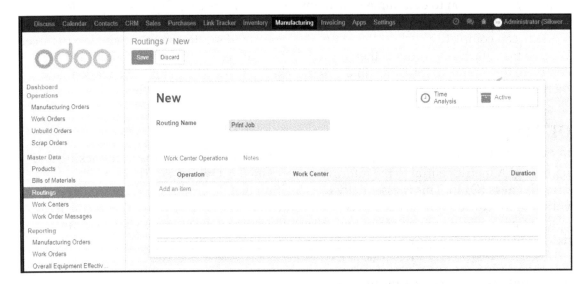

In our example, we have named the routing `Print Job`.

Next, we will define our work station operation by clicking **Add an Item** and bringing up the **Operation** form:

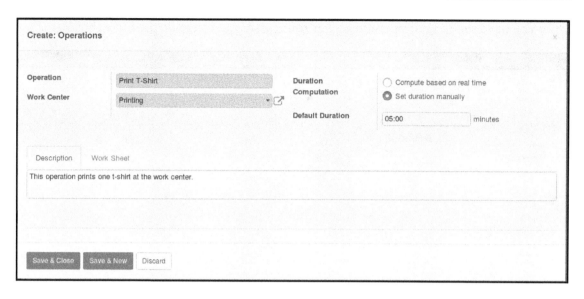

When defining our operation, we can name it whatever we wish, but in this case, I picked **Print T-Shirt**. This indicates that this operation is more specific than the simple **Print Job** we are assigning to the routing order.

For complex routings, you can specify the sequence of the operations. We could, for example, have a **Design** operation and a **Build Screen** operation before the print job operation. Then, we could specify a **Quality Assurance** operation and a **Packing** operation after the **Print Job**. You would handle all these exactly the same way you set up the printing work center and created the required operations to produce the product. By starting simple and adding additional operations and complexity over time, you can often get up and running much more quickly than trying to track every little task right from the beginning.

Once you have set up your operation, your routing should resemble the following form:

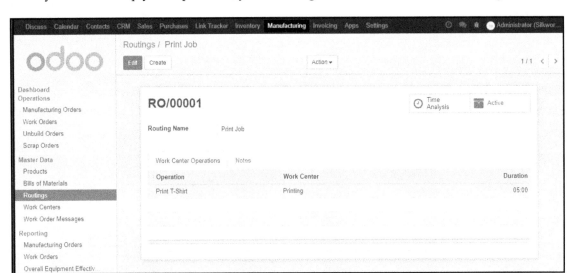

Here, we can see the finished routing along with the operation details.

Assigning the routing to a bill of materials

Now that we have created a routing, we need to tell the bill of materials to use our newly defined routing. In previous versions of Odoo, it was possible to assign a routing right on the work order. In Odoo 11, if you don't set up the routing on the bill of materials, it will not be available to you when you create a manufacturing order.

Pull up the **Bill of Materials** for our **Class of 2017 T-shirt** and set the routing to the **Print Job** we just created:

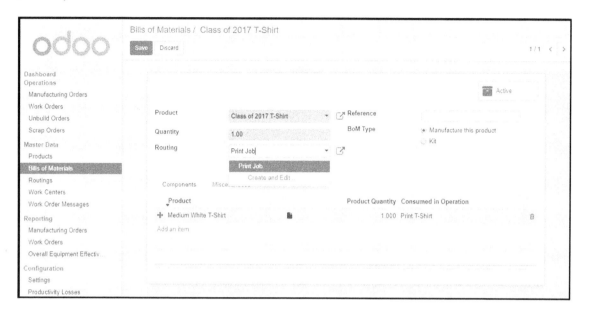

Creating a Manufacturing Order with routing and work center

Now that we have defined our work center and our routing operation, we can create a manufacturing order that will utilize our new production steps. In this example, we are going to produce fifteen **Class of 2017 T-Shirts**.

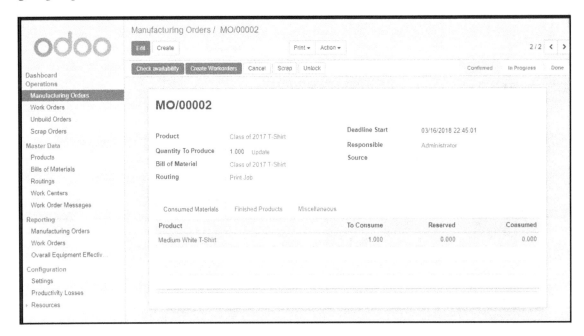

When we select the product, Odoo will now automatically assign the associated bill of materials for the product. You will notice in the manufacturing order that Odoo automatically selected **Print Job** for the routing of this order. This is the key field that will send this job to the printing work center to be produced.

When you click **Save**, you will notice that Odoo has not automatically created work orders. There is a separate button in Odoo 11 to trigger the creation of work orders.

Click the **Create Work orders** button to create the work order.

You can now go to the **Work Orders** option under **Operations** to view the work order in the default Kanban view:

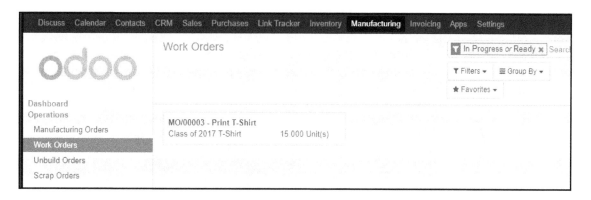

Clicking on the **Class of 2017 T-Shirt** would then bring up the work order for you to review:

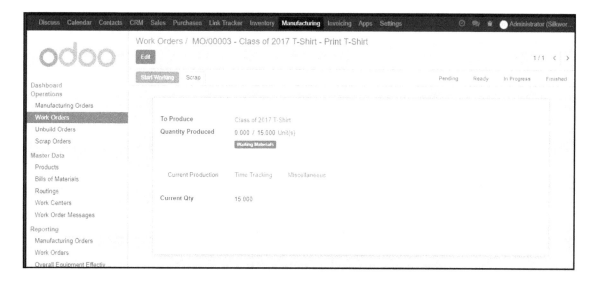

As you can see from the red **Waiting Materials** label, we are warned that we lack the materials to produce the product. Still, we can ignore this message and click the **Start Working** button at the top of the form to start producing the product. If you choose, you could use what you have learned in Chapter 4, *Purchasing with Odoo*, to purchase enough raw products to get rid of the **Waiting Materials** label.

At this point, Odoo considers this to be a real-time tracking system. That means that when your worker begins the job is when they should click the button. When the workers have completed the job, they should click the **Done** button. By implementing tablets or other workstations capable of running Odoo, you can create a manufacturing environment that automatically tracks the time of your operations.

If you click on the **Time Tracking** tab, you can see details on the current operations, as well as a timer that displays the updated duration of the operation in real time:

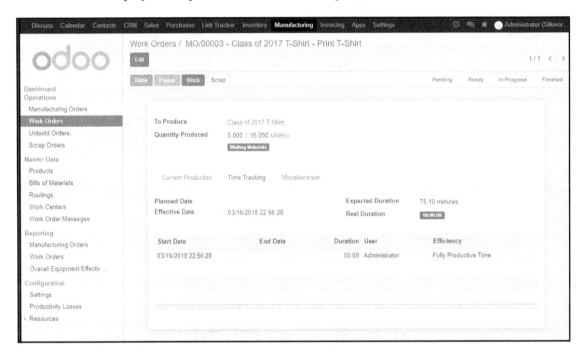

Now that you have had a chance to see the operation running, let's go ahead and click **Done** so we can see the results of our work in Odoo.

Odoo now refreshes the screen and moves the state of the workstation operation to **Done**. One thing that needs to be mentioned is that **Work Centers** can perform their operation, to completion regardless of the quantities in the inventory. This means that you would most likely have an internal process in which the worker would first check the availability of the manufacturing order before the worker even bothers to pull up the work order.

Let us now go and look at the manufacturing order:

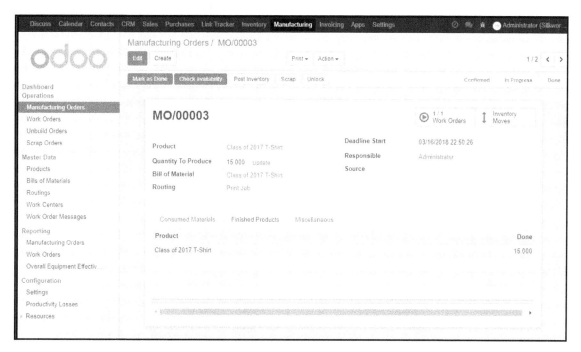

Here, we can see that because that was the only work order required to complete the manufacturing order, the **Finished Products** tab already shows the fifteen T-shirts as being produced. The order will continue to stay **In Progress** until you click the **Mark as Done** button. At that point, the **Manufacturing Order** will simply drop out of the list.

If you now go to your **Inventory Valuation**, you will see the results of these operations. Remember that, while we did not have enough inventory of the **Medium White T-shirts**, we went ahead and completed the work order anyway. Fortunately, Odoo keeps complete track of everything so we can properly reconcile the inventory later. We therefore see a negative number of **Medium White T-Shirts** in our inventory, as well as the sixteen **Class of 2017 T-shirts** produced from the two manufacturing orders in this chapter:

We have also set the cost of our **Medium White T-Shirts** to $5.00 and our **Class of 2017 T-Shirt** to $8.00 inside their respective product records. This allows us to calculate the value of our inventory. Next, we click **Attributes** and set up the variants we wish to use.

Creating routings based on product variants

Odoo allows you to create products that have variants. For example, we can have T-shirts that come in various sizes and colors. In manufacturing operations, it is common to require different processes based on variants of a product. Screen printing is no different. You may need to alternate the process if the shirt is white versus a shirt that is black or you may have a different press for large t-shirts as opposed to small t-shirts. Let's see how you can configure Odoo to change the routings based on product variants.

First, you must go into the **Sales** application and under **Settings,** check the **Attributes** and **Variants** options. Now, you can click **Attributes** to set up some variants for us to use for our example.

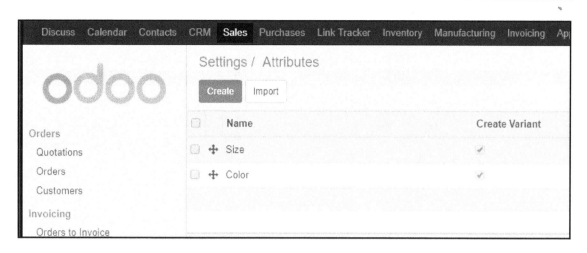

Now that we have set up our **Attributes**, we can go to our product and specify the variant values our product comes in. In this example, we have specified the shirt can come in **Black** or **White**:

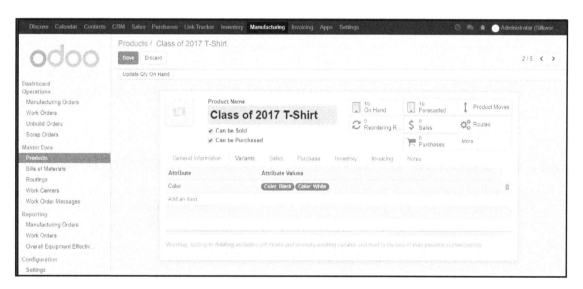

Now, we can configure a bill of materials and routing based on which color we need to produce:

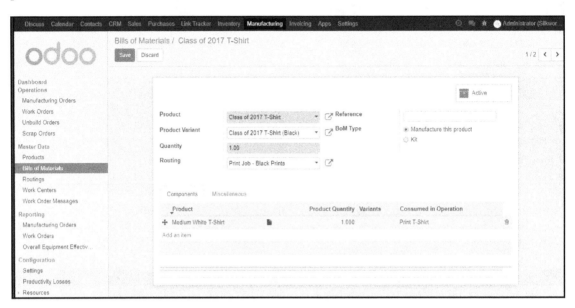

Notice how we were able to specify an alternate **Routing** for the **Black** product variant. Using this method, you can get a great deal of control over how you manage the production of your products.

Using Unbuild Orders or reverse bill of materials

Sometimes you have a situation in which you purchase products that then must be broken down and taken into inventory as their parts. One example may be a returned product that then you wish to disassemble back into its raw parts. Note that you must have an existing completed manufacturing order to create an **Unbuild Order**.

Here, we have created an **Unbuild Order** for a **Class of 2017 T-Shirt (Black)** manufacturing order:

Once you click the **Unbuild** button to confirm the order, the **White Medium T-shirt** used in the production of the original manufacturing order will be returned to the inventory.

Creating a kit using a bill of materials

Up to now, our **Bill of Materials** has been used to manufacture products. This process consumes the products in the bill of material to produce an all-new product. There is, however an entirely different way to use a Bill of Materials to create product kits. For example, let's say we have a **Fan Appreciation Bundle** that includes a **Hat**, **T-Shirt**, and three **Bumper Stickers**. When the customer purchases the **Fan Appreciation Bundle**, we don't want to create a new product, but instead want to ship the individual products to the customer.

Here, we have created a **Bill of Material** that has a kit with our example:

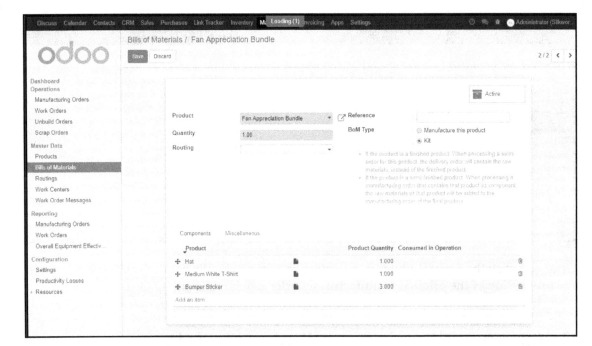

Notice that under **BoM Type**, we have chosen **Kit**. We can also see that Odoo provides a detailed explanation as to how it will handle the kits. As our example is a simple kit, the delivery order will simply contain the **Components** we have specified.

Summary

In this chapter, we installed the MRP application to begin setting up our manufacturing process. A bill of materials was created to define what products would be consumed when our product was manufactured. We manufactured our final product and looked at the inventory analysis report to verify our results. We then turned on the Work Center feature so we could explore how to set up work centers and routings to get more control over our manufacturing operations.

In the next chapter, we will take a closer look at accounting and other reporting options. Setting up your chart of accounts is an important step that we'll cover, as well as reviewing journal entries, creating invoices, and receiving payments. We will also be defining sales taxes and managing fiscal periods. Yes, there is a lot more to cover!

6
Configuring Accounting and Finance Options

One of the nice things about Odoo that is you can get up and running quickly, without having to spend a lot of time setting up complicated accounting and finance options. Odoo does a reasonable job of creating a basic chart of account structure as a starting point, helping you to get familiar with Odoo. When setting up a production system for your company, however, you will want to take the time to properly define your accounting requirements.

In this chapter, we will learn how to configure accounting in Odoo, covering the following topics:

- Enabling the user to see all accounting features
- Examining the chart of accounts
- Learning how the other applications create transactions in accounting
- Adding new custom accounts
- Configuring fiscal years and periods
- A quick overview of the available accounting reports
- Creating journal entries

What's new in Odoo 11?

Like many of the other applications in Odoo 11, the default accounting functions have been further simplified. Most significant is that there is no accounting application to install in the community edition. Instead, you must turn on settings within an individual user to enable the full accounting features. This is explained in detail later in the chapter.

Defining the chart of accounts for your business

The backbone of an accounting system setup is the chart of accounts. Wikipedia defines a chart of accounts like so:

A **chart of accounts** is a created list of the accounts used by a business entity to define each class of items for which money or the equivalent is spent or received. It is used to organize the finances of the entity and to segregate expenditures, revenue, assets and liabilities in order to give interested parties a better understanding of the financial health of the entity.

It is very likely that, if you are setting up Odoo for an existing business, you will be asked to configure the chart of accounts in Odoo to match the account structure the business is already using. Even if you are not tied to any existing chart of accounts, it is inevitable that you will need to have a firm understanding of how the accounting functionality in Odoo works if you are going to have a successful implementation.

If you are completely unfamiliar with accounting, then this chapter may prove somewhat challenging. It is important to get familiar with the basics of accounting if you want to succeed in implementing any ERP system.

Configuring a user to see all accounting options

Odoo configures a basic accounting structure when you install base modules such as **Sales and Purchasing**. To access all of the accounting configuration options in previous versions of Odoo, you needed to install the **Accounting and Finance** application. In Odoo 11, you do not install an application to access accounting options, but instead must take a few steps to properly configure any user to whom you wish to provide those options.

We begin by navigating to the **Settings** menu and then clicking **Activate the Developer Mode** on the far right of the dashboard:

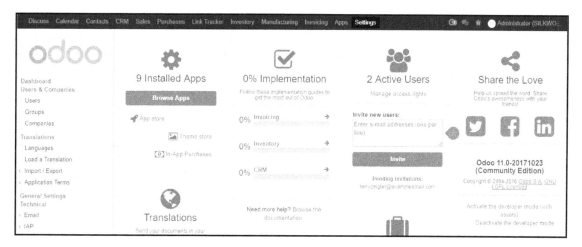

In this case, we are turning on Developer Mode just so, we can see all the options that are available for a user. Without Developer Mode turned on, we would not see the necessary options for a given user.

Next, you need to click the **Users** menu on the left and select the user for whom you wish to allow access to the full accounting features. In this case, we have selected the **Administrator**:

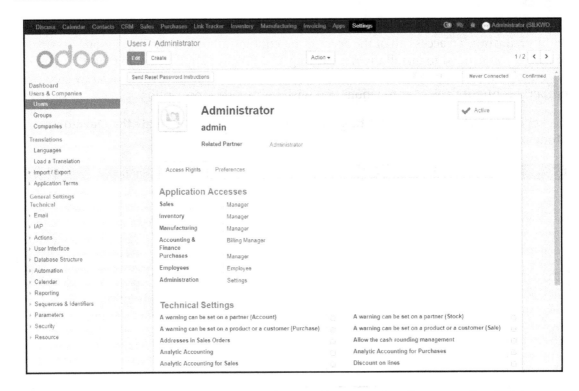

Scroll down and you will find the option **Show Full Accounting Features**. Check this option to enable the full accounting options in Odoo 11:

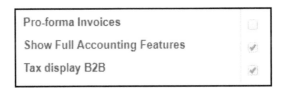

After you have configured the user to access the full accounting features, the contents of the **Invoicing** menu will change to include far more choices. Like when changing other settings, it's possible that you may need to use *Shift*-refresh in your browser to see the changes. Unlike previous versions of Odoo, the menu will remain **Invoicing** even when all of the options are enabled.

Viewing the current chart of accounts

We will begin by learning how to view the current **Chart of Accounts** in Odoo.

Go to the **Invoicing** menu and choose **Chart of Accounts** under the **Configuration |
Accounting** submenu. You will immediately see the chart of accounts sorted by the **Code** column:

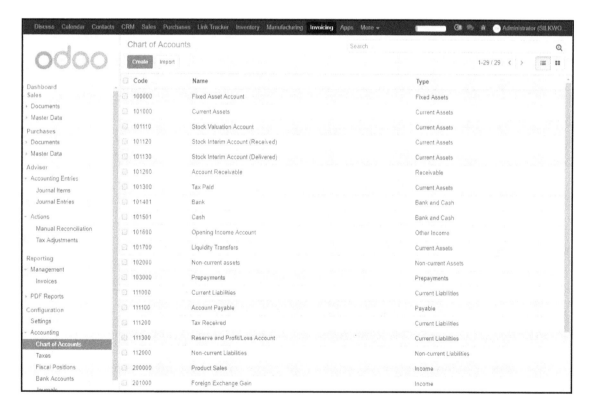

In the preceding screenshot, we see the currently configured **Chart of Accounts**, including the **Code**, **Name**, and **Type** of account.

Getting more information on a specific account

In Odoo 11, the type of account is used by the various reports to determine whether that account should be included, and if so, where on the report to include that account. Clicking on one of the accounts will bring up the account, along with an example report structure so that you can see just how that account type will be represented.

Click on the **Account Payable** account in the **Chart of Accounts** list view:

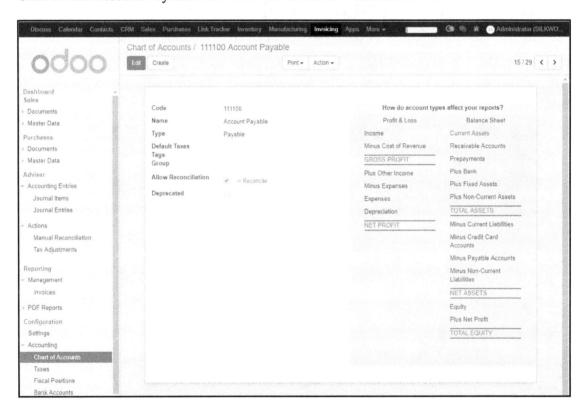

You can see on the far right of the preceding screenshot that payables are on balance sheet reports, and that they are subtracted from the total assets to give you your net assets. Understanding how account type affects your reports is critical to setting up a successful business system. Odoo simply makes this a little easier to understand by providing a quick reference. The panel on the right will not change, no matter which account you choose.

Learning how transactions in Odoo get posted to accounts

All transactions that take place in Odoo create **Journal Entries** that either credit or debit a specific account. Each journal entry must balance. This means that the debits must equal the credits. Odoo makes it very easy to examine your **Journal Entries** so that you can see exactly where each transaction is posted.

To view the **Journal Entries**, go to the **Invoicing** menu and, under the **Adviser** submenu, click **Journal Entries**. By default, Odoo applies a filter restricting the journal entries to only **Miscellaneous Operations**. Clear this filter to see all the journal entries:

In the preceding screenshot of the listing, you can see two journal entries.

If you do not see any journal entries in your list, make sure that you have cleared the **Miscellaneous Operations** filter; Odoo applies it by default.

You can see that in the journal listing, you get a summary including the amount and the status indicating whether the journal entry is posted or unposted. You can also see that, in the invoice journal entry, we have a reference provided to the original sales order.

Note that the journal entry summary does not contain any references to specific accounts in **Accounting and Finance**. To see these details, we must click on a specific journal entry. Click on the invoice for **$18.98** assigned to our customer/partner **Mike Smith**.

You will now see the details of the transaction and each account that was involved:

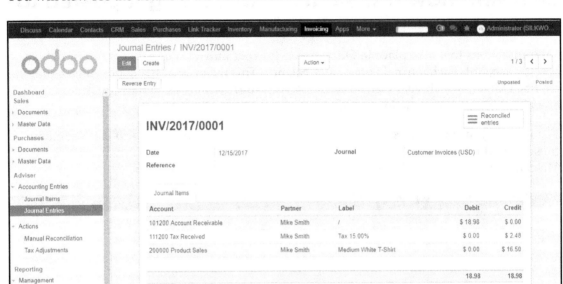

When we open the account, we see all the postings to the specific accounts that were involved. In the first row, we can see that **Accounts Receivable** was debited **$18.98** for the invoiced T-shirt order. Next, in the second row, Odoo has posted a credit of **$2.48** sales tax on the order. This goes into **111200 Tax Received**. Finally, in the third row, we see that a **$16.50** credit was posted to **200000 Product Sales** for the T-shirts themselves. Note how the **Debit** column matches the **Credit** column. Debits and credits must always be equal in a journal entry.

More details of the transaction are displayed under each item. Click on the first posting to **101200 Account Receivable** to pull up more details on that posting:

Open: Journal Items

Label	/	
Partner	Mike Smith	

Information

Amount

Account	101200 Account Receivable
Debit	$ 18.98
Credit	$ 0.00
Quantity	1.000

Accounting Documents

Journal Entry	INV/2017/0001
Invoice	INV/2017/0001

Dates

Due date	12/30/2017

States

No Follow-up	

In the preceding screenshot, you can use the links to quickly find the partner, account, journal, and journal entry related to the posting.

If this is still a little confusing, don't worry. We are now going to go through a set of transactions from the **Accounts Receivable** side so that you can better understand how Odoo handles accounting transactions.

Following transactions through the sales and accounts receivable process

In the previous example, we were looking at the chart of accounts and determining what transactions created the entries. Next, we will sell an item to a customer and see exactly how that transaction affects the accounting entries in the journal.

Let's begin by creating a new sales order.

Go to **Sales** and click on **Orders** to bring up the sales order listing. Click on **Create** to create a new sales order:

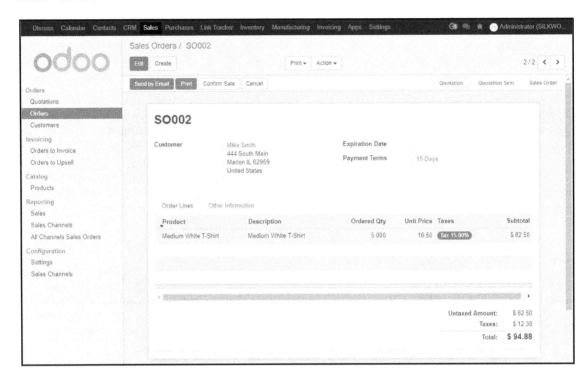

If you have followed along with our examples then you will already have the customer and product entered to create the sample sales order. Otherwise, you will need to add a customer and a product if you wish to follow along on your computer. In this example, we have created a sales order for five **Medium White T-Shirts**. Make sure, you click **Confirm Sale** to create the sales order.

Odoo will automatically number sales orders and other documents. In the preceding example, there have already been two sales order numbers used by the Odoo system. Therefore, depending on what you have already done with your current system, you may not have the same sales order number for your sample.

At this point, if you were to go and look at the journal entry listing, you will not see any additional journal entries. *Why is this?* The way Odoo is currently configured means that we must manually create an invoice. As long as you are in the **To Invoice** status, you will not see any transactions in accounting.

Only when we click on the **Create Invoice** button at the top of the screen will Odoo actually create accounting transactions.

Click on **Create Invoice** to generate a draft invoice for this sales order:

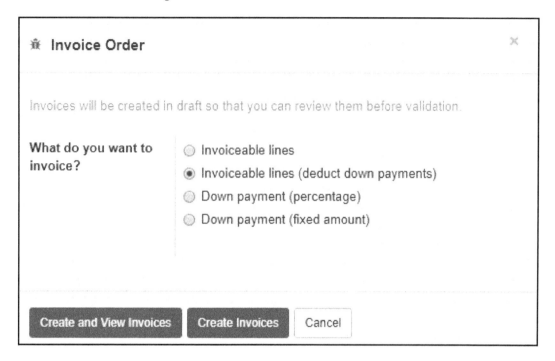

Odoo will present you with a wizard that allows you to determine how you wish to invoice. Please note that the primary difference is in how down payments are handled. As we have no down payments, we are fine to take the default option of **Invoiceable lines** (deduct down payments). If we did have a down payment, then it would be deducted automatically from the invoice total.

Click on **Create and View Invoices**:

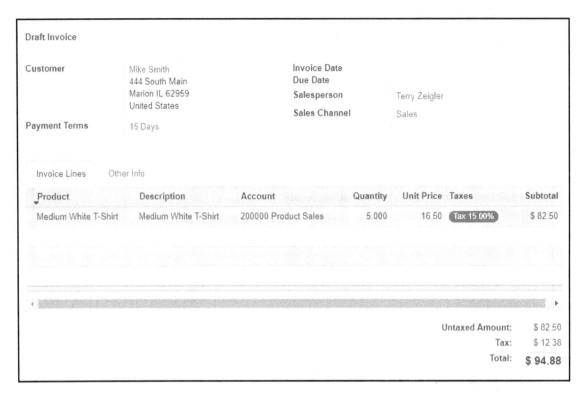

Because this is just a **Draft Invoice**, if you look at the journal entries, you will see no changes. However, if you look at the **Draft Invoice**, you can see the transactions that will be created once you validate the invoice.

In the line item of the invoice, you will see the **200000 Product Sales** account. This will be the account that will be credited for the sale of the medium white T-shirts the customer has purchased.

Choose the **Other Info page** on the **Invoice** form. Note that under **Account**, it reads **101200 Account Receivable**; this account will be debited to record the amount the customer owes to the company once the invoice is generated.

You can also see that this invoice will post **$12.38** to the **111200 Tax Received** account:

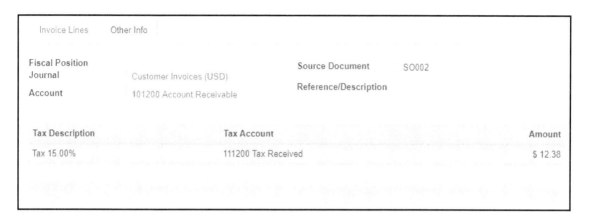

Click on **Validate** to post the invoice and create the transactions.

Viewing the transactions created by validating the invoice

Now that we have validated our invoice, Odoo has automatically created the accounting transactions to increase our **Accounts Receivable** assets and the accounting transaction to record the sale. We can now open the journal entries back up and see the newly posted transaction:

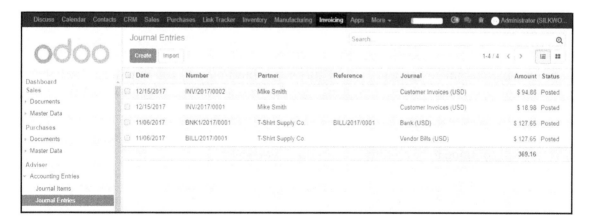

The number assigned to this specific invoice is **INV/2017/0002** for the amount of **$94.88**.

We can now click on this journal entry to see the details of the transaction:

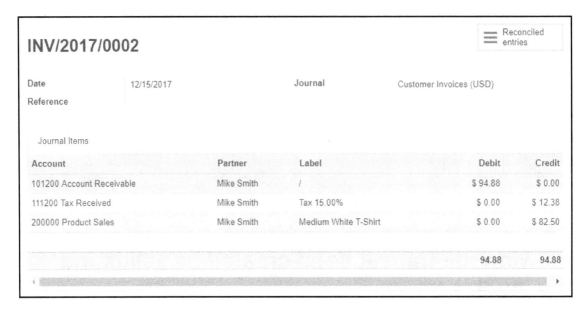

In the **Journal Items**, you can now see the same figures we examined on the invoice posted with the correct accounts. The **101200 Account Receivable** account has been debited by **$94.88** to show the new current asset that represents this customer invoice. The customer owes the company **$94.88**. As you create invoices and customers owe you money, **Accounts Receivable** will continue to grow.

Next, you will see that the tax for the invoice is a credit to the **111200 Tax Received** account. Typically, you will then use this **Tax Received** account to later send that money on to the appropriate government agency. This, by the way, would require you to write a check that would credit your bank account (reducing its value) while posting a debit to the **Tax Received** account.

Finally, note that the **200000 Product Sales** account has been credited with **$82.50**. This account will continue to be credited for products you sell.

 For our example, we are using only one sales account to keep things simple. In most companies, you will have far more sales accounts to organize the various types of products sold.

Now, let us see what happens to these accounts when a customer pays their invoice.

Go to **Accounting** and choose **Customer Invoices**, then click on the invoice to bring up the form. Click on **Register Payment** to bring up the **Register Payment** form:

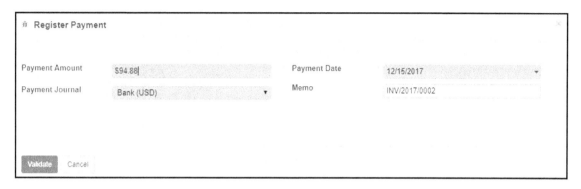

For our example, we have chosen the **Bank (USD)** payment method. You have the option to provide a memo to document the invoice payment. By default, this will include the sales order number, but many businesses may wish to include a check number as well.

Click the **Validate** button to pay the invoice and create the appropriate accounting transactions.

The invoice is now paid and the journal entries have been automatically created, and we can now see the payment listed as a new journal entry.

Like you have done previously, use the **Accounting** menu and choose **Journal Entries** to bring up the list of journal entries:

Note that we now have an entry number of **BNK1/2017/0002** that is also for **$94.88**, the same amount as the invoice. The **Journal** allows you to more easily organize transactions and identify exactly which accounts will be affected.

Let's examine the details of the payment that has been posted by clicking on the journal entry:

In this cash receipt, you will notice that we can see the details as to exactly which accounts will be affected when we post the entry:

- **101401 Bank** is debited with **$94.88**. This will increase this asset account.
- **101200 Account Receivable** is credited with **$94.88**. This will decrease this asset account.

Essentially, this journal entry transfers the potential asset the customer owes the company from **Account Receivable** into the bank account. The customer's account balance is reduced to reflect their payment.

Practicing posting transactions and tracking the results

Remember that people spend many years, learning about and even get full university degrees in financial accounting. It is important that you take the time to learn how each process you implement affects the accounts in Odoo. When implementing an ERP system for your company, take the time to get this right. It will save you a lot of pain in the long run.

Setting up your own accounts

For default English installations, Odoo installs the standard **United States Chart of Accounts** template. Most companies, however, will need to modify this chart of accounts or even set up an entirely different chart of accounts to match the needs of their business. As an example, we are going to add an additional sales account specifically for T-shirts so that we can better organize our sales into types of products.

To set up a new account, go to the **Invoicing** menu and then down to the **Configuration** section and, under **Accounting**, choose **Chart of Accounts**. Odoo will present you with a list of all your current accounts in Odoo. Click on **Create** to add a new account:

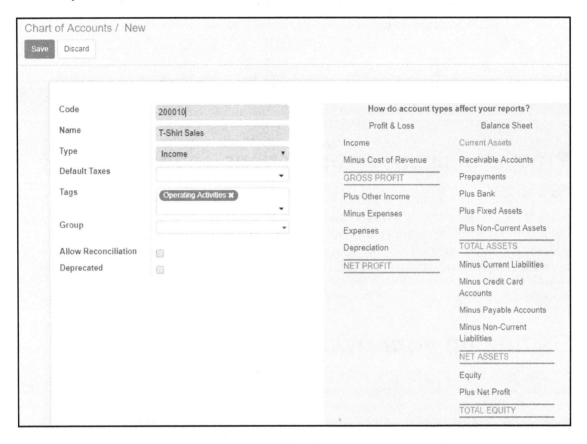

Note that in our screen, we have specified the account code as 200010. *Why did we choose this as the account code?* Odoo had already provided 200000 for the general **Product Sales** account, therefore 200010 was an appropriate account code to choose for our T-shirt sales. For the name of the account, we have named it simply T-shirt Sales.

The other important setting is the **Account Type**. Odoo needs to know the type of account you are setting up. So, for example, if you were setting up an account that was to track the costs of products you must purchase to produce your products, you would specify an expense account type.

Take the time to plan your chart of accounts in Odoo. Even if your company has already been using an existing chart of accounts, it is always a good idea to evaluate the current chart of accounts and make any improvements, depending on the current state of the business.

Specifying a new account for your product category

With Odoo, you can manage accounts at the product category level. Therefore, all products in a given category can utilize the same account settings. Let's create a new product category, T-shirts, for our Medium White T-Shirt, and assign that category to the **200010 T-Shirt Sales** account we created. Later, we can add all T-shirt products to this category.

Go to the **Inventory** menu, and in the **Configuration** section, choose **Product Categories** from the **Products** submenu. This lists the current product categories:

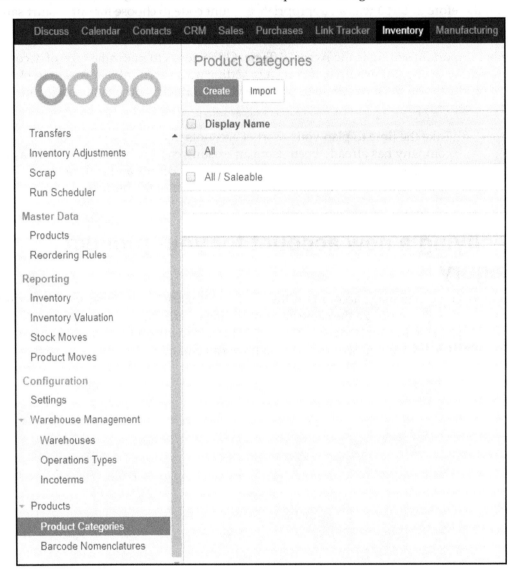

At this point, you will see that we only have two categories. Click **Create** to create a new category for our T-shirt products:

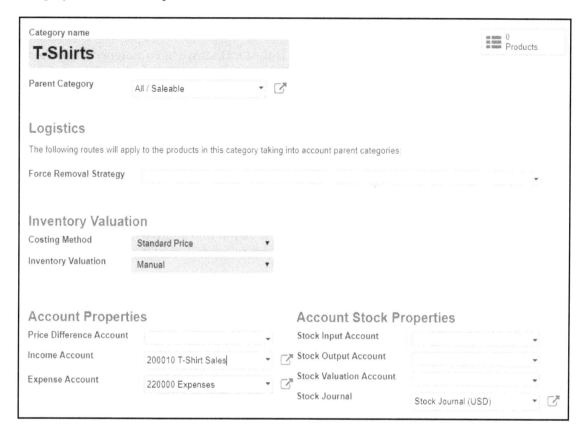

We have named our new category `T-Shirts`. All T-shirt products can now be grouped under this category. Also notice that we have set a parent category of **All / Saleable**. This allows you to view the T-shirt products along with all the other products when you choose the parent category.

Most important from an accounting standpoint is the fact that we have assigned the **Income Account 200010 T-shirt Sales** that we set up in the chart of accounts. When an invoice is posted that has a line item attributed to this product category, the amount for that line item will be posted to `200010 T-Shirt Sales`. For the **Expense Account**, we have specified the built-in **220000 Expenses**. This will post our expenses related to products in this category to that account.

Practicing with another product

Now, try going into the product record for the `Medium White T-Shirt` and setting the product category to `T-shirts`. Create a sales order, turn it into an invoice, and validate it. View the **Journal Entries** and you will see the income for your T-shirt in the specified income account.

Remember that it is important to practice using Odoo until you are comfortable setting up accounts and understand clearly where the transactions are posted. A little bit of time and effort put in during the configuration will save you a lot of time later.

Examining the available legal reports in Odoo

Like nearly all accounting and finance systems, Odoo provides the standard reports you would expect, including the following:

- **General Ledger**
- **Trial Balance**
- **Balance Sheet**
- **Profit and Loss**
- **Financial Report**

These reports are a bit buried near the middle of the **Invoicing** menu in the **Reporting** section and then accessed via **PDF Reports**:

Each report you select will bring up the corresponding wizard to specify the criteria for a given report. After you have made your selections and generated the report, you will be prompted to download the PDF file that contains the results. While going through each of these reports with all the screenshots is beyond the scope of this book, you are encouraged to spend some time examining each report and make sure that you understand how it fits within the reporting requirements for your business.

As you add more and more data to your system, some of the accounting reports will take additional time to process. As part of the testing process before you go into production, you should take the time to make sure all your accounting reports run at acceptable levels of performance using data that will simulate real-world conditions.

Creating journal entries

While Odoo will create many journal entries automatically when you perform various operations in the system, it is inevitable that, at some point, you (or your accountant) will wish to create a manual journal entry. A manual journal entry allows you to adjust account balances in a way that can be easily tracked and audited.

For our example, we are going to create a journal entry that will account for a small investment by one of the company owners. When someone puts money as an investment into a company, they are not buying anything and they are not selling anything. While there are other potential methods that can be used to reflect an investment, a simple journal entry is a straightforward way to accurately record the transaction.

To enter a journal entry, go to the **Invoicing** menu, select **Journal Entries** in the **Journal Entries** section, and click the **Create** button:

When you first create a new journal entry, you will need to pick which journal to post to. For this situation, we used an example of how we can post to the **Bank** journal to represent the owner's investment into the company.

We are considering the $5,000 investment as a cash investment by the owner, so we have posted this into the **Bank** journal.

Whenever you create a journal entry, you will add at least two line items. Furthermore, the line items must balance out. In our example, we are putting $5,000 in funds from the owner into the company bank account.

Typically, any investment the owner puts into the company must also be recognized as a liability for the company. *Why?* The money really does not belong to the company. Instead, the money, in our case $5,000, is considered the owner's equity. The owner is entitled to get that money back, and therefore it is booked as a liability. You can verify this by opening up the chart of accounts and looking at the list of main accounts. **Liabilities and Equity** are grouped together and are then divided out as you drill down into the account hierarchy.

Odoo sets up a **Capital** account that allows us to post the $5,000 we have put into the bank as capital stock for the owner. Once you save your journal entry, it is in a draft form. To post the journal entry and have it appear in your reports, you must click the **Post** button.

Summary

In this chapter, we examined how Odoo generates transactions and how you can use the chart of accounts to look at how those transactions originated. We examined both the **Accounts Payable** and **Accounts Receivable** accounts, and looked at how an invoice is posted. There are certainly more advanced Odoo topics, such as bank reconciliation and recurring entries, that are beyond the scope of this book.

In the next chapter, we will look at the **Human Resources** (**HR**) application. HR allows us to keep track of employees, the hours they work, and the services they provide. Staff can be assigned to user-defined departments and be designated as managers of other employees. And since your employees will also often be users of the Odoo system, the HR module is tied tightly to the user administration system, which manages access rights and messaging.

Administering an Odoo Installation

7

One of the greatest advantages of Odoo is that it is easy to get up and running with very little setup. Within just a few minutes you can have several applications installed and you can begin working with the system right away. In the previous chapters, we covered a great deal of functionality without having to spend a lot of time on configuration, access rules, languages, or other administrative topics.

Now, we will take a closer look at some important topics to consider when administering an Odoo installation. Topics that we will cover in this chapter include the following:

- Basic administration of an Odoo installation
- Backing up and restoring Odoo databases
- Creating users and assigning access rights
- Internationalization, including currencies and language translation
- How to manage document sequences
- Multi-company configurations

Basic considerations for an Odoo administration

Like most IT installations, successful Odoo installations require proper planning and maintenance. Care must be taken in documenting important configuration details, and you must always have a business continuity plan in place that focuses on getting your Odoo installation back up and running within an acceptable period of time.

Having an implementation strategy

While you are learning Odoo and prototyping how you may use it for your business, you may not care much about a clear implementation strategy; however, once you have made the decision to use Odoo for your business, it is important to plan your implementation strategy. While you may not have the time to write out a 150-page detailed strategy, it is important to take the time to document your overall strategy and have a plan in place before you begin setting up servers and installing Odoo.

While the total breadth of project management and administration that goes into an ERP system is beyond the scope of this book, there are several basic implementation considerations which you will always want to think about.

Development, staging, and production servers

One of the first considerations you will need to keep in mind when contemplating an Odoo installation is how you will configure servers for various Odoo instances that may be required during planning, deployment, and final production operations. For example, you don't want to be making modifications to Odoo's functionality in your live production system. Instead, you should always make changes and modifications in a development instance of Odoo, where you can test your changes outside of the live database.

In addition to a development server and production server, it is often desirable to have an Odoo installation that users (and in some cases, business partners) can use to learn the operations of the system. Sometimes, this installation is known as the staging server. This server will typically have all of the tested changes and functionality of the live system, but will be loaded with test data and configurations that are useful for training.

Each installation will have its own requirements and constraints. What is important is that you make these decisions early on in your Odoo configurations, so that you can properly administer the installations all the way from development to production.

Clear documentation of all Odoo configurations

Once you have decided what Odoo servers you require and how those installations should be configured, it is important that you create a clearly defined method for documenting all the details that go along with the setup. This can be as simple as a text or Microsoft Word document that is in a known place and kept up-to-date, or it can be as complex as a full-blown *Project Manager*. Using cloud organization tools, such as Dropbox, Evernote, and Google Documents, provide you with a lot of options for how you can document your Odoo installations.

It will be up to your own business policies to determine exactly where you store this information and how much detail you keep. It is important to note, however, that it is almost always better to err on the side of having too much detail rather than too little. You will need to be aware of how you secure usernames and passwords, and have a clear policy on how that information is securely stored.

Focusing on business continuity

Any business information system is only as good as its ability to recover from something going wrong. Despite having more reliable hardware and software, data can still get corrupted. Even the most dedicated employee can accidentally post bad data. The best security can be defeated. Despite Odoo's best efforts, there are probably bugs still lurking in its applications. No amount of planning can prevent a problem from occurring. This is why one of the most important tasks when administering an Odoo installation is making sure that you always have a clear recovery strategy.

Here are a few important considerations to remember:

- Regularly test your backups for recoverability. Just because you are backing up your data does not mean that it is quickly recoverable. All too often, businesses can go months, or even years, without testing if the data they are backing up is recoverable.
- Have a strong archive of backups. Perform daily backups along with weekly and monthly snapshots as well. Often, data can be bad, deleted, or corrupted long before anyone knows anything has gone wrong. Someone might accidentally delete a set of old entries, and it may not be until a few months later that a manager doing a report finds critical holes in the data.

- Have contingency system options. Even if you plan on hosting locally, consider having a cloud server configured where can run your Odoo installation in a pinch. Too often, you can have the backups ready to go but you are still waiting on hardware to be fixed or a part to be delivered, which is going to extend your downtime. If you plan to use your development server as a backup production system, make sure that you have the proper procedures in place and tested. Don't make optimistic assumptions about your system contingencies. Test them at least once or twice a year.

- Make sure that you know how long it takes to fully recover your Odoo installation and what data would need to be re-entered into the system. If you back up nightly, and it takes you four hours to get your installation back up and running, make sure your internal business processes are clear on exactly what steps are required.

- Know exactly how much downtime costs your business and plan accordingly. Companies such as eBay and Amazon are in crisis if they are down for even a few minutes; more than an hour of downtime for them would make international news. While you may not have their uptime requirements, it is important that you understand exactly what risks your business faces if your Odoo installation goes down for two minutes, two hours, or even two days.

Backing up your Odoo database

It is critical in a production environment that, at minimum, you back up both your working Odoo application directories and the associated Postgres databases. Ideally, you will have server snapshots and a clear business continuity plan in place and tested. Still, it is valuable to know that Odoo provides a built-in database backup tool. I use it frequently in a variety of Odoo installations.

Before going ahead, it should be noted that this function will not be applicable to all Odoo installations. If you are running in a hosted Odoo environment, where you have been provided login credentials to your database, then you will be provided with a specific backup procedure. Make sure that you fully understand how it works and have a way to test and make sure that it functions as expected.

The easiest way to get to the backup database function is to navigate directly to the database manager by adding `/web/database/manager` to the end of your Odoo URL:

Here, you will see all the databases in your Odoo installation with the option to **Backup**, **Duplicate**, or **Delete** each of the databases.

 Sometimes, if you are having trouble with an Odoo installation, such as getting Internal Server errors and other system-related issues, you can navigate directly to the database manager to back up your database and perform operations that may help you recover from the problem.

Clicking the **Backup** button will bring up a simple wizard that will allow you to back up the database in a ZIP format that will contain all the filestores associated with that database, or as a `pg_dump` file. A filestore could contain things such as document attachments or pictures associated with your products. The `pg_dump` format is a standard Postgres database operation that will generate a backup of the database only, without the associated filestore.

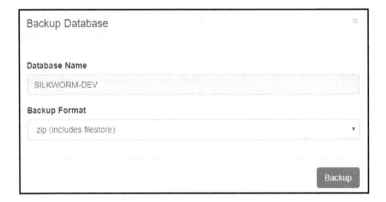

Click the **Backup** button to begin backing up the database. The database will then begin downloading. (If your database is extremely large, there is a chance that the file may not be easily downloaded.)

Restoring an Odoo database

The ability to back up a database does little good unless you have the ability to restore the database and get it back up and running. You can click the **Restore Database** button to bring up the **Restore Database** form, shown as follows:

Here, you specify the **Master Password** and choose the file you wish to restore. Once you have the file selected, you will need to specify a new database name to restore the database into it.

You also get the option to choose either **Backup Restore** or **Copy of an existing database** as the **Mode** for restoration. As the instructions explain, Odoo will handle the restore slightly differently if you are restoring a database that has been moved rather than copied. A moved database would be one in which you do not intend to have another instance running, whereas a copied database would assume that the other database stays in use. Use the appropriate mode for your situation.

Administering users in Odoo

In any ERP system, it is important that you completely understand how users and user access rights are managed. When Odoo is first installed, an admin account is created automatically. This is a superuser account, and it is the only one like it. In some systems, any account can be specified to have full administration privileges. Odoo, however, gives permissions to the administration account that no other user in the system has.

Specifically, all access rights are bypassed when using the administrator account. Much like the root account in Linux or Ubuntu, you always need to protect your administration account by using a strong password and keeping it secret.

Selecting a user to administer

Let's begin looking at a user in Odoo and see how they are tied to partner records within Odoo applications.

To access the list of users, click **Settings** in the main menu and then choose **Users** from the **Users** section in the left-hand menu, as follows:

We can now click on `Terry Ziegler` to bring up the user, and to look at the additional options available:

When you pull up a user in your own Odoo installation, it is unlikely that your screen will look exactly like the preceding screenshot. Depending on the exact applications that are installed, the available application accesses will change. It is also common to see specific modifications to this screen depending on the Odoo build you are running.

Managing user preferences

Now, click on the **Preferences** tab and take a look at the available options:

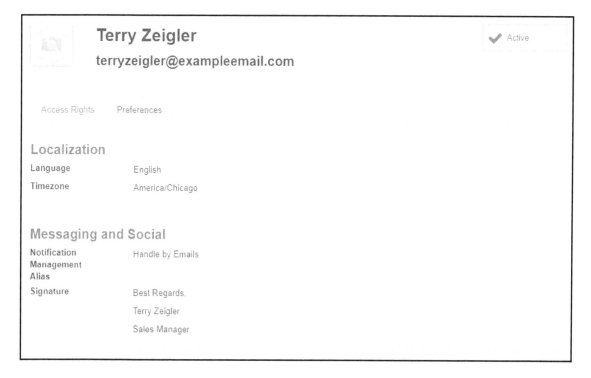

In this section, we have the ability to specify important localization options that can dramatically change the user experience. We can specify one of the many languages that Odoo supports, as well as the timezone and default sales team of the user.

Additionally, the **Preferences** section lets you manage your **Messaging and Social** options for a user.

Currently, there are only two options for receiving inbox notifications by email: either a user never receives notifications or receives all of the notifications.

The **Alias** option will allow administrators to configure an email alias for the user. By creating an alias, the user can receive incoming messages from an email that is different to the one assigned to the account.

Finally, you can use the **Signature** rich text area at the bottom of the page to specify a signature footer for emails sent by this user. If desired, the user can change their own signature at any time by choosing **Preferences** from the menu in the upper right-hand corner of the screen, shown as follows:

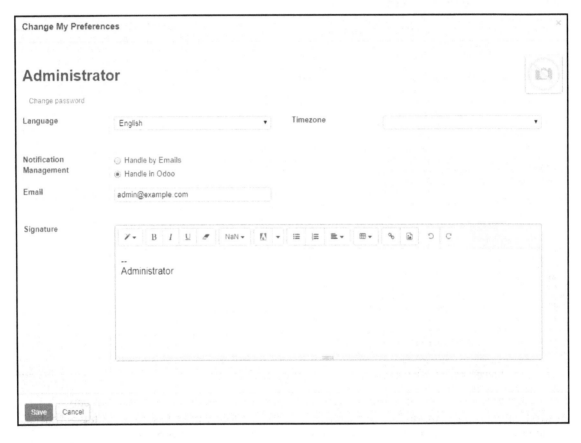

Remember that if you are an administrator making these changes for another user, changing these settings will require that user to log out of the system before their session can be updated with the changes.

If you are setting up a lot of users, don't forget that you can use the **Duplicate** option under the **More** menu at the top of the form to make a copy of a user. This can be handy if a worker has left and has been replaced with another worker. You can deactivate the old employee and duplicate their profile for the new employee.

Understanding groups in Odoo

In Odoo, you give users permissions by assigning the users to groups. Once a user is assigned to a group then the user has all the permissions and options that are associated with that group. Users can belong, and often do belong, to more than one group. To see the list of groups that are currently available in your Odoo installation, you will need to turn on the developer settings. To do this, go to the **Settings** menu at the top of the page and then choose **Dashboard**, as shown in the following screenshot:

Dashboard

At the bottom-right-hand side of the page, you will find a link to **Activate the developer mode**. Clicking this link will then refresh the settings menu and provide you with many more options for administering your Odoo installation.

Once you have successfully entered developer mode, you can manage the user groups in Odoo by clicking the **Groups** link under the **Settings** menu:

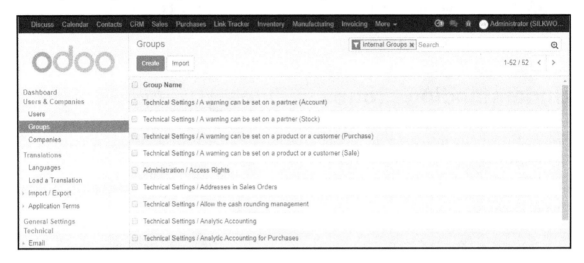

As you can see, Odoo has a lot of groups. Fortunately, once you understand how groups work, you will easily be able to determine exactly what options are available to a user when you put them in a specific group.

For our example, let's examine the **Sales / Manager** group. You can find this group by scrolling down the list of groups or by using the search function to narrow the list until you can find the group that you are looking for.

Like other lists, clicking the **Sales / Manager** group brings up the following form:

At the very top of the form, on the left, you can see that a group is always associated with a given application. In this case, the group is associated with the Sales application. On the right is the name **Manager**. Odoo automatically adds a slash (/) between the application and the name when displaying a full name in the list.

As you can see, the first page lists the users that are assigned to the group. Naturally, you can add and remove users from this group as required. You will also notice that there are seven pages on this form that allow you to configure exactly what permissions a group will offer to its users.

Understanding group inheritance in Odoo

Managing access permissions in any ERP system is always a challenge. Odoo makes managing user permissions a little easier by allowing you to inherit permissions from multiple groups and then define a new group that automatically includes all of the permissions from those groups. With proper planning, this allows you to create groups that provide your users with the permissions they require.

Let's take a look at the groups **Inherited** by the **Sales / Manager** group:

Application	Sales		Name	Manager
Portal			Share Group	

Users	Inherited	Menus	Views	Access Rights	Rules	Notes

Users added to this group are automatically added in the following groups.

Group Name

Sales / User: All Documents

The **Sales / Manager** group has **Sales / User: All Documents** included in the **Inherited** list. Just like the instructions say, users added to the **Sales / Manager** group will automatically be added to the **Sales / User: All Documents** group.

With this in mind, manager groups such as this will most often include all other groups that have more restrictions in the system. For example, looking at the **Sales / User: All Documents** group allows you to see the most restrictive group permissions for the **Sales** group.

Defining menus for your group

Groups provide a direct way of determining what menus users in that group have access to. In the case of the **Sales / Manager** group, we have additional menu options listed, however members of the **Sales / User: All Documents** group would not see these menus unless they are also members of **Sales / Manager**, or if they are added specifically to the **Sales / User: All Documents** group:

Application		Sales			Name		Manager
Portal		☐			Share Group		☐

Users	Inherited	Menus	Views	Access Rights	Rules	Notes

Sequence	Menu
1	CRM/Configuration/Opportunities
2	Contacts/Configuration
3	Sales/Configuration/Sales Orders
5	Sales/Reporting
6	Sales/Configuration
6	CRM
6	CRM/Reporting/Activities
15	CRM/Configuration/Leads & Opportunities
20	CRM/Reporting
25	CRM/Configuration

If, for example, you wanted to allow users in the group **Sales / User: All Documents** to view the **Activities** report, you could remove the menu from the list in the **Manager** group and add the menu to the **Sales / User: All Documents** group. Because the manager group inherits from **Sales / User: All Documents**, its users will still be able to see the menu—as will those who are only in the **Sales / User: All Documents** group.

Understanding access rights in Odoo

So far, we have seen how groups can inherit from other groups and how menus can be assigned to a specific group. Now we will look at what access rights determine which models a group has access to and what permissions they are assigned.

In the following screenshot, you will see the **Access Rights** page for the **Sales / Manager** group:

| Application | Sales | | | | Name | Manager |
| Portal | | | | | Share Group | |

| Users | Inherited | Menus | Views | Access Rights | Rules | Notes |

Object	Read Access	Write Access	Create Access	Delete Access	Name
Sales Channel	✓	✓	✓	✓	crm.team.manager
Invoice	✓	✓	✓	✓	account_invoice manager
Quotation	✓	✓	✓	✓	sale.order.manager
Sales Orders Statistics	✓	✓	✓	✓	sale.report
Contact	✓	✓	✓	☐	res.partner.sale.manager
Product UoM Categories	✓	✓	✓	✓	product.uom categ salemanager
Product Unit of Measure	✓	✓	✓	✓	product.uom salemanager
Product Category	✓	✓	✓	✓	product.category salemanager
Information about a product vendor	✓	✓	✓	✓	product.supplierinfo salemanager
Pricelist	✓	✓	✓	✓	product.pricelist salemanager
Contact	✓	✓	✓	☐	res_partner group_sale_manager
sale.layout_category	✓	✓	✓	✓	report_layout_category_1
Pricelist Item	✓	✓	✓	✓	product.pricelist.item salemanager
product.price.history	✓	✓	✓	✓	prices.history sale manager

Access Rights is where you define exactly what models the group has access to. In Odoo, the term **Model** represents a business entity object and its related operations. You can determine if a group has any combination of **Read Access**, **Write Access**, **Create Access**, or **Delete access** for each group. For example, in the preceding list, if you scroll down you will find that the **Sales / Manager** group has the ability to read, write, and create meeting types, but they cannot delete meeting types.

Now let's take a quick look at the access rights of the **Sales / User: Own Documents Only** group:

Application	Sales			Name	–	User: Own Documents Only
Portal	☐			Share Group	☐	

Users   Inherited   Menus   Views   **Access Rights**   Rules   Notes

1-40 / 49 ⟨ ⟩

Object	Read Access	Write Access	Create Access	Delete Access	Name
Sales Channel	✔	☐	☐	☐	crm.team.user
Quotation	✔	✔	✔	☐	sale.order
Sales Order Line	✔	✔	✔	✔	sale.order.line
Invoice Tax	✔	✔	✔	☐	account_invoice_tax salesman
Invoice	✔	✔	✔	☐	account_invoice salesman
Invoice Line	✔	✔	✔	☐	account_invoice.line salesman
Payment Terms	✔	☐	☐	☐	account_payment_term salesman
Analytic Tags	✔	☐	☐	☐	account.analytic.tag.sale.salesman
Analytic Account	✔	✔	✔	☐	account_analytic_account salesman
Sales Orders Statistics	✔	✔	✔	☐	sale.report
ir.property	✔	✔	✔	✔	ir.property.sales
Journal	✔	☐	☐	☐	account.journal sale order.user
Contact	✔	☐	☐	☐	res.partner.sale.user

The manager group we looked at previously allowed users to create and write records, but the **Sales / User: Own Documents Only** group only has read access for many objects, such as **Sales Team**, **Journal**, **Partner**, **Product Template**, and so on. This group can see the information, and it can be selected on forms and reports, but they do not have permission to modify records in those objects.

Understanding group rules in Odoo

Sometimes in a system you want users to have access to a particular model, but not to all records in that model. For example, you may want users to have access to phone calls within the system, but only to records of their own phone calls rather than all calls from the whole system. When you need to control user access based on the contents of records within a model, you can define **Rules**.

For this example, we are looking at the rules for the **Sales / User: Own Documents Only** group. Because this is a very restricted group, there are many rules that limit users in this group, meaning they only see records that are associated with them personally:

Application	Sales		Name	User: Own Documents Only
Portal			Share Group	

Users	Inherited	Menus	Views	Access Rights	Rules	Notes	

Name	Object	Global
Personal Orders Analysis	Sales Orders Statistics	
Personal Order Lines	Sales Order Line	
Personal Invoices Analysis	Invoices Statistics	
Personal Leads Analysis	CRM Opportunity Analysis	
Personal Activities	CRM Activity Analysis	
Personal Orders	Quotation	
Personal Leads	Lead/Opportunity	

Typically, manager groups will have little or no rules because they do not have restrictions on what records they can access. Groups such as **Own Documents Only** have quite a few rules so that users can't see records that do not belong to them. Let's take a quick look at the **Personal Orders** rule so we can see how to construct a rule that limits what records a user can access:

Odoo provides a pretty good description at the bottom of the form on how rules interact. If no groups are specified in the list, this means that this rule will apply to everyone-all groups. As you can see in the preceding screenshot, you can specify the access rights for this rule. So, you could have a rule in which a user can access (read) certain records, but they would not be able to create, write, or delete records.

The most important part of the rule is the **Rule Definition** or **Domain Filter**. This is the filter that is applied to each record to determine if that record should be available. While the syntax may look a bit cryptic, you can see that the system is checking that **user_id** is equal to the current **user_id**. Specifically, this filter will be true if you are looking at your own records, or records that have not been assigned to any specific user.

When making your own rules, copy and paste rules from a similar rule to make it easier to get the syntax right. Also, be careful about changing rules in a live system. It is possible that an error in your syntax could make it impossible to access certain parts of the system.

Internationalization in Odoo

Even with a conventional English installation of Odoo, it is possible to configure Odoo to work with a variety of languages, time zones, and currencies without downloading any additional add-ons. Odoo has very robust features for configuring a global ERP system that can meet the demands of today's multicultural business environment.

As with most Odoo features, you only need to configure the international features that you require for your business. For example, you may do business entirely in US dollars but would like to offer Odoo in Spanish for some of your workstations, users, or portal customers. On the other hand, if you are purchasing from a supplier in an alternative currency, you may choose to create a special price list that allows you to do business in that currency.

Configuring language translation

Like many of the other options in Odoo that we have discussed, business requirements should drive how you configure your system. For our real-world example, we want to be able to offer a native Spanish Odoo interface for some employees. Let's see how we can configure Odoo to provide other language alternatives.

Fortunately, Odoo makes this very easy. Simply go to the **Settings** menu and choose **Load a Translation** in the **Translations** section, as shown in the following screenshot:

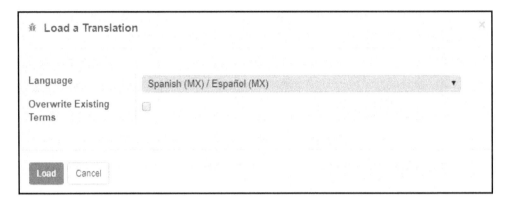

You will find quite a few languages to choose from in this list. At the time of writing, there are more than 80 languages to choose from.

Many of these languages are community supported, and translation will certainly vary. Furthermore, ERP systems can often be confusing, even for users that speak the language fluently. Take the time to train users so they understand all their processes well.

You would use **Overwrite Existing Terms** if you have made custom modifications to a language translation and now wish to overwrite them.

After the language is loaded, you will get a confirmation message and instructions on how to begin using the installed language, shown as follows:

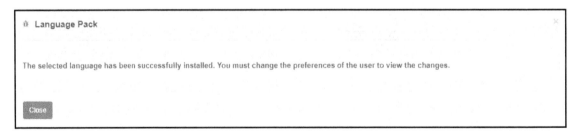

Now that we have installed the new language, we can assign that language to our users, customers, and even our suppliers. In the following screenshot, we can see that we have set language choice of `Mike Zeigler` to Spanish. Odoo also allows you to specify the time zone by either the GMT offset or by common regions. In this case, we have chosen Cancun as the **Timezone**:

After the changes have been saved and the user has logged back in, we will see that their interface has changed to Spanish:

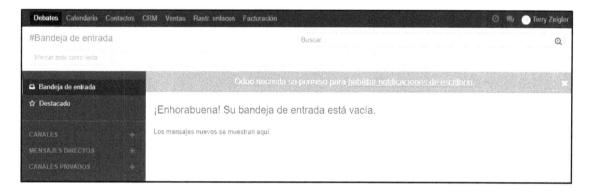

Using translation features to customize Odoo for your business

Even if you do not plan to use Odoo's translation features, they can be great for changing forms to better fit a given business requirement.

Starting in Odoo 10, the base language is no longer loaded into the translation framework. Therefore, you will need to synchronize terms for the English language if you wish to make any changes to the translations it uses. Synchronizing the terms loads the terms for the specific language into Odoo.

To synchronize terms, go to **Settings**, and then under **Translations** choose **Languages**. In the row for the **English** language you will see an icon at the far-right side of the screen that will bring up a confirmation to synchronize the terms when clicked:

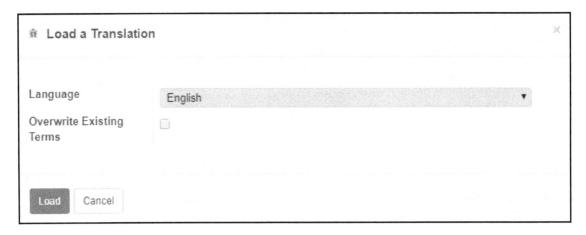

Once we have loaded the translation for **English**, we can examine the terms.

To see the translated terms for a given language, go to **Settings**, and then under **Translations** choose **Application Terms / Translated Terms**:

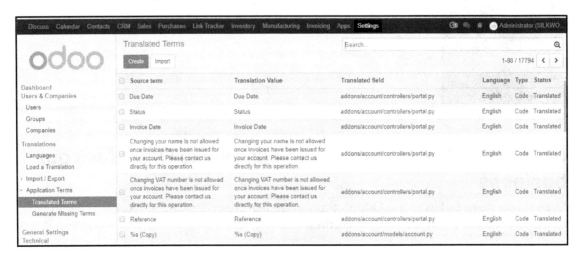

Notice that in the second-to-last column, we can see that the first page has all English translations and that the record count is **16,737**. Nearly every message, menu, and label in Odoo is driven by the translations in this table. Odoo easily adapts and supports dozens of languages, but we can also use these translations to change terms to make them more business-friendly for our requirements. For instance, you could change **Due Date** to **Date Due**, or change **Invoice Date** to **Date of Invoice**. Neither will affect how the system works as they are just labels.

 It is often the case that businesses have different terms for certain fields and models inside of Odoo. Use these translation features to customize an Odoo setup for a given industry.

International currencies

As have seen, it is quite easy to configure Odoo for multiple languages. Currencies, however, will require more planning and testing during system configuration. Unlike languages, multiple currencies have the ability to directly modify the amount of money you are receiving or paying out. If the system has misconfigured currency settings, you are almost guaranteed to have inaccurate transactions within your system at some point. Make sure that you thoroughly test all scenarios when working with multiple currencies in Odoo or any other ERP system.

To set up multi-currency in Odoo, go to the **Accounting** menu and select **Settings** in the **Configuration** section, as shown in the following screenshot:

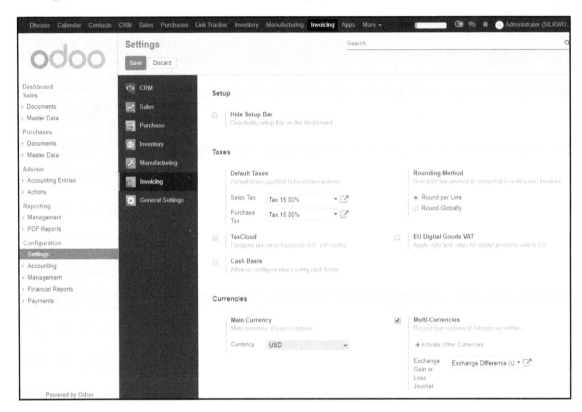

Under **Currencies**, you will find **Multi-Currencies**. Check this and you will get the option to select the accounts to which the differences between exchange rates are posted. When setting up a full production system, you will want to assign appropriate accounts, as discussed in Chapter 6, *Configuring Accounting and Finance Options*, we can post to the default account, **Exchange Difference**, as an appropriately-typed income or expense account for demonstration purposes.

After clicking on **Multi-Currencies**, the screen will refresh and give you the option to **Activate Other Currencies**. Clicking this option will bring up all the currencies that are available in your Odoo installation:

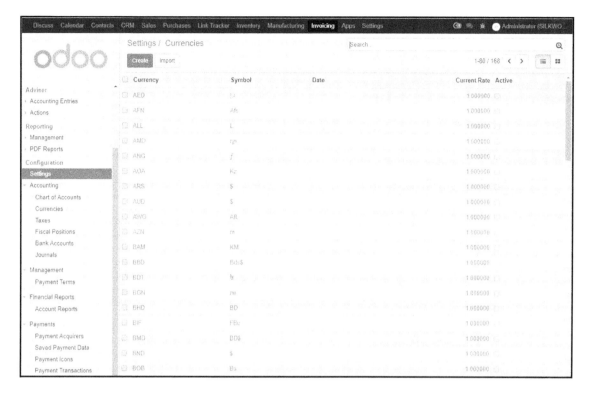

When you turn on **Multi-Currency**, Odoo specifies that both the USD and EUR currencies are active. You can activate any other currency by editing the appropriate record and checking the Active option.

Let's go ahead and activate the currency for the Mexican Peso by finding the **MNX** currency record and setting it to Active, as shown in the following screenshot:

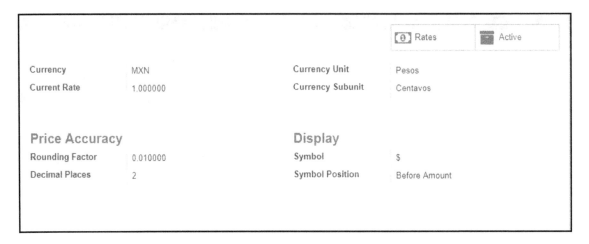

You will notice that this screen also contains the option to specify the rounding factor that will be used in converting the MXN currency to the base Odoo currency. In this installation, that is the US currency.

You will not notice the changes from multi-currency until we look at how some of our documents now appear in Odoo.

 As when configuring other Odoo options, it is a good idea to *Shift*+refresh your browser to force Odoo to load any new menus or settings resulting from your changes.

Purchasing in a different currency

Create a new purchase order and observe the new currency selection available at the top of the form, as shown in the following screenshot:

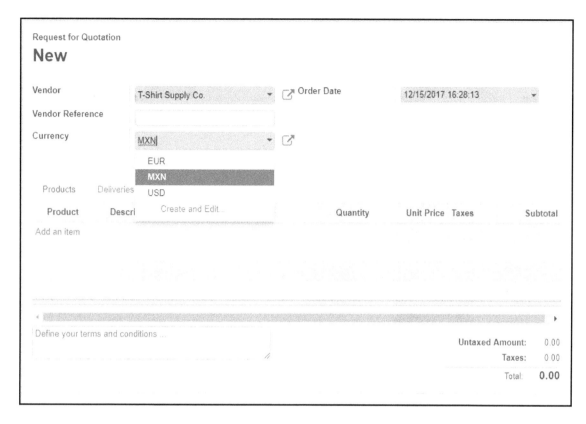

Once you have chosen a currency, you will see the symbol change at the bottom of the purchase order to show that you are now purchasing in the new currency.

However, if you then try to add a product to your purchase order, you will quickly discover that the unit cost does not auto-populate from the cost we specified in the product file. As we are now using multiple currencies, we either need to provide more detailed pricing information, or we must enter the amount on each purchase order we create.

Managing supplier price lists

Now that we know we are going to have suppliers from whom we need to purchase in a different currency, let's see how we can set up a price list for an alternative currency so that when we order products we do not have to re-enter our costs.

We must first turn on multiple vendor price lists. Click on the **Purchases** menu and then click **Settings** within the **Configuration** section. There, you can check the **Allow using and importing vendor pricelists** option under the **Vendor Price** section, and click **Apply**:

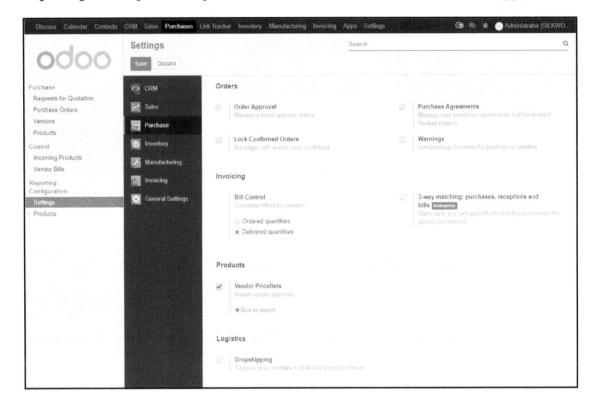

After we have turned on the option to manage pricelists per supplier, we can go to the vendor and set the currency for the vendor under the **Sales & Purchases** tab:

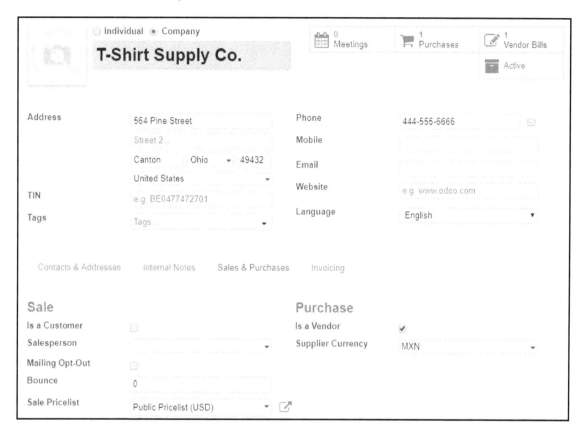

Once you save the vendor record and go to create a new purchase order, the currency will automatically default to the new supplier currency we specified.

Let's see what happens when we add the line item for the Medium White T-Shirt:

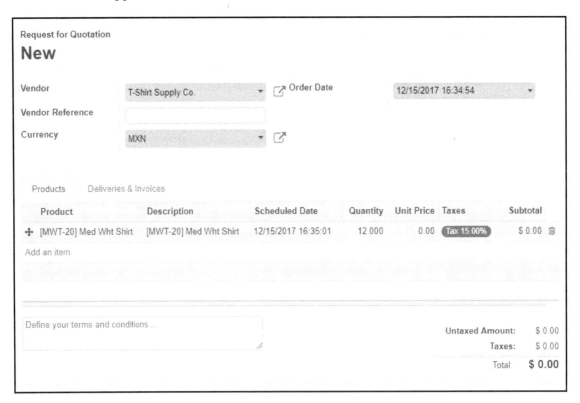

If you look carefully at the preceding screenshot, you will notice that the **Unit Price** for our Medium White T-Shirt is still set to 0.00. What's happened? While we have configured the vendor to use the MXN currency, we have only specified a cost for US currency. Let's see how we can fix that.

Under the **Purchases** menu, select the **Vendor Pricelists**, shown as follows:

Let's make it so that this t-shirt is now priced by the Peso (MXN):

Once you **Save** and create a new purchase order, the product will then be picked up and priced correctly in Pesos.

As you can see, pricelists are flexible, but you must be careful to properly configure and test your configuration. It's very easy to end up pulling the wrong currency into a document.

Managing sequences in Odoo

When you are setting up a system for your business, there is a good chance that the default naming conventions of documents and number sequences used by Odoo are not ideal. A simple example is that you're unlikely to want your invoices starting at 00001 if you've already produced thousands of invoices. In this case, you would want the number to start where the old system left off.

Additionally, sequences in Odoo don't just manage the numbering of your documents. They also manage how the document name looks inside Odoo. To see the current sequences defined by Odoo, go to the **Settings** menu and choose **Sequences | Sequences & Identifiers**. In Odoo 11 this is only accessible through developer mode:

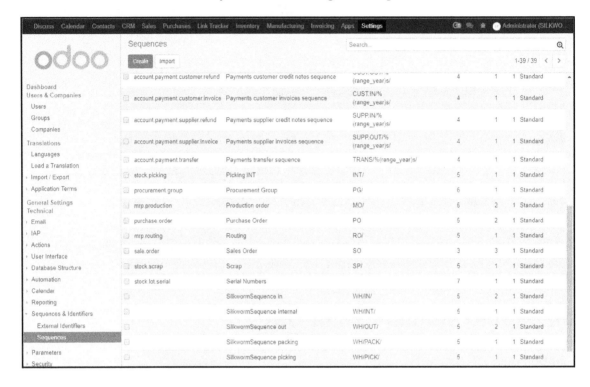

Here, we have scrolled down so that you can see the **Sales Order** sequence. Click on the **Sales Order** sequence to bring up the details, as shown in the following screenshot:

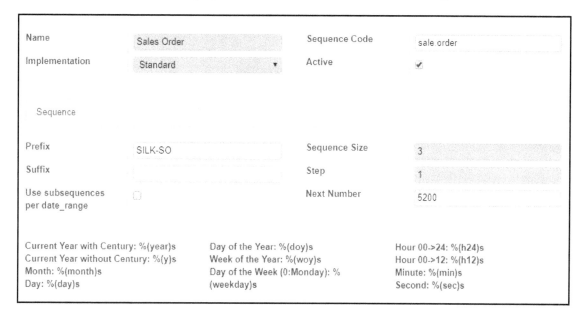

Simply using **SO** is generic and could potentially match a document identifier from another company.

So, for this example, we have changed the **Prefix** of the **Sales Order** in our Odoo installation so that it begins with SILK-SO. It is common in a business situation that you'll want to prefix your documents with a notation that identifies that document specifically to your company. Also notice that we have bumped up the **Next Number** to 5200.

After you save the changes to the sequence, any new documents will now use the new sequence definition, as shown in the following screenshot:

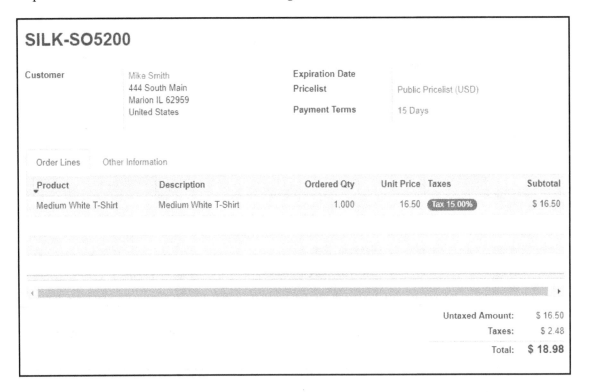

Multiple companies in Odoo

Odoo has the ability to manage multiple companies within the same database. This feature allows you to consolidate some of your system administration and manage more complex operations. As a general rule, multiple-company configuration is an advanced topic. You should be very comfortable working with single-company configurations before you begin looking into multiple-company configurations. When managing operations, Odoo's warehouse management and analytic accounting abilities are often preferable to configuring multiple companies.

A good general rule is that if a company is not a separate legal entity then it should not be set up as part of multiple companies in Odoo. However, every business requirement is different, and the ability to use multiple companies in Odoo may allow you to easily implement a solution that otherwise may have been difficult.

To set up Odoo so that it uses multiple companies, go to the **Settings** menu and then choose **General Settings**, as shown in the following screenshot:

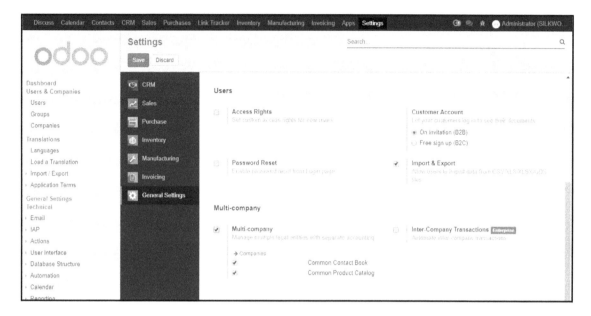

After you have checked **Manage multiple companies** and clicked **Apply**, Odoo will configure the installation for multiple companies. Please note that this operation will take a few seconds, and sometimes longer on some systems.

By default, Odoo does not turn on multi-company operations for a user even if you have configured multi-company operations through its general settings. Even in the case of the administrator, you must go in and manually set multi-companies.

Setting up a second company in Odoo

Now it's time to create a second company. With Odoo, you can have multiple companies that are all independent of each other, or you can have child companies in which you can link a chart of accounts and other operations to a parent company. For example, we have created a new company named `Euro Shirts` and have set `Silkworm Inc.` as the parent company.

Go to **Settings** and then choose **Companies** and click **Create** to create a new company.

In this example, we are choosing **France** as the country and have selected **Silkworm** as the **Parent Company**:

In the following screenshot we have assigned the user a second company.

Once you have added the second company, you may need to *Shift*+refresh your browser. At that point, you can choose which company you are working with by a drop-down box on the right side of the window.

Now that we have defined a second company, we need to setup the **Fiscal Localization**.

Setting up the Chart of Accounts for your second company

When we created our database in Chapter 2, *Installing Your First Application*, Odoo installed the United States Fiscal Localization based on the country we chose in the setup. Go to the **Invoicing** menu and choose **Settings** under **Configuration**. At the top left you will see the option to choose the **Fiscal Localization** for **Euro Shirts**:

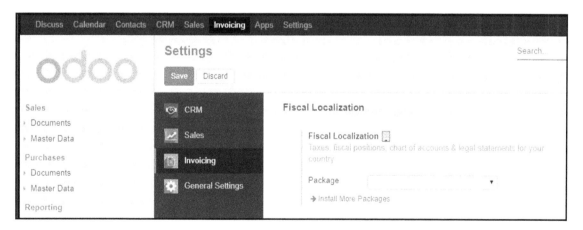

As we have not set the **Fiscal Localization,** yet the **Package** drop-down has no current selection. Click **Install More Packages** to bring up a list of available **Chart Templates.**

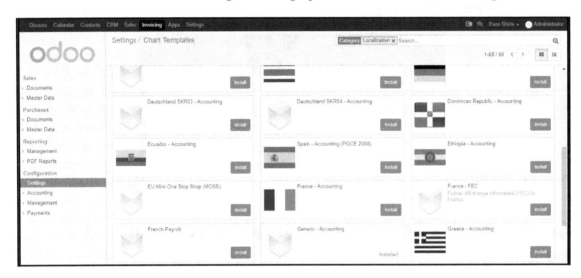

Now, you can search for the **Chart Template** that you require for your second company. In this case we will choose the **Chart Template** for **France.** It will take a few moments for Odoo to complete the configuration. Now when you look at the settings for Euro Shirts, you will see the new template has been applied.

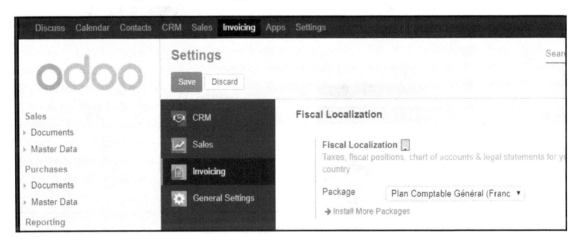

We have now completed several of the basic steps that are required to implement a multi-company solution in Odoo.

Implementing a multi-company solution

As previously stated, setting up a multi-company system is complex. While the system will work in much the same way as it did previously, it is important that you understand how a multi-company system impacts every operation within the system. Customers, users, suppliers, and the chart of accounts all tie into multiple company operations. This chapter has provided the very basics of how to configure a multi-company setup, but final configurations will take a great deal of planning and fine-tuning if you want a truly successful installation.

Summary

In this chapter, we examined some of the things that you should consider when administering an Odoo installation, such as planning your server configuration and establishing good practices for ensuring business continuity in the case of failure. We discovered how to back up and restore databases, as well as manage user access and group permissions.

Later in the chapter, we looked at internationalization and configured Odoo to handle multiple languages and international currency. We learned how to change Odoo sequences, so your documents will use formats and numbering systems that work for your business requirements. Finally, we took a brief look at how to set up a multi-company configuration in Odoo.

In the next chapter, we will take a look at human resources and how you can apply Odoo to make recruiting, interviewing, hiring, and managing employees easier.

8
Implementing the Human Resources Application

Over the past few decades, companies have had increasing demands placed upon them to keep track of employee-related information. Odoo has a variety of modules that can help your company organize information concerning your employees. Some of these applications, such as timesheets and applications that monitor attendance, can become critical processes that help a company contain costs. In this chapter, we will look at how you can integrate Human Resource applications.

In this chapter, we will cover the following:

- The functions of the employee directory
- Creating timesheets to track time on projects
- How to use leave management to manage employee vacations and time off
- Recruiting new employees to fill job vacancies

What's new in Odoo 11?

The applications covered in this chapter have very few changes in Odoo 11. Aside from some very small interface improvements, there are really no functional changes between Odoo HR applications in Odoo 10 and Odoo 11.

The modular approach to Human Resources

Like the rest of Odoo, **Human Resources** (**HR**) applications allow you to implement the functionality you need today and then later add additional modules. This approach makes it much easier to start using Odoo right away to solve specific company needs. The best way to be successful in implementing a system is to plan ahead and implement it in stages. Once you are successful at putting one application in place, then you can move on to putting additional applications in place.

Installing the Employee Directory

When you install the base Odoo applications, you get the ability to manage system users, but you will notice that there are no menu options for entering and managing employees. To begin working with Human Resource applications, you will need to install the base **Employee Directory** application.

Go to the **Settings** menu and install the **Employee Directory** application using the same process as the previous Odoo applications:

After you have installed the **Employee Directory** application, you will see a new menu at the top named **Employees**. Clicking on the **Menu** will take you to a dashboard that displays the **Employees** in a **Kanban** view:

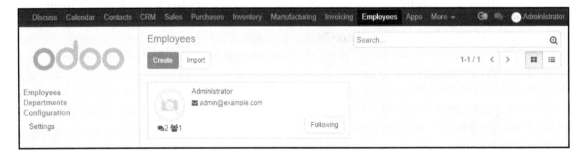

What you may notice first is that, for better or for worse, Odoo does not consider users to be employees. The only employee that is in the current Odoo installation is the administrator. On top of that, there is no built-in mechanism to automatically turn your users into employees.

Creating a new employee

First, let's go ahead and see how we can add a new employee to our system.

Click the **Create** button to bring up the form for you to begin entering a new employee into Odoo:

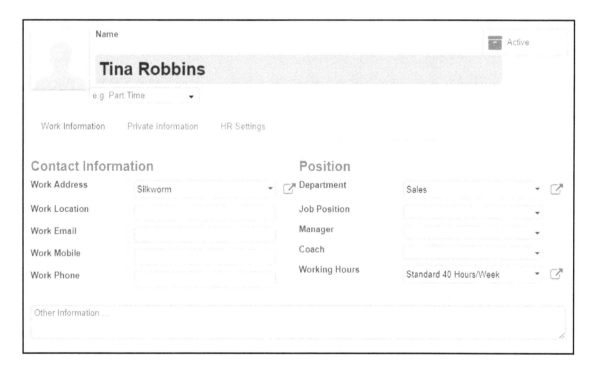

The only required field in the employee form is the name. All the other fields are optional. Odoo will set the default working address to the company address. While most fields are self-explanatory, we will go over several of the more important fields in order to take them into consideration.

Department

The employee department is a common way for a company to organize employees. While we currently have Tina assigned to the sales department, we can move her to another department. In our example, we are going to create a production department and assign Tina to that department:

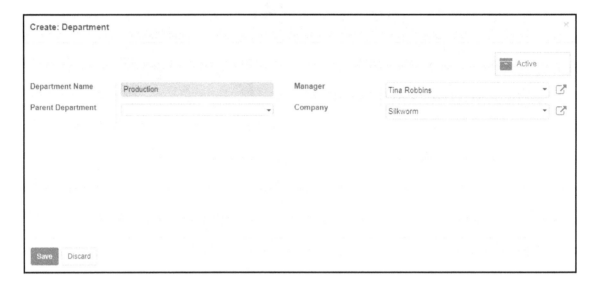

In this screen, we have set the **Department Name** to Production and set the **Manager** of this department to Tina Robbins. Please be aware that you must save the record first before you can assign Tina as the manager.

Also, note the **Parent Department** field. This field allows you to create a hierarchical structure of departments for your company. Typically, you will want to look at the organization chart of a company and take some time preparing the company department structure.

Job Title

The **Job Title** field allows you to manage job titles for employees inside of Odoo:

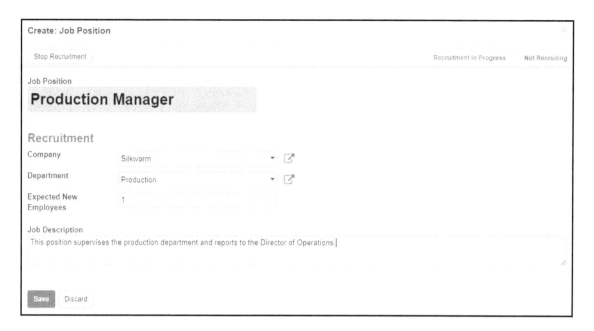

In this screenshot, we have created a job title of Production Manager for Tina Robbins. As you can see from this form, job titles are tied to departments. This means that to properly configure Odoo, you would need to create job titles across departments. Therefore, you do not necessarily want to name a job simply Manager. That would make it difficult, when looking at the list of job titles, to know within which department that manager may be associated.

Note that there is a place to enter the new employees that are to be expected, and it has a default value of **1**. You can also see that the status of this job title shows **Recruitment in Progress** as well as a **Stop Recruitment** button, which we will cover later in the chapter.

If you try to save the record, you may get an error, reading **Error! You cannot create a recursive hierarchy of employee(s)**. It appears because Odoo knows Tina is in the Production Department and that the manager of that department should be Tina, and fills in the Manager field. Clear the **Manager** field to proceed.

Manager and Coach

The **Manager** and **Coach** fields in the employee screen can be used to specify any other employees that are already in Odoo. The manager is often called the supervisor in some companies, and may be involved in approving the employees' timesheets, leave requests, performance appraisals, and so on. The coach is just an optional field that you could use to specify another relationship the employee has that is valuable to the position.

Employee Private Information

The **Private Information** tab on the employee screen contains the individual's private details that are of interest to the HR department, such as **Private Address**, **Date of Birth**, and citizenship status:

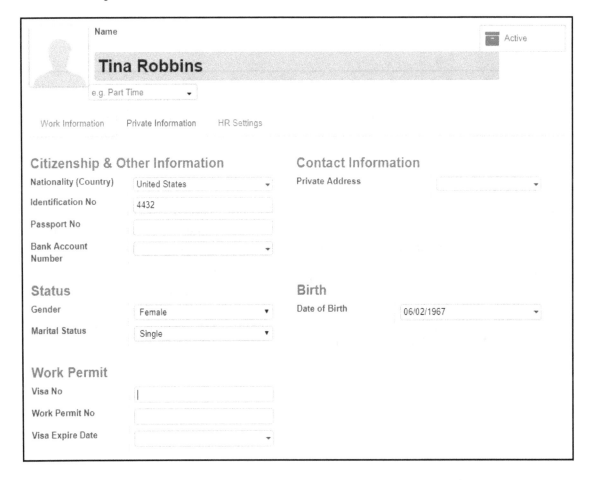

The nationality field allows you to select from the entire country listing that comes pre-loaded in Odoo. Typically, the **Identification No** field would be used for an employee badge. Odoo includes a **Passport No** on the form, which may be required in some cases where a company is required to report citizenship information to the government.

If you do decide to enter a home address for the employee, you will be taken to another screen. Near the bottom of the form, you have the ability to specify **Gender**, **Marital Status**, and **Date of Birth** for the employee.

HR settings

On the **HR Settings** page, the **Related User** field will allow you to associate the employee with an existing user account in Odoo. Simply select the user from the pop-up list and choose which user you want associated with the employee. It is also possible to add users on the fly by choosing **Create** from the **Related User** popup:

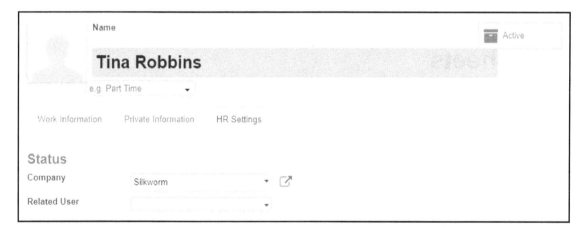

If the employee is not a user in the system, you can simply leave this field blank as we have in the preceding screenshot.

Managing Departments

Earlier, we saw how we can add a department on the fly as we are entering an employee. Odoo also provides a dedicated **Department** dashboard that lets you see and add departments to the system.

Click on the **Departments** link to bring up the form:

The default installation of the **Employee Directory** application comes with two departments, **Administration** and **Sales**. We added the **Production** department in the previous section when we added Tina Robbins as an employee. Clicking the **Employees** button under either department will take you to the appropriate list of employees for that department.

Timesheets

Odoo allows you to install a HR module that will allow you to track employee time and attendance. Timesheets are most useful when you have jobs that require you to account for employees' work hours and assign those hours to projects or customers. To utilize this feature, install the **Timesheets** application:

Once you have installed the **Timesheets** application, the menu bar will be expanded to include two new main menus called **TimeSheets** and **Attendances**. Currently, after installing the **Timesheets** application, Odoo just takes you to the standard **Discuss** menu, just as if you have logged in.

You should be aware that installing the **Timesheets** application requires the installation of the **Project Management** application as a dependency.

Click the **Timesheets** menu to pull up the application. If you are using the enterprise edition of Odoo, you will have an alternate method for creating a new timesheet.

To begin recording employee activities, click on **My Timesheets** and then click the **Create** button:

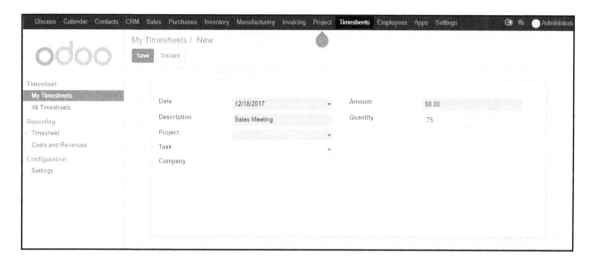

As you can see, we are presented with a form that allows you to enter the activities line by line. Each line has four required fields. The **Date** is filled in with the current date by default, and the **User** defaults to the current user in the system. You must then enter a **Description** and provide a **Project** to attach the activity to.

In Odoo 11, the **Amount** field is where you would put the actual dollar amount that you would bill for the task. The **Quantity** field is where you specify the number of hours related to the task.

A project is how Odoo ties the duration of the activity to the appropriate accounting entries. We will learn more about projects in the next chapter on project management.

For now, we will simply create a project to attach the activity to:

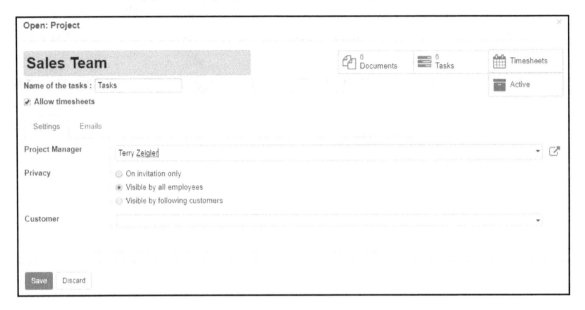

One thing you will notice is that you can assign a customer to the project as well. This can then allow you to more directly invoice customers based on a given project or activity. We are going to leave this blank for now and consider this an internal project that we need to track the time for.

After you save the project and timesheet, you can come back to the main Kanban view to see your new timesheet displayed. In the screenshot that follows, you can see the timesheet we created for the **Sales Team** as well as another timesheet for a **Sales Meeting**. As you can see, both timesheets are tied to the **Sales Team** project:

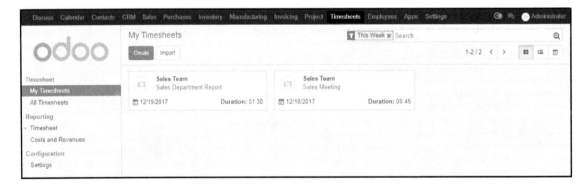

Implementing Leave Management

In addition to managing and approving daily timesheets, it is also possible to install an Odoo Human Resources application that will manage holidays, leave, and other information related to employee time off. We install **Leave Management** in the same way as we installed the other Odoo applications:

After you have installed the **Leave Management** application, you will have yet another new menu, the **Leaves** menu. One departure from earlier editions of Odoo is that now Odoo installs many of the Human Resource applications as separate menus. This leads to having more and more main menus within the Odoo application. Fortunately, however, the menu automatically collapses down into a drop-down list when there is not enough room to display the menu horizontally across the screen:

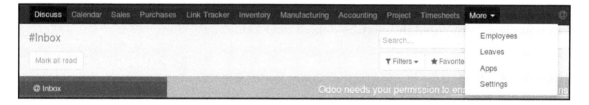

The primary purpose of this **Leave Management** application is to provide an easy mechanism for employees to request leave and for their managers to approve or deny the request.

Creating a leave request

When you click on the **Leaves** menu option, you are taken to a monthly calendar that will show you your current leave requests. Naturally, if there were no prior leave requests made, or there are none for the current month, then the calendar is empty.

Click on a day in the calendar to tell Odoo to schedule a leave request beginning on that day:

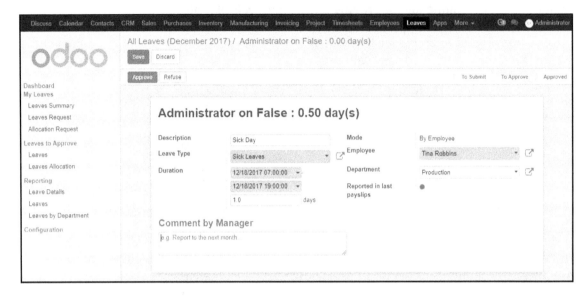

In this example, we have requested a **Sick Day**. It's possible to configure leave types to only allow a specific number of days or a specific length of time. The **Personal Days** leave type, for example, is configured this way by default in Odoo.

Leave type

For our example, we have chosen the **Sick Day** leave type. This implies that the employee is taking this leave with pay. Alternative leave types can be managed for reporting purposes.

Duration

When you change the **Duration** using the **Date Range** fields, Odoo will automatically re-calculate the **Days** field.

Mode

When entering a leave request like we are in this example, the **Mode** field is read only as you are specifying the actual leave for a specific employee. For our example, we are submitting the leave request for a single employee. When you use the **Allocate leave** option instead of just doing a leave request, you have an additional option. By using the **By Employee Tag** mode, you can allocate leave days that match all employees who share that same employee tag. So, for example, you could easily allocate 7 days of vacation time to all employees that had the *full time* employee tag. They would then use up this time by submitting leave requests.

Employee

The **Employee** field lets you set the employee for whom leave is requested.

Department

The **Department** field lets you set the department from which leave is requested.

Submitting for approval

When requesting leave, clicking the **Save** button is all that is required to save the information and send it on to the assigned manager of the employee for approval.

Once you have saved the leave request, the form will close and you will see the updated calendar:

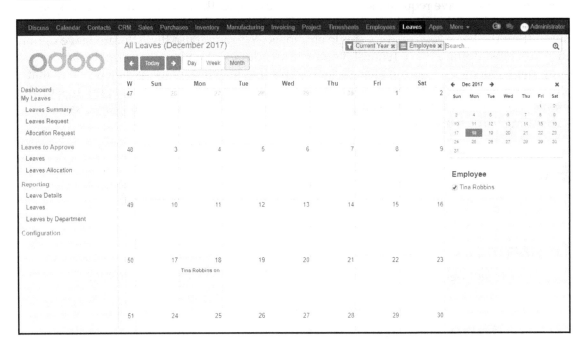

As you can see, our leave request is presented on the calendar with the appropriate information.

Approving leave requests

Clicking on the **Leaves** option in the **Leaves to Approve** section of the **Human Resources** menu pulls up the list of leave requests to approve. You may have to clear the **My Department Leaves** filter if the leave request is not showing in the list. In our example, we can see the leave request we have submitted for Tina Robbins:

To approve a leave request, simply click on a request and then choose **Approve** to approve it, or **Refuse** to deny the request.

Recruitment process

Many Human Resource departments spend a great deal of time managing the recruitment process. Odoo provides an application that can help organize the information and make it easier to keep track of the communication required when hiring new employees.

Install the **Recruitment Process** application as you have the other Odoo applications:

After the **Recruitment Process** application has been installed, you can access the application by selecting the newly added **Recruiting** menu.

You are then presented with the **Job Positions** form:

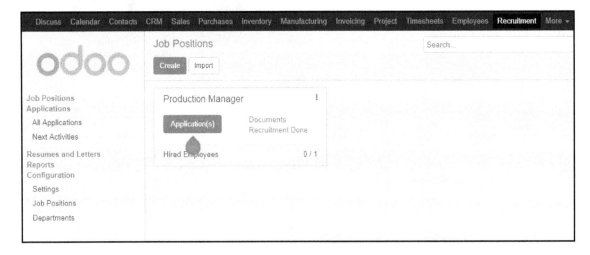

You will then see the **Production Manager** job position we added early in the chapter. Like the other Kanban setups in Odoo, each position provides various options to color the panel and perform other common operations.

Recruiting for a new job position

Tina Robbins has been very busy in her position of Production Manager. It has been decided that there is a need to hire a Production Assistant to assist her in her duties. With the new recruitment application installed, we can now create a new job position and start the recruiting process.

Click on **Job Positions** under the **Recruitment** menu and click the **Create** button:

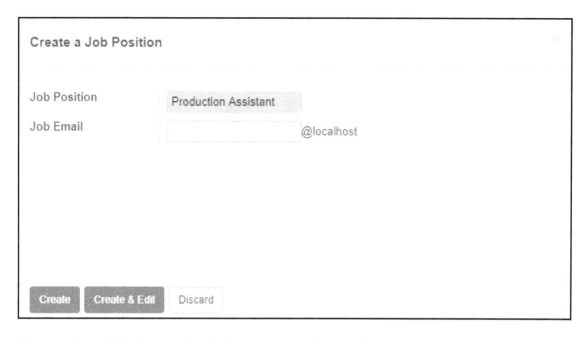

Here, we have filled in the details for our **Production Assistant** and assigned the position to the **Production department**.

When we go back and look at the **Job Positions** in Odoo, we will find that the Kanban view now displays details about the job position we created:

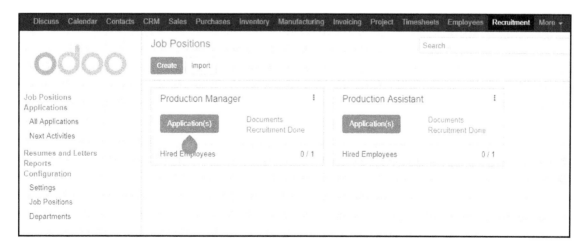

Creating an employment application

When a potential employee sends in an application, resume, or another document that will allow you to record their interest in working for your company, you can create a recruitment application.

Click the **Application(s)** button for the **Production Assistant** to bring up the application list for the job position:

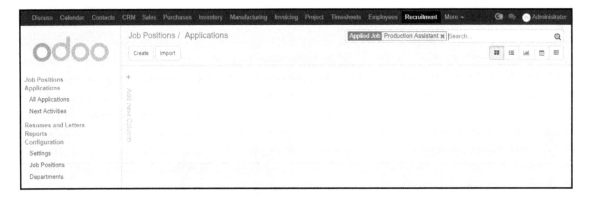

Because there are no applications, naturally this list will start out empty. Also, note that there is a filter applied that is restricting the applications to only those that are associated with the Production Assistant position.

Click **Create** to add a new application:

This form has a lot of fields to be filled out. By default, the only required field for the application is the subject. The rest of the information can be collected throughout the recruiting and interviewing processes.

Hiring employees

Let's go ahead and hire this Bob Nelson guy. Thankfully, Odoo's Recruitment module will create the employee for us by simply clicking the **Create Employee** button near the top of the form.

Looking at the **Employees** list, we can now see that `Bob Nelson` is an employee in the **Production** department with the title of **Production Assistant**:

Summary

In this chapter, we examined the various Human Resource applications available in Odoo. We installed the base **Employee Directory**, followed by applications that managed time and attendance, as well as leave requests. Finally, we installed an application that allowed us to manage the process of recruiting new employees. We walked through the completion of an employment application and finally turned the potential applicant into an employee.

In the next chapter, we will look at the **Project Management** application in Odoo and how it can be used to improve service quality for customers. **Project Management** allows you to organize anything, from the simplest projects to complex projects involving multiple tasks. Furthermore, you can even track the time related to these projects and display project information in a variety of graphical formats to make it easier to track your deadlines.

9
Understanding Project Management

In this chapter, we will explore a very flexible application that allows you to manage projects and tie them into other applications in Odoo. The **Project Management** application allows your company to manage project stages, assign teams, and even track time and job costs related to projects. Analytical accounting features give you even greater control over how project costs can be tied to your company's general ledger.

This chapter covers the following topics:

- Discovering the various uses for Project Management
- Linking projects with customer accounts
- Assigning teams to projects
- Creating custom project stages
- Adding, assigning, and organizing tasks
- Tying into analytical accounting and employee timesheets

What's New in Odoo 11?

Project Management in Odoo 11 has undergone some minor interface changes that simplify some operations. In addition, **Project Management** now ties into Odoo 11's new activity menu.

Basics of Project Management

Depending on your industry and the types of project you may encounter, the **Project Management** application can be set up to manage independent projects; or, instead, it can be configured to manage projects related to customers or sales orders. With additional modules, it is possible to tie the **Project Management** application in to virtually any aspect of Odoo.

For example, you could simply use the **Project Management** application to track the various stages and tasks involved with a company event. Who is going to be responsible for finding the location? When will you need to order the invitations? Who is going to set the agenda? When is an employee going to go and pick up the sound system? In this instance, the **Project Management** application is simply being used to track a single project that is not associated with the customer.

In other instances, you may wish to utilize the **Project Management** application to track projects that are organized around your customer records. A common example would be a construction firm. After assigning a project to a customer, you can track various stages of the project life cycle. Employees can be assigned tasks and, using the Odoo messaging system, you can share project details with your customers. It is in this configuration that the Odoo **Project Management** application can add real value to an Odoo installation, and provide better integration with your accounting system with less effort than a standalone project management tool.

Installing the Project Management application

To access project managing features, if you have not followed along in Chapter 8, *Implementing the Human Resources Application,* you will need to install the **Project Management** application. In Odoo 11, **Project Management** is automatically installed when you install the **Timesheet** application.

If **Project Management** is not installed, go to the **Settings** menu and install the **Project Management** application using the same process as the previous Odoo applications:

Understanding the Project dashboard

After installing the **Project Management** application, the screen will be refreshed and you will see the **Projects** dashboard. The dashboard provides an overview of the active projects and comes with the project we added in the previous chapter, **Sales Team**:

We can see in the summary that the project we created in the previous chapter has **0 Tasks**, as we never added any tasks to the project. If you click on **Timesheets**, you will be taken to the two activities we created.

While this project was useful for an internal example of using a project to time various employee activities, let's see how we can use the **Project Management** application to manage various tasks for a customer.

A real-world project example for a customer

As in other chapters, we will use a real-world example to demonstrate the functionality of Odoo's **Project Management** application. In the silkscreen industry, it can be common to have extremely large projects that span many different types of apparel and print designs. For this example, we are going to create a project to manage creating an entire line of sports jerseys for an organization called Lil League.

In defining our project, it is important to look at the scope of our project and why it will be valuable to use the project manager to organize the various tasks involved. With our Lil League organization, we have multiple teams that can vary in terms of the logo design for the team, the number of players, the sizes of the apparel required, and the printing of different players' numbers and even players' names. There are often multiple deadlines to manage and a number of people that may need to approve various phases of the project as they are completed. Using the **Project Management** application, we can better track this information and tie it in to sales orders and other Odoo functions.

Creating our first project

After the **Project Management** application has been successfully installed, we can go to the **Project** application and create a new project.

The basic steps we will follow are:

- Creating a new project record
- Giving a name to the project
- Assigning the project to a specific customer
- Assigning team members to the project

To begin, under the **Project** application, select **Dashboard** in the menu on the left, then click the **Create** button:

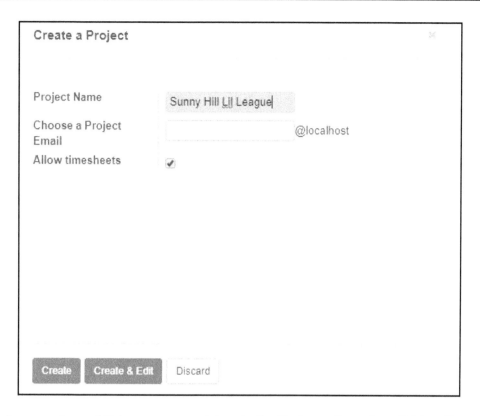

In previous versions of Odoo, you were taken to the Project editor after clicking **Create**. Like many processes in Odoo 10, this is now greatly simplified, and you are presented with a very simple wizard that prompts for a **Project Name** as well as a project email. For our example, we will use `Sunny Hill Lil League` as the name for our project.

The **Project Email** is useful when you want a specific email assigned to the project. If you leave the project email field blank, Odoo will automatically create an email based on the project name. Leave the **Project Email** field `blank` so that Odoo will create our email address for us automatically. As this email is only used for potential incoming emails, there will be no harm in this as long as the email does not conflict with another you may be using for a different purpose.

As you may expect, checking the **Timesheets** checkbox will allow you to associate timesheets with the project like we did in the previous chapter. We will go ahead and leave this checked so that our project can manage the labor that is spent on the project, and then bill it to the customer when required.

Once you create the project, the dashboard will refresh, revealing the project you just created.

Understanding project stages

Project stages allow you to track a given task through different phases of its completion. These stages often will vary from project to project depending on the types of task involved. For example, a project involving software development would likely have different task stages from one that involves planning a real-estate development seminar.

In Odoo 11, a new project does not provide default stages for your project. Fortunately, it is very easy to create new stages. Let's go ahead and create some stages for our new project.

Click the **Tasks** button at the top of the new project you have created to bring up the tasks:

Naturally, we have not added any tasks to the project yet. We can, however, begin defining stages for the project by clicking the **ADD NEW COLUMN** button. A small panel will come up for you to enter the description for the stage.

For our example, we are going to create stages for `Specifications`, `Art Design`, `Approval`, and finally, `Production`.

Simply type in the stage, in this case `Specifications`, and then click the **Add** button:

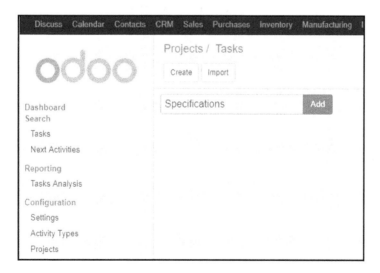

The screen will refresh to show the new column added. Use the same process to add the additional stages to the project:

New column added

When you are finished adding them, your project stages should look similar to the preceding screenshot. Now, we are ready to begin adding tasks to our project.

Defining project tasks

The main unit for tracking the various activities involved in a project is a project task. Odoo provides a quick way to add a task to the project by clicking the large plus button under the appropriate project stage.

Click the plus button inside the **Specifications** stage, and create a task for Determine Team Names:

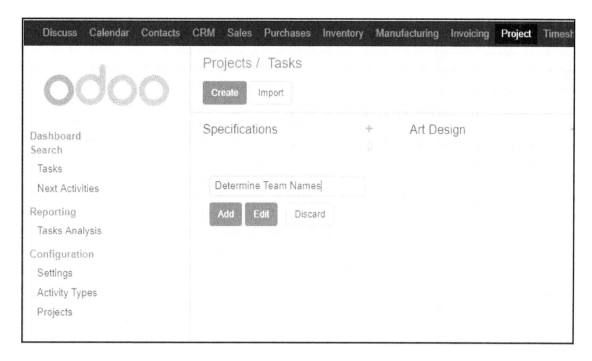

Similar to adding a stage, you simply enter the title of the task and then hit the **Add** button. The screen will then refresh, and you will automatically be prompted to add the next task. Once you have created the task, you can click on the task to open it or you can use the menu on the task to pull the task up to edit it. Once you have opened the task you can now provide additional details.

Here, we'll define additional aspects of the task:

- Name of the task (which is required)
- The **Project** to which the task is assigned
- The **Deadline** date of the task
- The responsible party **Assigned to** the task
- Any **Tags** you would like to associate with this task
- A **Description** of the task

For our example, we have filled out the task as shown in the following screenshot:

At the top of the form, you will see all of the project stages, with the current stage highlighted in blue. In this example, **Specifications** is the currently selected stage. When in edit mode, you can click on these stages to directly assign the task to a given stage. This can be changed as the project progresses, so you are not locked into keeping a task assigned to the same stage throughout the project.

One of the important aspects of good project management is assigning responsible parties for each task. The **Assigned to** field allows you to specify who is ultimately responsible for the completion of the task.

The **Tags** field can be valuable for more effectively tracking and organizing tasks. In our example, we have defined an **information collection** tag. This tag can then be assigned to any task that is related to collecting data regarding the project.

Creating additional tasks

For our real-world example, we are going to define several tasks at various stages. When creating your own list of stages think about the flow and order of your tasks. Ideally a task will move from left to right and stages are completed. For our example, our tasks include:

- Specifications about out the details of the project.
- Creating the art design
- Approval of the design
- Producing the product

Now that we have created generic tasks for the entire project, let's go ahead and assume we have received a draft list of team names. This will allow us to track the progress of each team as it goes through the various stages in the project. For our example, we will use the following team names and leave them in the **Specifications** stage to start.

- `Bulldogs`
- `Falcons`
- `Wolf Pack`

After entering our tasks and assigning them to the various stages, the result should look something like this:

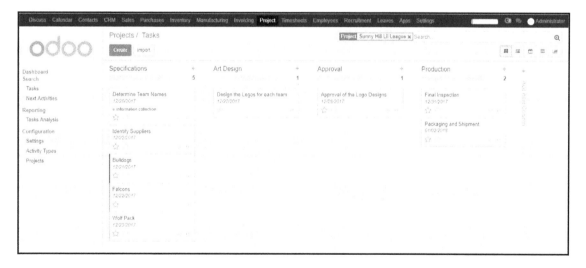

Specifications stage

The Kanban interface allows you to pick up a task and move it to another stage, or reorder it within a current stage, by just clicking and dragging. You can reorder the stages by clicking on the title of the stage and dragging it to the position you like.

Also, notice that we have added in deadline dates to the tasks. We can then view the tasks in the calendar view for the project.

Click on the Calendar icon on the right of the form to bring up the Calendar view.

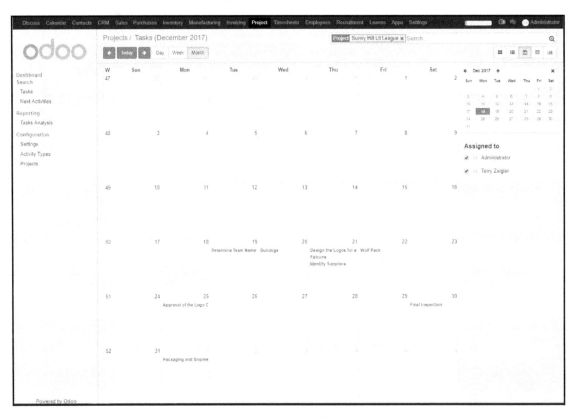

Calendar view

Completing project tasks

As you complete project tasks, you can bring them up and mouse over the **Active** button. It will then change to **Archive** as you hover over it. When you click the button, the task will be archived. This method will remove the task from the project entirely and hide it from view.

 If you ever need to see tasks that have been archived, there is a search view already created for Archived that you can apply to your searches. Alternatively you can use the advanced filter skills you will learn in `Chapter 10`, *Creating Advanced Searches and Dashboards* to set a filter that displays records in which active records are false.

Previously in Odoo, a **Done** status was provided by default. If you need to keep track of completed tasks and not have them fall off the project, you will need to set up a **Done** or **Completed** stage for your project.

Scheduling an activity

In addition to managing task deadlines you can also directly schedule activities related to a project task. When you schedule an activity it can then be centrally managed through Odoo 11's **Activities** menu. Pull up the task you wish to schedule an activity for then click the **Schedule activity** link to pull up the form to schedule the activity. You can find this link just under the description of the task.

Now you can enter the details for the activity you wish to schedule. In this example we have scheduled a call to discuss approval of the art for a specific phase of the project:

When you click **Schedule,** you will then be able to see the task under the **Activities** menu.

Monitoring task completion

Odoo uses a simple set of flags to determine if a task is ready to move between stages. In the top left corner you will find a small round icon that can allow you to specify if the task is ready to go to the next stage (green), or if the task is blocked for some reason from moving to the next stage (red).

So for example, when a task moves to the approval stage the person responsible for performing that task can choose to mark it in red. This will tell anyone looking at the task that it is held up:

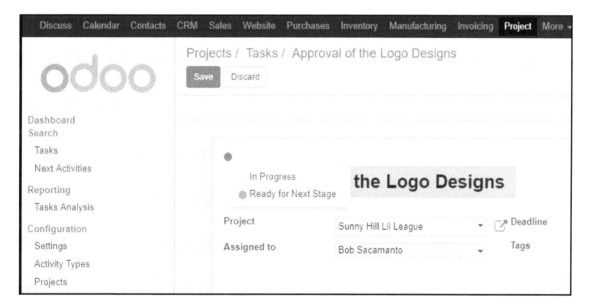

Here we have marked an approval task as blocked, so the icon shows red. As you can see you can set it to gray to show it in progress (the default setting) or set it to green to specify the task is **Ready for Next Stage**.

Using these flags you will see at a glance on the Kanban view whether a task is ready to move forward or if it requires some sort of special attention.

Calculating project costs and time

To assist the process of calculating project time and costs, you can install the **Human Resources** application, **Timesheets**. This application lets you create timesheets for your employees that let you specify hours worked by day. If you have been following along, this application should have already been installed in Chapter 8, *Implementing the Human Resources Application*.

If you click the **Timesheets** page on a given task, you will get a list view in which you can create new timesheet entries. In this example, we have attributed one hour to **Determine Player Names** in the **Bulldogs** task.

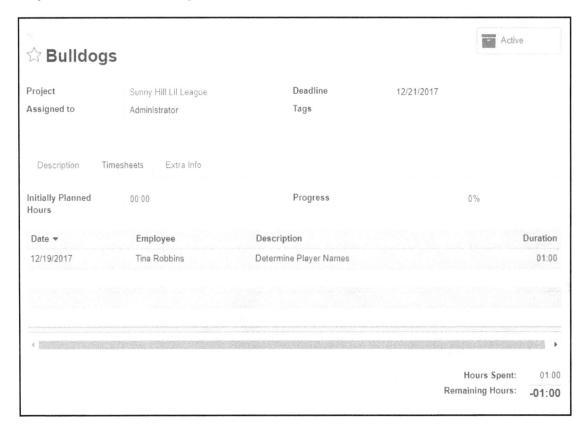

You can learn more about using timesheets and analytical accounting in `Chapter 8`, *Implementing the Human Resources Application*.

Summary

In this chapter, we examined the **Project Management** application by taking a look at the Project dashboard. We then created an example of a real-world project involving our Lil League organization. After setting up our project and assigning team members, we defined the various stages that will be involved in completing the project. With the stages defined, we were able to go through and assign various tasks to the stages, along with their dates of completion. Finally, we looked at the various ways you can view the tasks and how you can complete them.

In the next chapter, we will explore how you can create advanced searches and custom dashboards in Odoo. As a company uses its system from day to day, the amount of collected data can grow quite rapidly. Being able to locate pertinent records in a speedy fashion is vital for optimum business operation. We'll discover how to utilize all of the handy searching, filtering, and dashboard presentation tools that are at our disposal within Odoo.

10
Creating Advanced Searches and Dashboards

In this chapter, we will cover advanced searching, custom filters, and dashboards. We begin by looking at how Odoo searches the various datasets within the system. Next, we explore more advanced searching options and discuss how you can save these filters so that they can be easily accessed when you need them. Finally, we discuss the Odoo dashboard capabilities and how we can improve usability for users.

The topics covered in this chapter include the following:

- Identifying users' search requirements
- Understanding default filters versus custom filters
- Grouping items in a list
- Setting and saving advanced search conditions
- Creating dashboard content and layouts

What's New in Odoo 11

There are no noticeable changes in how advanced searches or dashboards are handled in Odoo 11 vs Odoo 10.

Determining the search requirements for your business

One of the tasks that can often be frustrating and time-consuming for users is trying to find the information they need. When datasets are small and simple there is not much of an issue. As the number of records in the system grows, it can become increasingly hard to find information.

When implementing an ERP system, you will want to take the time to work with users and get familiar with the data that they use each day. If you are working with a purchasing system that only produces an average of 10 purchase orders a day, you will have far fewer concerns raised over advanced searching in that application. However, if you have 20 purchasing agents cutting 450 purchase orders a day, it will be critical that the users have a firm grasp on the search functionality of the system. Trying to locate a specific order can be like trying to find a needle in a haystack.

 Take the time to sit with users and watch them use the system. Often, users will need to look up the same types of data repeatedly in their daily interactions with the system. These are the activities that you will want to set up custom filters for and perhaps even include on the user's dashboard.

Fortunately, Odoo offers a robust searching mechanism, as well as the ability to create dashboards for displaying information that the user may need to look at frequently.

In this chapter, we will create a new database with demonstration data so you can better see the searches in action.

Creating a database with demonstration data

It can often be valuable to test certain features in Odoo without having to enter a lot of data. Odoo offers an option to populate a database with demonstration data when you create it. Since this chapter is focused specifically on searching for and displaying data, we will load up a database with the sample data provided by Odoo.

Accessing the database manager

While it is possible to access the database manager by clicking on a link in the login screen, there are times when that link is not available. One reason could be because the website application has been installed and the **Manage Databases** link is hidden from the home page.

 Sometimes, if your Odoo server is throwing internal server errors, or you are having other problems with your database, you can resolve the issue and make backups of your data by going directly to the database manager.

To access the database manager directly in the default installation of Odoo, you can use the following link: `http://localhost:8069/web/database/manager`.

You will then be presented with the database manager screen:

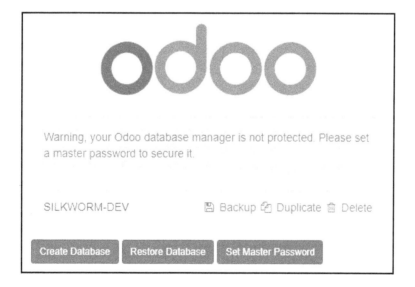

Naturally, you will need to change the server address and port to match your Odoo installation:

1. Click the **Create Database** button to create a new database.
2. When creating our database, we check **Load demonstration data** so that our database is prepopulated, making it easier to present example search techniques:

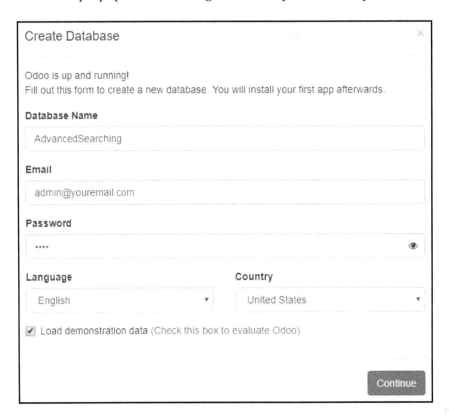

3. After you click **Continue**, Odoo will set up the new database. So, now that we have an application to work with, we will install the **Sales Management** application:

Searching in Odoo

Odoo provides a standardized search box in the upper-right corner of the form. Depending on the menu item, some forms come with predefined filters already set for the list.

If you navigate to **Sales** and select **Customers**, you can see the search box in the upper-right corner with the **Customers** filter preassigned:

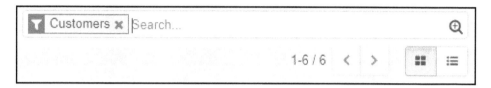

Some lists open with a predefined filter that will limit the primary dataset. In the prior screenshot, you can see that the list view, **Customers**, has a customer filter applied by default when you open the form. Odoo stores customers, vendors, and employees in the same central database table. The **Customers** filter prevents those other types of data, such as vendors or employees, from displaying in the list:

The Customers filter

In this instance, if you clear the **Customers** filter by clicking on the small close box in the tag, you will have a list with not only customers, but partners, users, suppliers, and contacts as well. The **Customers** filter is applied by default in this view.

Sometimes, users can get confused if they accidently remove the filter. If you are not getting the results you expect, always double-check the filter in the upper-right corner and, if necessary, navigate away from the view and back again to refresh the default filter.

Basic searches are handled easily in Odoo. Just go into the search box, begin typing, and press the *Enter* key. Odoo will then look at the primary search fields for the type of data you are searching for, and show you the results in the list or Kanban view.

In the following screenshot, you can see a simple search:

A simple search

In this example, Odoo has returned all the customers that have `camp` in their name.

Now, we can see that there are two filters applied: the default filter, **Customers**, that was there when we opened the customer list, and the **Name** filter that will limit those customers to just the names that include `camp`.

 The small space between the two filter tags means that both conditions are required for a record to be included in the results list (A and B).

When two filter tags are next to one another without a space between them, it denotes that records may meet either condition (A or B).

Odoo will remember your search criteria as you move between list, Kanban, and form views. Once you go to another menu item, the search criteria will reset to the default search when you return.

As you type in the search box, before hitting the *Enter* key, Odoo will display the available filters in a small drop-down list directly under the search box:

Type the letter R into the search box. You will notice how the **R** is now in bold where it will be applied to the filter. Also, note that, to the left of **Search Salesperson for: R**, there is a small triangle. Clicking on this triangle will expand the results in the list:

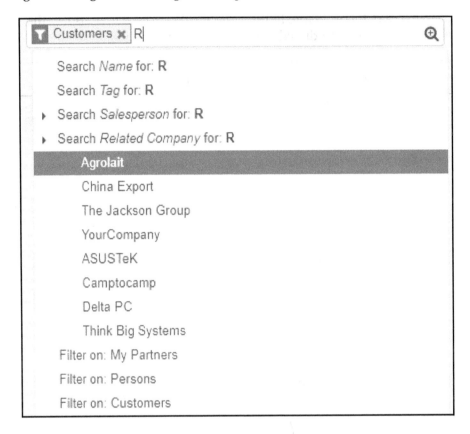

Using filters in list views

Odoo provides default filters for all of the list views. Applying a filter will limit the records that Odoo is displaying. You can apply one or more filters depending on your needs. The available filters will vary depending on the data that you are viewing.

For example, the **Products** view will have a completely different set of filters and group options than the **Customers** view:

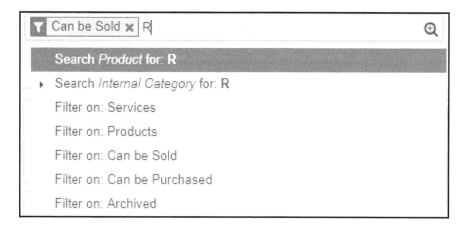

While each search box will have different default filters and **Group By** options, the functionality will be the same. In Odoo 11, you can access all the search features by clicking the small magnifying glass with the + sign in it to the right of the search box:

When you click this, Odoo will expand the search area to show all the search features. Let's return to the customer list and click the small triangle to bring up the advanced search options:

In Odoo 11, the advanced search tools have been consolidated into **Filters**, **Group By**, and **Favorites**. Let's first explore the data using **Filters** to limit the records that are displayed:

In the example dropdown in the preceding screenshot, you can see the check mark next to the filter that has been applied—**Can be Sold**. The tags for the currently selected filter are also displayed inside the search box. Clicking on a filter applies the filter immediately and refreshes the results list.

Naturally, the list of available filters will change depending on which set of records you are viewing. You can add multiple filters and Odoo will return the records that match all of the filters which you have applied. Clicking on a filter that is already highlighted will remove that filter from the search.

Grouping information

In addition to filtering your results, you can also group data in most Kanban and list views by using the **Group By** option. When you group data in a Kanban view, you will get a column for each category. You can then use the horizontal scrollbar at the bottom of your window to look through the items. This will be ineffective for items with a very large number of groups:

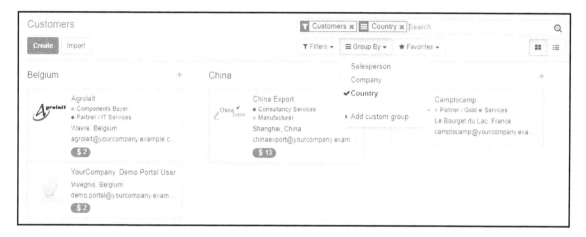

The Group By option

The preceding screenshot shows **Customers** in a Kanban view, demonstrating how a user will need to scroll not only up and down, but also left and right to get a view of all of the items.

Grouped data is often more easily represented in a list view.

When you group data in a list, a little triangle appears to the left of each group header. Clicking on this triangle will display the rows grouped under that header:

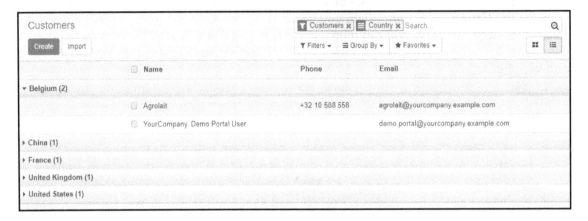

As shown in the preceding screenshot, we have filtered by customers that are companies by selecting the **Companies** option in the **Filters** menu. We also grouped our data by category by selecting **Country** in the **Group By** menu. Next, we expanded the **France** country section by clicking on the small triangle to the left. You can then see the list of companies that are in France. As with filters, clicking on **Companies** again will remove the grouping. You can also nest groups inside of other groups simply by selecting additional items under **Group By**.

Grouping can be a great way to look at data. Unfortunately, with extremely large datasets, grouping lists can be very slow because far more records must be processed if you are filtering and browsing data.

Performing a custom search

While the default filters may help us find most of the data records we seek, it is inevitable that there will come a time when we will need a more customized search. To create a custom search, open up the **Filters** drop-down menu and then click on **Add Custom Filter** to expand the available options. Here, we will get a drop-down list of fields that can be used to set our search criteria:

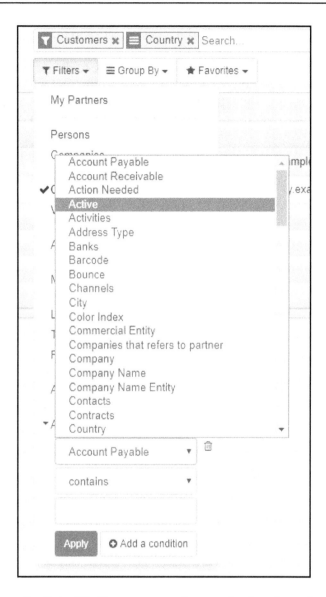

Choosing a field from the list will allow you to select a criterion from the available search operators, as well as specify the data for which you wish to search. Click on **Add a condition** to enter further criteria. Clicking on the small **x** to the right of a search condition will delete that condition from your custom filter.

In Odoo, you will often find it a best practice to make records inactive when they are no longer required. For example, if you discontinue a product, you will often find yourself unable to delete that product because there are transactions tied to it. Therefore, you will wish to deactivate that product record. By default, Odoo will hide inactive records. If you need to retrieve inactive records, use a custom filter to create a condition where the **Active** field is false and then apply it to this filter.

You can continue to add additional criteria to your custom filter. When you have specified all the criteria you wish to use in your search, click on the **Apply** button to apply the custom filter:

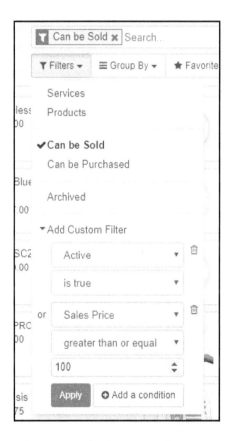

In the custom filter option, we have specified two conditions: **Active** must be **is true** or the **Sale Price** for the customer must be **greater than or equal to** a value of **100**. Many users can get confused and believe that this filter would imply that both **Active** and **Sale Price** must meet our criteria, but this is not so. Note the **or** to the left of the second condition.

Specifying multiple advanced searches

As you can see in our previous example, Odoo will always use an **or** operation between each of the conditions you add to the search. But what if we wanted to have a search where the record is active and the sale price is greater than **100**? To accomplish this, you must first apply the custom filter with only the active condition defined. This will limit the results to only active products. Then you can go back and add a second custom filter that only contains the **Sale Price** greater than **100** condition.

Just remember that if you want both conditions to be true, then they must be applied separately. If you want either of the conditions to be true, then add them together in one search:

Advanced search

In the previous screenshot, we created a search that will return **Products** that can be sold and are active or have a sale price greater than or equal to $100, and the cost of the product must be less than $50.

Saving your favorite filters

While advanced searches are quite powerful, they can often take a bit of time to configure to get the results in the manner in which you want them. Fortunately, Odoo allows you to save your searches so that you will not have to build them from scratch each time. To save a custom search, click on the **Favorites** dropdown-which is the little triangle next to **Save current search**—provide a name for the search, and then click on **Save**:

Once you click on **Save**, the filter is added to your list of **Favorites** and can be applied just like the default Odoo filters. In addition, you also have the option to save the custom filter for all users, and even set a custom filter as the default filter to be applied when you bring up the list:

Custom filter

In the preceding screenshot, we applied the custom filter that we just saved—**Special Products**. As you can see, the criteria at the top no longer shows all the detail in the advanced search, and instead it uses the name you provided when you saved the custom filter.

> There is no easy way for an end user to see what the criteria of their search is after they have named and saved their search for later use. Like in our example, credit customers are all we will see when returning to the search later. Until Odoo provides an easier method, users should be encouraged to document their searches.

The ability to save advanced searches into your own custom filters and make them available for other users allows you to better customize Odoo for your business requirements.

Creating custom dashboards in Odoo 10

Dashboards allow you to take information that you need to look at frequently and put it together in one place. In previous versions of Odoo, the installation came with dashboards, even if you never used them. In Odoo 11, you can add custom dashboard support by installing the **Dashboards** module:

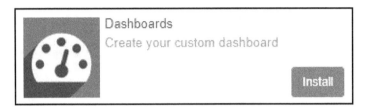

Odoo has a very flexible dashboard system. Each user has a personal dashboard named **My Dashboard** provided when you install the Dashboards module. Initially, this dashboard will be empty except for some useful instructions on customizing your dashboard:

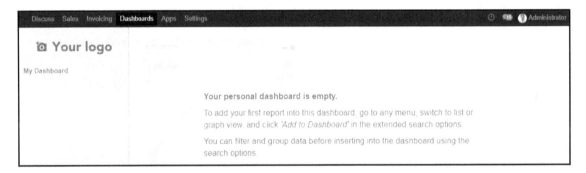

Let's see how we can add our custom filter from the previous section to our dashboard. Return to the products, choose the list view, and apply the custom filter:

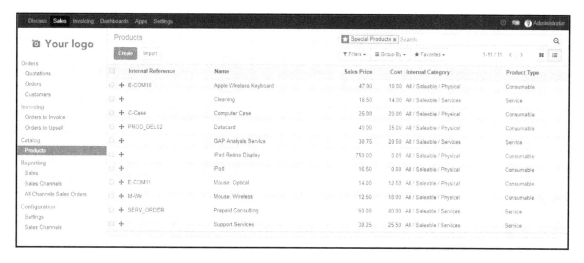

Applying the custom filter

To add a new result set to your dashboard, open up the **Favorites** drop-down menu and simply click on the little triangle next to **Add to my Dashboard**. By default, Odoo will prompt you to add the search list to your own personal dashboard. However, if you wish, you can add the results to any dashboard by selecting the name of that dashboard in the list and clicking on the **Add** button:

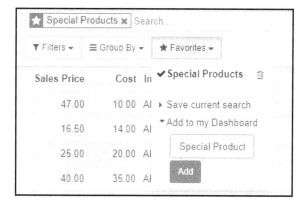

In this example, the current **Special Products** filter we created in the previous step will be added to **My Dashboard**, which can be found as the first option under the **Dashboards** menu.

The build of Odoo 11 that we were running required that you *Shift* + refresh your browser for any new additions to the dashboard to show up:

Odoo provides a variety of layouts, so you can customize the appearance of the dashboard according to your preference. For example, you may wish to have two columns of lists summarizing your sales, or, if there are view columns, you may choose to have a column of three lists.

Clicking on the **Change Layout** button will bring up a small pop-up window to allow you to select an alternative layout:

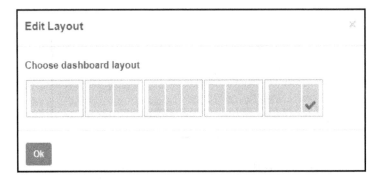

In the top-right corner of each item added to the dashboard, you can click on the little underscore icon to collapse the report area down to just its title. To arrange an item on your dashboard, simply click and drag the item to drop it in the desired location. Finally, you can remove an item from the dashboard by clicking on the close box in the upper-right corner of the item:

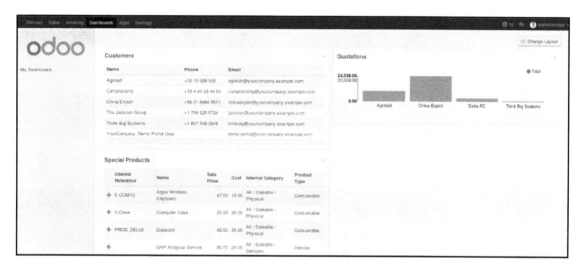

Removing an item from the dashboard

In this example, we have added a few more items to the dashboard and arranged them into two columns. Adding a graph is just as easy as adding a list view to the dashboard. In this example, we went under **Opportunities**, changed the view to **Graph**, and then added it to our dashboard.

Looking at Odoo's Business Intelligence Features

In addition to powerful search features and dashboards Odoo also provides a robust Business Intelligence framework that allows real-time reporting from most applications. You can see an example of Odoo's Business Intelligence features by opening the Sales application and clicking Sales under the Reporting heading.

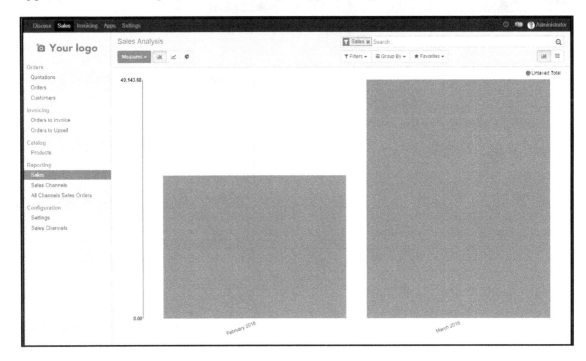

Sales application

As you can see, by default Odoo has provided a bar graph of our sales by month. We can then go under Measures to change the data the graph displays.

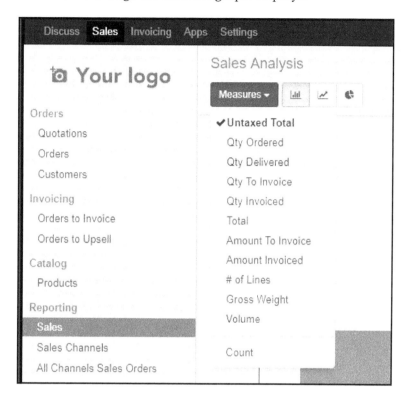

As you can see we are currently viewing the Untaxed Total, but you can change it to any of the others to your graph by just choosing from the list. Let's change the graph to display Qty Ordered instead.

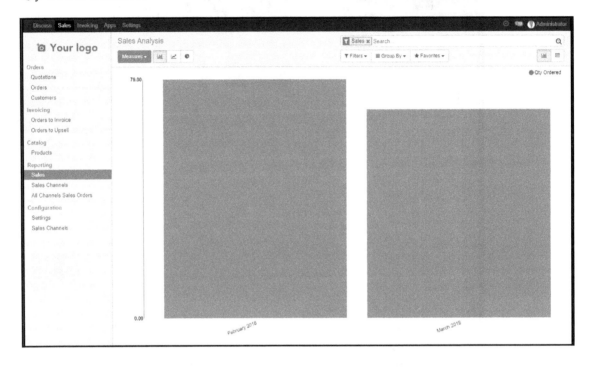

You can see that the description on the far right has changed to show the measure that we have selected. Also, notice that you can still apply Filters and save Favorites as well. Finally, if you wish you can look at the data as a line graph or a pie chart using the icons next to the Measures drop-down. Here we are have changed the graph to be a pie chart.

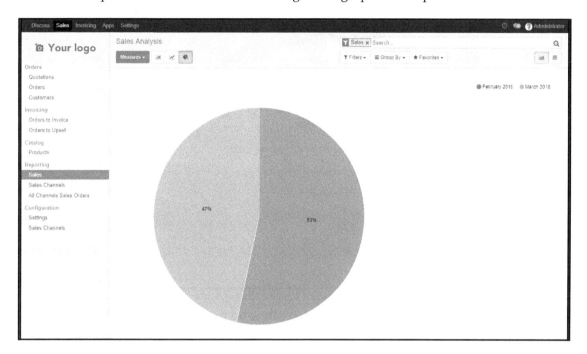

pie chart

The available Measures will of course change depending on the application and specific report you are working with. In addition, you can also look at the data in a grid view instead of graph. For many reports this is a more practical way of viewing the data. Here we have clicked on the icon in the far top right corner of the view to display the data in a grid instead of a graph.

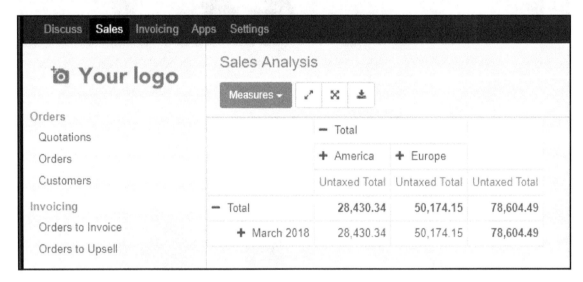

As you can see there are also plus and minus controls on the rows and columns that let you add and remove data items in the grid. When showing the data grid you also have access to a small download button to export your data into an excel file.

Summary

In this chapter, we examined Odoo's advanced searches and dashboards. Advanced searching allows you to search based on a variety of fields and save your searches so that you can easily pull them up later. Using these features, you can more easily find the data you are looking for and place data that you need frequently into your own personal dashboard.

In the next chapter, we will begin to take a look at how you can customize Odoo to meet the specific needs of your organization. We will discover how to activate Developer mode, which will allow us to append fields to Odoo's screens. We'll then begin adding our own fields to forms for collecting data, to lists for finding and displaying the data, and to models, which handle all the rules and methods for storing the data in the underlying PostgreSQL database. But first, what is the single most important thing that we need to do before customizing our system? That's right-we need to know how to back up and restore our data, just in case.

Building a Website with Odoo

11

In this chapter, we will look at perhaps the most important business application that was added to Odoo in version 8-the Odoo **Website Builder** application.

The topics covered in this chapter include the following:

- A brief introduction to **content management systems** (**CMSs**) and how they make it possible to manage websites
- Modifying pages with Odoo's website builder
- Inserting and customizing blocks
- Important Odoo website blocks and how to use them
- Editing the menu of your website and organizing pages
- Selecting themes for your website
- Promoting your website

What's new in Odoo 11?

On the surface, there are few enhancements between Odoo 10 and Odoo 11. The functionality between the two versions is very much the same. There are, however, technical improvements that make Odoo's web application more responsive. It should also display better on most mobile devices.

What is a CMS?

The **Website Builder** application available for Odoo 11 is commonly known as a CMS (or content management system). A CMS is a collection of tools that allows you to structure, organize, and manipulate your website without having to interact directly with the inner workings of your website. A key feature of a CMS is the ability for nonprogrammers and those with little technical expertise to create and edit content on the website once the initial structure of the site has been designed.

In many ways, Odoo is coming into a very crowded market that has a great variety of both open source and paid CMSs that you can choose to build your website with. Here are a few popular website CMSs, all of which, at this point, have considerably more configuration options and significantly more installs than Odoo.

WordPress

WordPress is arguably the most popular CMS that companies may choose to deploy their website with. More than a decade of maturity and a massive install base means that there are plenty of themes, add-ons, and professionals that can support a WordPress website. In addition, WordPress is open source, and continues to be developed aggressively, and, in more recent versions, is targeting improved social networking features.

Joomla

Joomla is also enjoying great popularity in the crowded CMS market, and is written in PHP and open source as well. This CMS, while perhaps not as often deployed as WordPress, has thousands of available plugins and can be found under some very prominent sites on the internet. A few of the more high-profile sites that use Joomla for their CMS include Harvard University and the Guggenheim Museum.

Drupal

No list of popular CMS solutions would be complete without including Drupal. Like the other two, this CMS is also PHP-based and open source. For the most part, Drupal has more advanced capabilities and would be considered for more complex sites than perhaps you would build in WordPress. While there are fewer available themes for Drupal than for Joomla or WordPress, that has not kept Drupal from being the CMS for very popular websites, including Popular Science and Sony Music.

Evoq or DotNetNuke

Evoq was previously known as **DotNetNuke** (**DNN**), and has recently been changed through its own rebranding effort, much like the way OpenERP became Odoo. So, according to their own news release, DotNetNuke is no more and is now to be known as Evoq. While not nearly as popular as the other three listed, Evoq has the distinction of being a Windows Server-based solution that uses Microsoft's .NET platform. Some big names using Evoq for their CMS include Hilton and Samsung.

Why use Odoo website builder for your CMS?

With so many CMS solutions available that have far better support and more mature features, a very valid question is why would someone use the Odoo website builder as their CMS? Not only is this a good question to ask, it is vital when building a website for your company that you pick the tools that work best for your given situation and requirements. So let's quickly look at some of the pros and cons of using Odoo as the CMS to build your website.

Potential advantages to using Odoo as a CMS

While Odoo is still new and does not have the same kind of proven track records and successful websites as the CMSs that have been previously mentioned, there are still some very compelling reasons to consider Odoo as your CMS:

- It has a one-click setup if you already have Odoo installed.
- It has very easy-to-use features, such as fast page editing and simple controls.
- It has great support for mobile devices.

- It has powerful built-in language translation support.
- It integrates seamlessly with Odoo to leverage many of the applications already available for Odoo. This is especially true for the ecommerce application that will be covered in the next chapter.
- A growing number of professional themes will make the Odoo website builder an attractive option in the years to come for those who are already using Odoo.
- It has good built-in promotional tools.

Current limitations of using Odoo as a CMS

Despite a growing list of positive reasons to consider Odoo, there are also some reasons why it may not be the CMS for every solution:

- It has very limited support among hosting companies, website designers, and consultants. If your Odoo website breaks, you are reliant on Odoo experts to fix your website.
- It has limited CMS functionality for version control of your web pages.
- It has complex and confusing security in its web pages and in the assignment of access permissions to content.
- It has a very limited set of themes available that work directly with Odoo, and the professional themes that are available are expensive.
- The immaturity of the CMS itself may cause volatility in the years ahead as new features are added, making it challenging to move your website between databases of various Odoo versions.
- There is no easy way to move websites or web pages between Odoo databases, which can add integration, testing, and deployment challenges.

Backing up the website you make in your Odoo database

If you do use Odoo's website builder for your website, as has been stated in many of the other chapters, back up your database often. All of the web pages that you create are stored inside your database, so you must back it up to make sure that you have a copy of your website. Additionally, you will want to make sure you keep your Odoo application backed up as well, because the static themes, images, and CSS files that are located there must be available to properly display your website.

In Chapter 13, *Customizing Odoo for Your Business*, you can find simple instructions on how to backup your database.

Installing the Odoo website builder

One of the greatest reasons to consider Odoo's website builder is that you can try it out in a matter of seconds. Just install the **Website Builder** application like you would any other Odoo application, go to **Apps**, and search for **Website Builder**:

Once you click **Install**, Odoo will install the required modules and take you to a new screen that will allow you to choose the basic theme for your website:

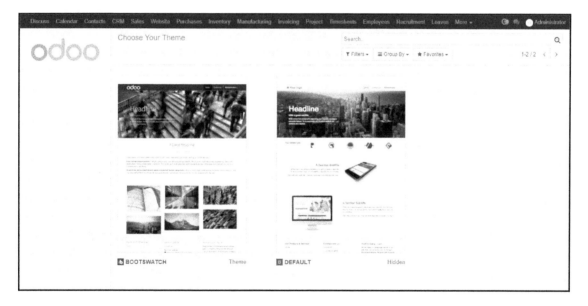

In this build of Odoo 11, you can choose between bootswatch themes or plain Bootstrap. You will also now be provided with a thumbnail preview of what the website will look like. We have decided to use bootswatch, which will allow more flexible theme selection than plain Bootstrap.

> The website builder installed for this chapter was Odoo 10 Community Edition. Depending on your specific Odoo build, you may have an alternative selection of themes, or may in fact get taken directly to your Odoo homepage.

Also, you should be presented with a website builder tutorial that will walk you through some of the basics of building your website.

Here, we can see initial web page presented by Odoo:

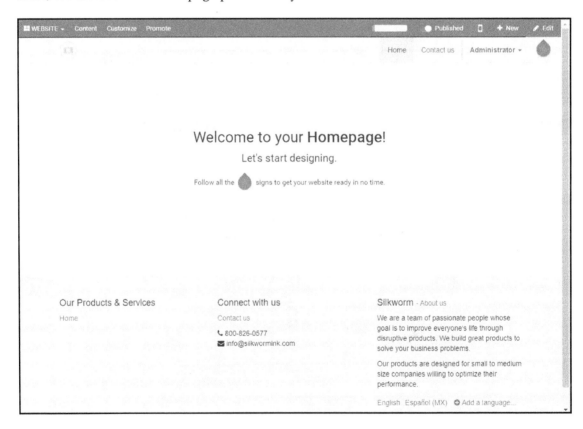

In the middle of the screen, you will see a **Welcome to your Homepage!** Title, along with an invitation to follow the ● signs for a simple walkthrough that will assist you in building your first website in Odoo. We will go ahead and use some of these tips to highlight the basic features of the Odoo **Website Builder** application:

Clicking the ● in the top-right corner directs your attention to the **Edit** page button at the top-left corner of the screen. This button is available on every page while you are on your Odoo website as an administrator. Clicking this **Edit** button will toggle your page into edit mode so that you can make changes to your website.

Click the **Edit** button to begin editing your home page.

After clicking the **Edit** button, your page should refresh to display the toolbars and options available for editing your web page:

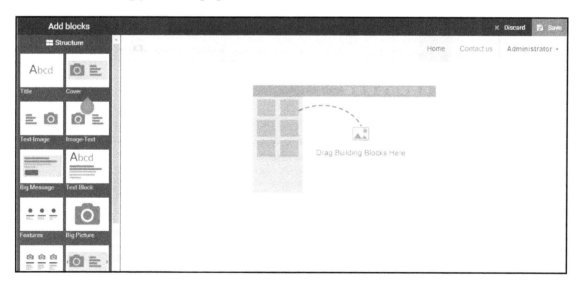

Here, we can see that the tutorial is prompting you to drag the **Cover** block and drop it into your page. This is the action that you will take any time you want to add additional content to your web page. Also note that the tips that walk you through each step are shown just for the tutorial that is run the first time.

Click **Insert Blocks** to add new content to your web page.

Click and hold your left mouse button over the **Banner** block and drag it out onto your web page. The web page will immediately update to show you the banner, along with a snippet of text with a button to the left:

Odoo's simple tips will still follow along, prompting you to now change the title of your text to whatever you choose. All of the editing is performed right in the page itself. Just use your mouse to select the text, like you would in any simple text-editing program. Also note that, at the top, you have the ability to modify the text to make it bold, underlined, or italic, or to change another property, such as color.

After a few changes, the Odoo website builder tutorial will come back once again, calling attention to the **CUSTOMIZE** toolbar menu at the top-left corner of the block. This is a very important menu that allows you to edit properties of the container as well as select the parent container of any object which you are editing:

Following the tip, we can use the customization menu to now change the background of the banner. There are several options, including uploading a graphic or changing the background to a color:

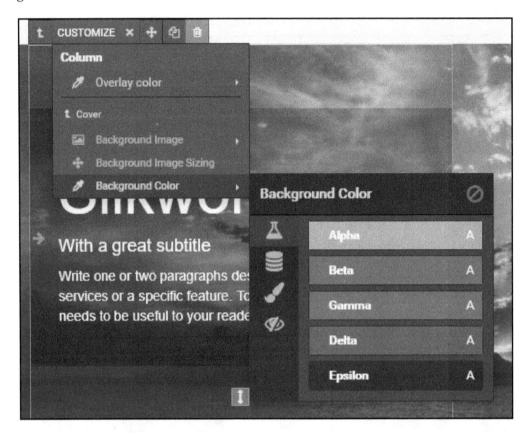

As you move your mouse over the colors, you will see the background change to reflect your choice. Pick a background that you like, and the Odoo tip will then prompt you to drag an image-text block onto the page:

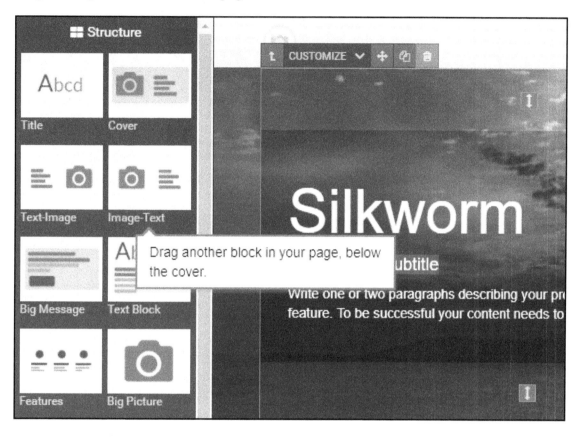

Image-Text block

Follow the instructions, and drag the block below the cover image in the previous step.

You can feel free to change the block as you wish and practice with the various options that are available:

Saving your web page

Once you have had a chance to practice editing your web page, use the **Save** button at the very top-right corner of your page to publish your changes:

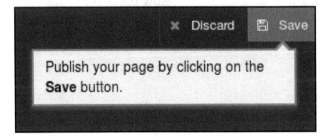

After you click the **Save** button, the page will refresh, and we can see our web page as it will appear to the visitors that come to our site, aside from the blue bar at the top which is always visible when you are logged in to Odoo :

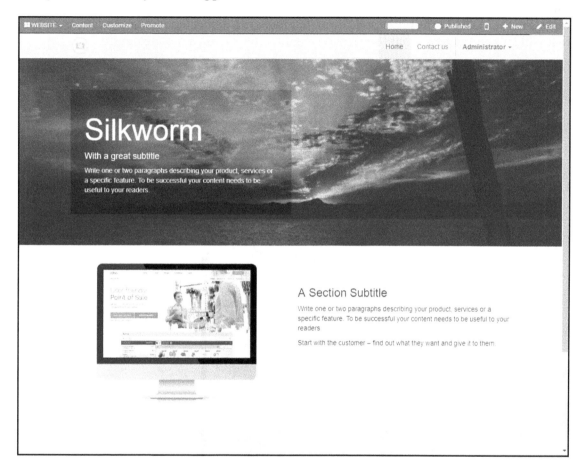

Odoo's tutorial will give you a little congratulation message for successfully saving your website and completing this part of the tutorial. We've now learned how to edit our web pages, add new content blocks to those pages, and save those changes. As you can see, it is pretty easy to create web pages in Odoo using the website builder. Still, expect to spend a bit of time learning how the various objects can be combined and edited to get the results you desire.

Previewing our website on a mobile device

Certainly, one of the most compelling reasons to consider Odoo's website builder for your CMS is that it was built, from the beginning, to support mobile devices. This feature is so central to the **Website Builder** application that there is a dedicated phone preview button that will let you preview what the website should look like on a mobile device:

Click the mobile preview button to see how your web page will look on a typical mobile device:

While you should still double-check all of your web pages on real mobile devices before you deploy your website, this feature is very valuable because it allows you to get an idea of what your pages will look like on mobile devices.

Adding new pages and menus to your website

Next, it is time to take a look at how we add new pages and menus to our website. It is a good idea to lay out your ideas ahead of time, and decide what pages you need and how the menu structure for your website should look. I personally believe that it is better to start out simple and add additional complexity as you go. Still, there are some pages you will already know that you must have on your website, so you may as well go ahead and add them.

From Odoo's top menu, use the **New** menu to add menus and pages, or the edit pages to make changes to an existing page:

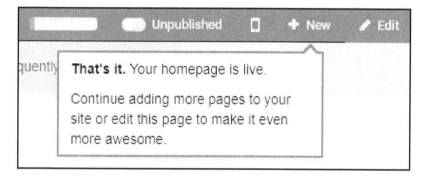

Adding a new page

Clicking **New** brings up a large icon in the center of the page to confirm that you wish to add a new page to your website:

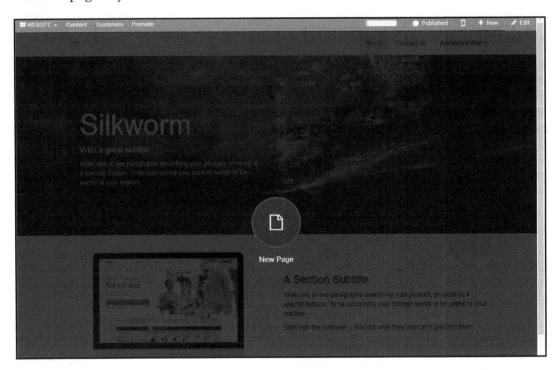

In this example, we will name our page `Frequently Asked Questions`, a page that is common on many websites. We will also leave the **Add page in menu** checkbox checked so that our page will be added to our menu automatically when the page is created:

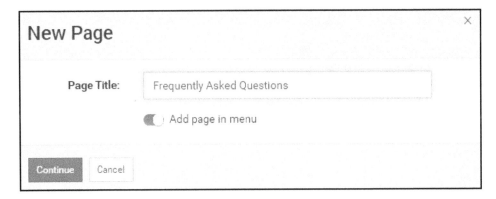

Simply click the **Continue** button and the web page will be added and will be ready to be edited, just like we edited the previous web page.

Creating our Frequently Asked Questions web page

In the following example, after creating the page, we inserted an **Accordion** block found under the **Feature** section in the **Blocks** area. We then edited the block with some of Silkworm's frequently asked questions content:

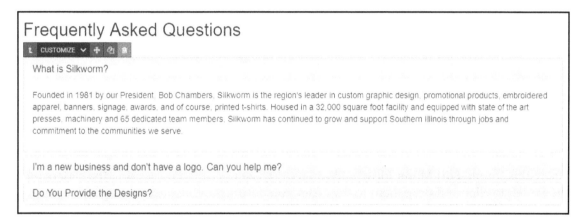

Once the page is the way you want it, click the **Save** button to publish your changes.

Managing menus on your website

In the **Content** menu, you can choose **Edit Menu** to organize the menu structure for your website:

Using this simple **Edit Menu** form, you can reorganize your menus by using the sliders on the far left to click and drag them to the order you desire. Any menu you drag to the top will automatically become the home page of the website and get the little icon of the house on the far right to designate the page.

Dragging a menu to the right will nest menus within other menus. Using these basic methods, you can create a hierarchy of menus to contain your pages in any structure that you choose.

Adding a new menu to your website

Click the **Add Menu Entry** link to bring up a form that will allow you to add a new menu item to your website.

In this example, we have added a new menu named `Silkworm Design Tool` and specified an external link to connect directly to the design tool that Silkworm currently uses for people who wish to design orders on their website:

The form allows you flexibility in assigning a menu to an existing page, creating a new page, or specifying a URL or email address to link to the menu. You also have the option to specify that the menu should open the page in a new window.

Changing themes in Odoo

One of the attractive features of most CMS solutions is the ability to change the theme of your website without having to modify your content. Odoo's website builder provides the ability to modify your theme by selecting the **Customize Theme** option from the **Customize** menu:

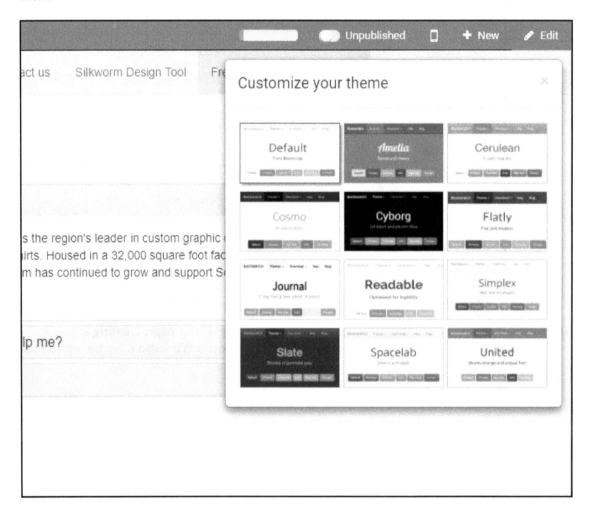

Customize Theme option

With this build of Odoo 11, you have the option to select from a variety of free Bootstrap themes. Simply click **Apply**, and your website will then be updated with the new theme.

Here, we can see how our **Frequently Asked Questions** page looks after we have applied the **Cyborg** theme and adjusted the font color of the main body text:

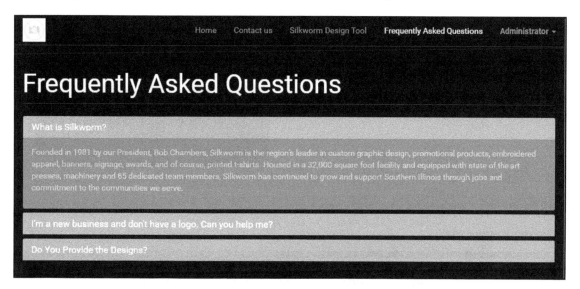

As you can see, simply by changing the theme of your website, you can create a dramatically different look.

Promoting your website

Some of the other nice features of Odoo's website builder are the built-in promotion tools for your website. Not only is it helpful to use the promotion option for each of your web pages, it is vital. If you don't go in and specify the title, keywords, and descriptions for your page, Odoo will provide default information to search engines such as Google. This is never a good idea. Be sure to take the time to at least provide a proper title and description for your web page.

To promote your web page, go to the web page you wish to promote, click **Promote** in the website builder menu, and choose **Optimize SEO**. Odoo will then bring up the promoting form:

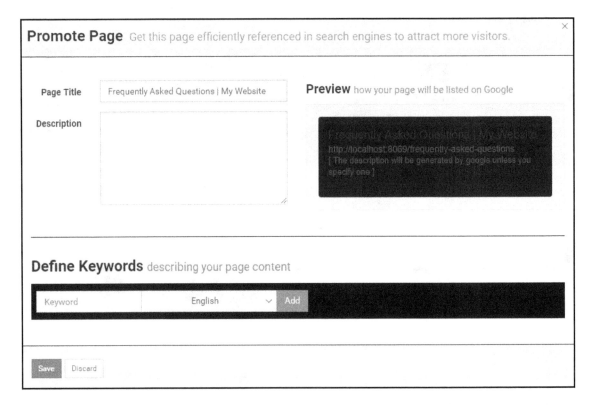

For this example, we have intentionally left the fields as they were when the form is brought up, so you can see why it is so critical that you specify the title and description for each of your pages. Note how Odoo has named our page and that the preview at the bottom is nothing like what we would want to have listed with search engines.

Specifying keywords for your website

Search Engine Optimization (SEO) is a huge topic that could fill an entire book all on its own. One of the major aspects of good SEO is that it knows what keywords which are most popular for the page you wish to promote. Odoo provides a handy little tool that ensures that as you specify keywords, Odoo will let you know the associated keywords that are also popular with Google.

In the following screenshot, we have entered the `t-shirt` keyword and can see associated keywords that may be good to include within the content of our web page to get better results in search engines:

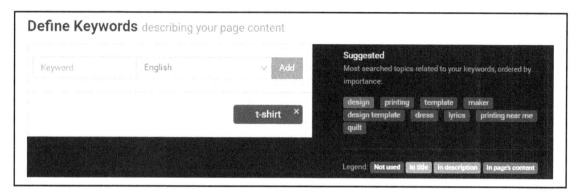

In the results, next to the keyword **t-shirt**, you will see **design**, **printing**, **template**, **maker**, **design template**, **dress**, and more. Note how **design** is shaded in purple. This is because Odoo is indicating that this keyword is located within our web page. If, for example, we added the word **dress** within our **Frequently Asked Questions** page, we would then see the keyword colored appropriately.

Creating a title and description for your website

Take time to make a description that includes good keywords and accurately describes the content of your web page. There are many good books available to help you better promote your website and provide advice on how you can get the best results in search engines.

In the example shown in the following screenshot, I have added a few keywords to the title as an example of how Odoo will color the keywords you have selected. We have also turned the theme back to the default to make it easier to read the text. The purpose is to try and have as many keywords as possible in your title and description so that you can get better results for your page. In this case, **design** and **printing** are important keywords that I have included in the title, based on the feedback from Odoo's keyword research:

Note that this is only an example, and it is far more important to have accurate descriptions than to simply make a title based on popular keywords.

Summary

In this chapter, we took a look at Odoo's exciting new website builder. We discussed CMS a little bit, and some of the other more popular options. We then demonstrated how to install the website builder and followed along this Odoo's simple but effective interactive tutorial to learn the basics.

We then learned how we could add new pages to websites, configure and edit menus for the website, and how to add additional blocks and content to our pages. Finally, we finished up by learning how to change themes to give our website a new look, and promote our web pages for good search results and a proper description within Google.

In the next chapter, we will look at how we can use our new website to host an e-commerce shopping cart that integrates directly with our products in Odoo.

Implementing E-Commerce with Odoo

12

In the previous chapter, we looked at the new *Website Builder* application and saw how it can be used to create a website with ease. Now that we understand the basics of getting a website up and running, this chapter will show you how you can extend a simple website to become a full e-commerce site that can take and manage orders. Even better, this functionality ties directly into sales management, which you learned about in `Chapter 3`, *Exploring CRM in Odoo 11*.

The topics covered in this chapter include the following:

- An overview of e-commerce and how it is implemented in Odoo
- How to install e-commerce and view the default web store
- Configuring and modifying your online store
- How to use product variants such as color and size to provide customized options for the products you sell
- Advanced product options such as alternative products, accessories, and categorizing your product
- How to set up a payment processor

E-commerce and Odoo

As you will probably be aware, e-commerce is a term that describes offering your products and services to customers electronically, typically on an internet website. Over the years, e-commerce has expanded to include more and more markets. There are an increasing number of ways to take payment on websites, and now many mobile applications include the ability to take micro-transactions. E-commerce now covers a very wide field of options.

Popular e-commerce platforms

Despite Odoo's late entry into the website builder/CMS market, Odoo is introducing e-commerce functionality into a mature market with several options. While there are hundreds, if not thousands, of viable e-commerce platforms out there, here are a few of the more popular ones.

Magento

A list of popular e-commerce applications would not be complete without Magento. Magento is open source, very popular, and is often a user's first choice when integrating with Odoo. Even with Odoo's new e-commerce option, Magento continues to be popular with those who need more advanced functionality.

Volusion

Volusion is also a very popular e-commerce platform, and it takes an entirely different approach. Instead of an open source solution, Volusion is a hosted solution in which you configure your website and cart. Volusion offers many different pricing models, as well as a free 14-day trial. While not for all companies, Volusion can be a fast solution for companies that need to get up and running without having to worry about installing software.

Shopify

While Shopify is very popular, and is a hosting solution like Volusion, it also directly markets Point of Sale solutions as well. This means that Shopify is often a good solution for companies that want to have an online presence but also have retail operations. Like Volusion, Shopify also offers a variety of pricing options and a 14-day free trial.

Yahoo Small Business

Also a hosted solution, Yahoo Small Business offers a straightforward online shopping cart; in other words, it is what you would expect in a basic e-commerce solution. With Yahoo, advantages include easy advertising integration, local marketing options, and robust e-mail handling options.

Odoo as an e-commerce platform

In Odoo, e-commerce is implemented within the website builder; the website builder is a dependency in Odoo e-commerce. Odoo will install the website builder if it is not already installed in the database. In addition to adding a great deal of functionality to the website builder, e-commerce also provides additional options applicable to products, such as variants, the ability to appear in multiple categories, associations with alternative products, and so on.

While other e-commerce platforms may have more features, there are some significant advantages to using Odoo e-commerce—especially if you are already using, or are planning to use, Odoo as your primary accounting/ERP system. For example, products that you enter into Odoo automatically integrate with your e-commerce website, and orders you receive will automatically come into Odoo.

Best of all, Odoo e-commerce is extremely easy to set up.

Installing Odoo e-commerce

You install Odoo e-commerce like other Odoo applications:

After clicking **Install**, Odoo will refresh the browser and you will be taken to the store page that Odoo has added to the website menu. As before, Odoo has a tutorial that takes you through the basics of the Odoo website. Here, you should see the basic Odoo shop setup that has been displayed using data that we've entered throughout the book so far:

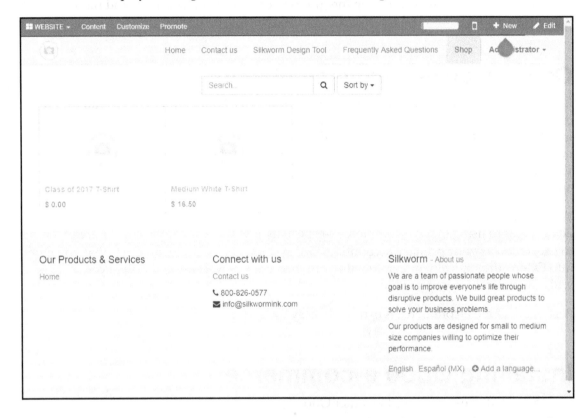

You will notice that there is a placeholder showing you where the pictures for your product will display once you've added images. We'll take a look at how to do that a bit later in the chapter.

Setting up Odoo is a straightforward task. The easy integration of your products and e-commerce's relationships with other Odoo applications means it is a much less complex approach than syncing Odoo to an external e-commerce system.

Basics of Odoo e-commerce

You will notice a few things about Odoo e-commerce right away. There is a search box at the very top of the page that will allow you to search for products on the store. It is also worth mentioning that the footer is shared between all pages on the website.

Odoo has a handy feature that allows you to enter products directly from the website. In other words, you don't have to go into the **Sales** menu in Odoo and click and add products there; instead, you can do it right from this shop page.

Click the **New** button at the top of the form and you will be prompted to either add a **New Page** or a **New Product**, as shown in the following screenshot:

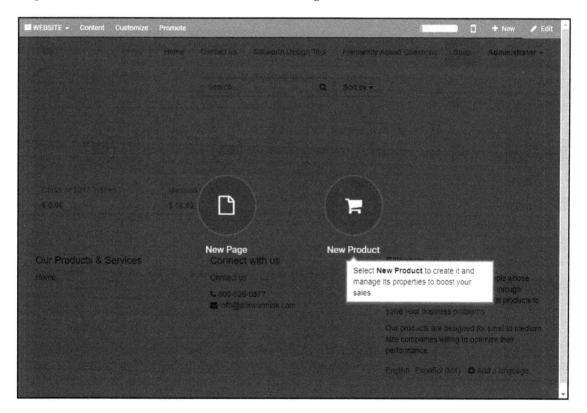

Let's go ahead and click the **New Product** button to bring up the form.

In this case, we have entered the name of a new product that we want to add to our store, and we are have been prompted to click the **Continue** button to add the product.

Odoo then refreshes the web browser to show the new product page that your users will see. Here, you can edit and add content to the product page, as you also saw in Chapter 11, *Building a Website with Odoo*:

Product page

While the page is not much to look at yet, you can see it includes the basics. The price is under the name of the product, as is the option to change quantity, and the button that will add that product to a shopping cart. Using what you have learned in the previous chapter, you can drag and drop blocks from the left-hand side to add content to the product page.

Setting the product price from the e-commerce page

Another nice feature of Odoo e-commerce is that you don't have to go all the way back to the product lists inside standard Odoo business applications. You can change the price right on the website, as shown in the following screenshot:

While it may seem like a small thing, the ability to change the price on the web page can help with your workflow.

Adding a picture to your product

If you are going to run an e-commerce site, you will need to have a picture of your product. After following Odoo's tutorial, you will be prompted to add a picture for the product, as shown in the following screenshot:

When you're presented with Odoo's picture selection wizard, you have the option to choose pictures from a gallery, your own computer, or even from a URL:

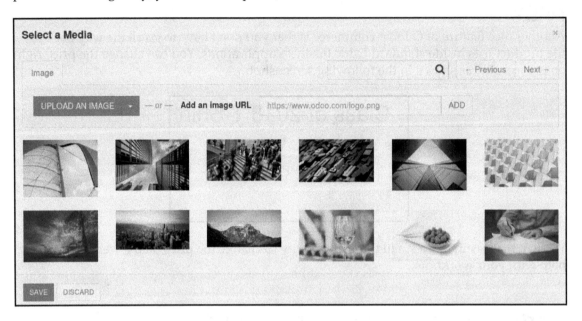

Notice the **UPLOAD AN IMAGE** and **Add an image URL** buttons near the top. You will probably use these more frequently than the built-in gallery pictures that Odoo provides.

We are going to use the **UPLOAD AN IMAGE** option to add an image of a simple blue t-shirt. We are using Chrome on Windows 10 to upload **Blue_Tshirt.jpg**, which was obtained from the creative commons image library:

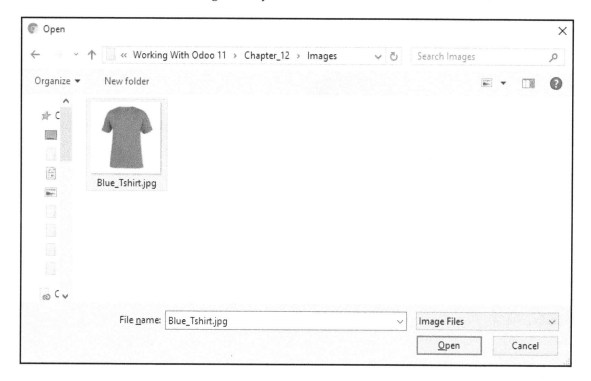

Once you click **Open**, the page will refresh and you should see that your product image has been successfully uploaded, as shown in the following screenshot:

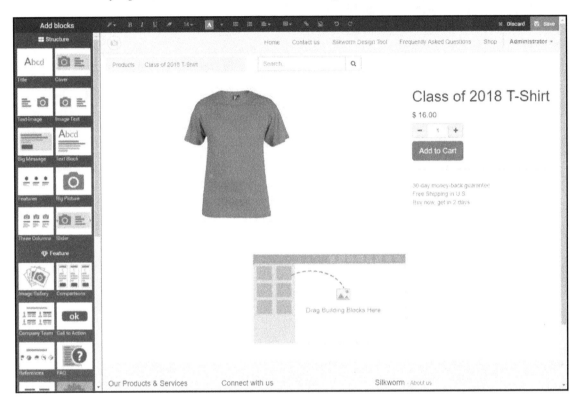

Product image

Describing the product

You should now also be able to add blocks and drag a **Text Block** onto the page. If you need to, take the time to learn what blocks are available and how to use them to make a product page that meets the needs of your customers. You can review Chapter 11, *Building a Website with Odoo*, to learn more about inserting blocks into web pages.

After you have finished inserting blocks and editing pages, click the **Save** button to commit your changes.

Publishing your product

By default, both new and existing products in Odoo are not published to the website. You can see them when logged in either as an administrator or a user with appropriate permission. Until you publish the product, they will not be seen by anonymous website users:

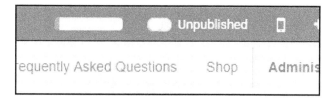

When you click the red **Unpublished** slider, the button will change to green and should now display **Published**, as shown in the following screenshot:

Your product has now been published and should be visible to anyone who accesses your website. By clicking the button again, you can set the product back to the **Unpublished** state.

Additional configuration options for your Odoo shop

When you first install Odoo e-commerce, it provides you with a default layout to get you started. However, there are several options available that you can use to alternate how your shop looks and what kind of information it displays. Let's take a look at a few of those options now.

Choose **Shop** from the main menu in order to see your changes. By clicking the **Customize** menu on the right, you will get a list of options that can be checked or unchecked to change the appearance of your online store.

 The **Customize** menu is available on every page, but the options that are available in the menu change depending on what page you are on.

Let's check the **Add to Cart** option to add a small image to each product that will allow visitors to add the product to the shopping cart:

In the previous screenshot, you can see the available list of options, as well as the shopping cart icon to the right of the price of each product. Feel free to experiment with the other options available inside the **Customize** windows to get the appearance you want.

Modifying the order of the products on the store

There are also other store options available for you to edit the shop page. One of them is the ability to re-order products. Click **Edit** at the top of the page and then hover over products to see the options available.

We will choose **Promote** | **Push to top** to send the **Medium White T-Shirt** to the top of the page, as shown in the following screenshot:

As you can see, it is possible to promote a product to the top of the page, but it could be time-consuming if you decide to move around a lot of products.

Inside Odoo 8's product page, you could quickly adjust the order of the products by setting sequence numbers directly. Unfortunately, this has been removed in Odoo 11. Using the skills you will learn in `Chapter 14`, *Modifying Documents and Reports*, on customizing Odoo, you will be able to add the sort order field to the product view.

Take a few minutes to explore the other options in the menu. The **Size** options allow you to change the size of the product when it shows up in the grid, giving you the opportunity to make more interesting shop layouts. The **Styles** options give you the option of adding a sale ribbon to the product, as we can see in the following screenshot:

Setting up product variants

Another nice feature that comes with the e-commerce application is the ability to create product variants. This is a particularly important feature for the business case that we have been using throughout this book. Product variants allow you to offer different options for the same product; for example, a t-shirt will often come in various sizes and colors, or a computer company may want to offer a product with different memory options.

In Odoo 11, product variants are not turned on by default in the e-commerce application. To turn on the product variants option, click on **Settings** in the **Configuration** section under the **Sales** menu:

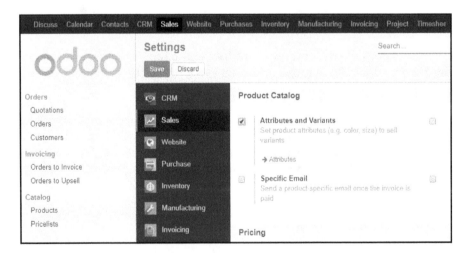

Under **Product Catalog**, select the option **Attributes and Variants.**

To create product variants, you need to navigate to the product you wish to create the variants for. Let's create variants for the `Class of 2018 T-Shirt`.

After you have exited the edit mode in the website builder, choose **Sales** from the **Website** menu in the top-left corner of your screen. Then, choose products and bring up the **Class of 2018 T-Shirt**.

Choose the **Variants** page, and you will see the grid where we will add the variants:

Notice on the right that there is a separate button that brings up a list of variants with the number 1 in the button. You always have one variant that is the base variant of the product.

Now click the **Edit** button at the top of the page and add some variants to the product.

To add variants, simply edit the product, choose the **Variants** tab, and click **Add an Item**. In the **Attribute** column, you provide the label you want to use for your attributes. We will create attributes for both **Color** and **Size**. In the product's **Attribute Values** column, you add each of the available values. Here, we will list the available sizes and colors for our product:

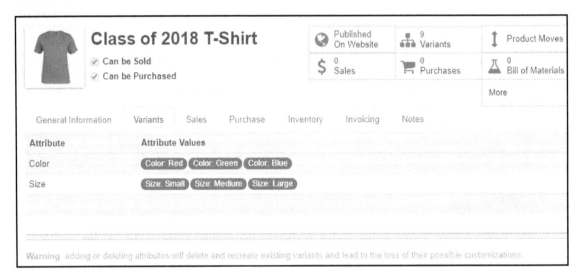

As you can see in the previous screenshot, we have created two attribute categories, one for **Color** and one for **Size**. For the color attribute, we have specified **Red**, **Green**, and **Blue**. For the **Size** attribute, we have specified **Small**, **Medium**, and **Large**.

Save the product, and then go back to the website shop and see the options as they now appear on the product page:

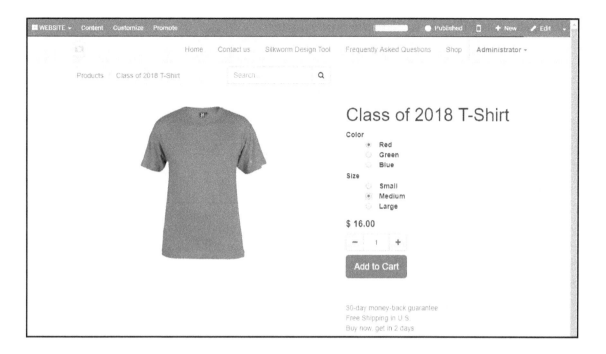

Advanced e-commerce product options

In addition to the basic options that we have covered so far, Odoo offers several advanced options that give you more control over how products appear in the store. These options include specifying multiple categories, alternative products, accessories, as well as direct control over the position of the item in the store.

Once again, you will need to go to the product page:

We can see in the preceding screenshot that we have specified a few advanced options. Instead of our product now showing up inside one category, it will show up in the **T-Shirts**, **School**, and **2018** categories. This gives us more flexibility when designing our e-commerce store.

> To see the categories on your website, you will need to go to the **Customize** tab on the store page and check the **Product Categories** option.

Alternative products

Often when customers purchase one product, it is likely there are alternative products that they may also want to buy. Perhaps it is another brand of product, or a deluxe version of the model that they are currently viewing. For our example, we have chosen the medium t-shirt as a potential alternate.

Now, when the user comes to the product page, they will see the alternative product displayed at the bottom.

Accessory products

These are products that may accompany or complement a product purchase. For our business example, we have chosen a sports logo that could be bought as a pin or a logo on the shirt. A more standard e-commerce example would be if you purchased a tablet computer, you would be offered a case, a stylus, or perhaps even a warranty.

The accessory products are presented when a product is added to the cart.

Looking at the shopping cart

While we have primarily been focusing on configuration, we also need to remember the website's users. Let's see how the shopping cart looks for them by adding the **Class of 2018 T-shirt (Red, Small)** to the shopping cart, as shown in the following screenshot:

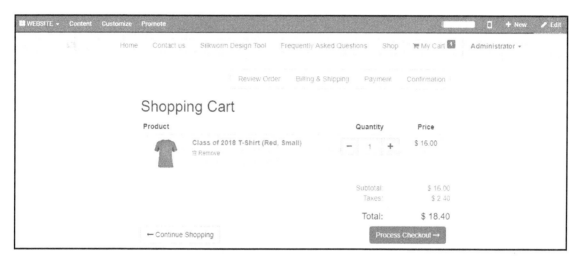

You will notice that the sports logo has been added as a suggested product to our shopping cart, along with a link to add it to the cart. Odoo's shopping cart works like most e-commerce shopping carts do. After you adjust your quantity and are finished shopping, you click **Process Checkout →**, which will take you to the form that collects your shipping and billing information. A progress bar at the top right of the form keeps the user informed of the steps in the process.

Because we are logged in as an administrator, you will see different items on the screen than if you were a guest who was using the shopping cart. One trick is to open an incognito window in your browser to see the exact look and feel for a potential buyer.

Seeing the draft sales order in Odoo

As soon as an item is added to the shopping cart, the order will appear as a draft within Odoo in real-time. To see this, go into **Sales** and look in the list of quotes, where you will see your e-commerce order listed at the very top. Click on it to see the details of the order so far:

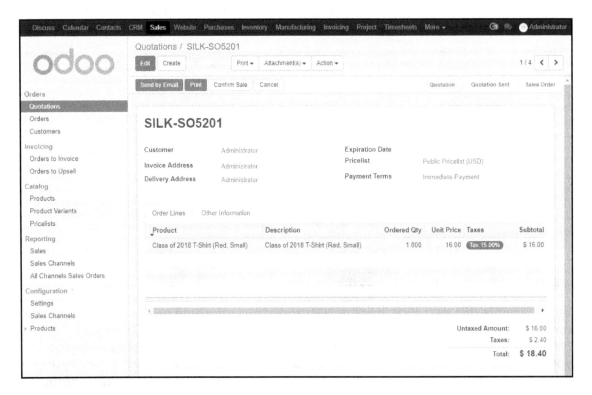

If the user abandons the order without checking out, it simply remains in draft mode and will be available to delete later. This is a good way of seeing how many of your users have added something to a cart but didn't make it all the way to the checkout.

Even if a user doesn't check out, this information can be valuable to see what customers are looking for.

Checking out

Providing a billing address and shipping address is an essential part of the checkout process. Odoo, by default, assumes that the shipping address is the same as the billing address:

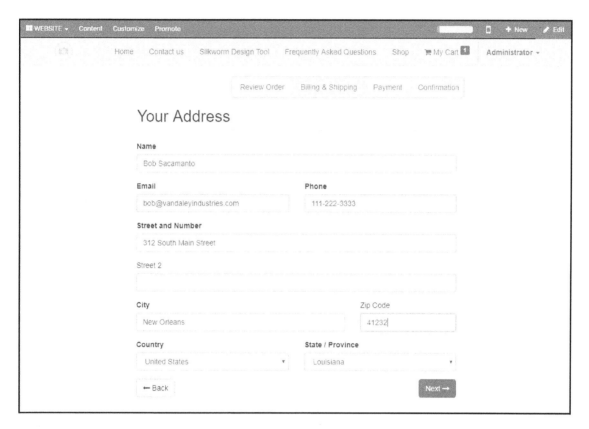

In Odoo 11, all of the fields on this form (in bold) are required except for the **Zip Code** and **Street 2** fields.

After clicking **Next→**, you will be prompted to verify your address information, as shown in the following screenshot:

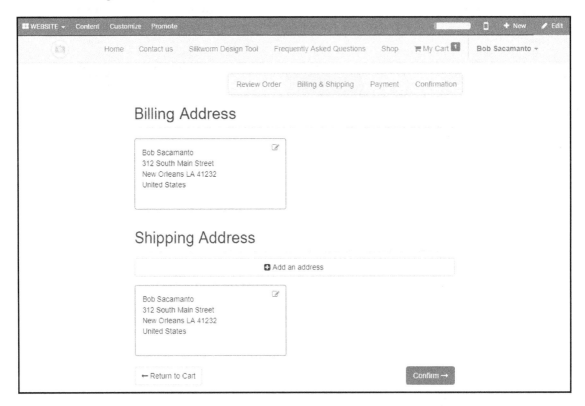

Here, you are presented with both the **Billing Address** and **Shipping Address** fields, which will both be the same initially. If you use the small icon in the upper-right corner of the address box to edit the address, those edits will apply to both the billing and shipping address. To add an alternate shipping address that is different to their billing address, the customer will need to click **Add an address**.

As customers are using these forms, they are, for the most part, easy to understand. Furthermore, Odoo automatically creates the customer record. All the work is done by the customer! It is important, however, for you familiarize yourself with the checkout process, as it is up to your company to make sure it works as you wish. Depending on your sales volume and the nature of your business, it may be necessary to customize the checkout process to maximize your sales.

Once a user clicks **Confirm**, the status onscreen changes to **Payment**, and they are taken to a page titled **Confirm Order**. By default, Odoo installs **Wire Transfer** as the one and only method of payment:

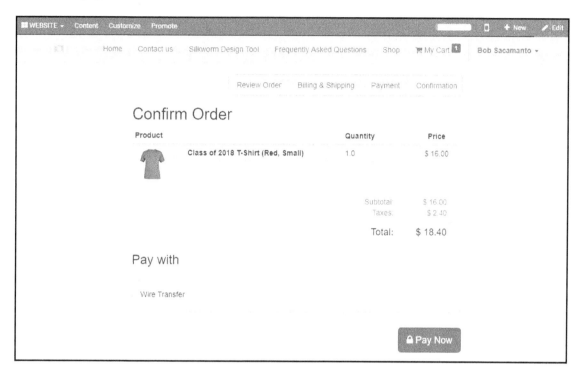

Now that we have reached this point, the remainder of the process is just like any other e-commerce system. You will notice, however, that the only payment method that is available is a **Wire Transfer**. Next, we will see how we can add PayPal as a payment processor.

Adding PayPal as a payment processor

While Odoo only includes **Wire Transfer** by default, the framework is modular and can be extended to include additional payment methods.

 One of the most popular e-commerce payment processors, PayPal, can be quickly installed and integrated into your Odoo e-commerce system.

We have to install a PayPal payment processor a little differently because it is not a full application, but rather a module. We still need to go to **Settings** and **Local Apps**, but we will need to uncheck the **Apps** filter from the search.

After clearing the **Apps** filter, simply type in `PayPal` to see the standard **Install** button:

Once you've clicked **Install**, the screen will refresh and you will be left on the **Apps** screen with the apps filter back in place. We now need to go to the **Website Admin** menu and choose the **Payment Acquirers** option in the **eCommerce** section to bring up the list of payment acquirers. You should now see the **PayPal** provider in that list.

 As you can see, it is possible to install a Payment Acquirer through this list rather than having to go into the **Apps** form and install it there.

Click **PayPal** to open the form and see the available options, as shown in the following screenshot:

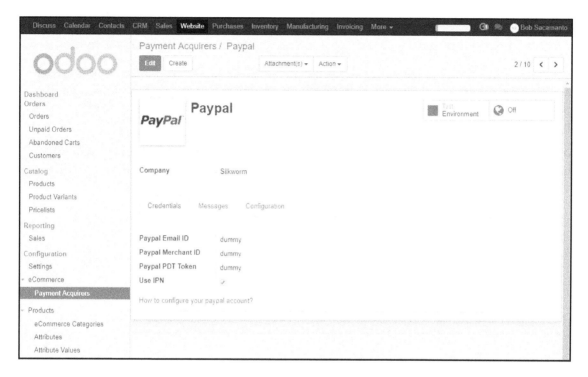

You should see, under the **Environment** option, that Odoo defaults to the **Test** environment, which PayPal calls the sandbox. This allows you to configure your **Paypal Email ID** and **PayPal Merchant ID** at the bottom and begin testing your store. Once you have everything worked out, you can turn the environment from **Test** to **Production**.

Naturally, you will need to set up a PayPal account and use the credentials they give you to fill out the form.

Summary

In this chapter, we learned how Odoo e-commerce fits in with the website builder, how to install it, and the basic configuration options. Next, we looked at product variants and how they could be used to make it easier to present products that come in multiple styles.

We also spent a little time learning about the advanced product options Odoo offers, such as alternative products, accessories, and defining multiple categories. After looking at the checkout process, we learned how to add an additional payment processor, PayPal, and where you need to go to set the options required to make it all work.

In the next chapter, we will look at one of the more exciting aspects of working with Odoo: how to use Odoo's developer mode to add additional fields to your models and modify views to customize Odoo to fit the requirements for your business.

Customizing Odoo for Your Business **13**

In this chapter, we will begin covering one of the greatest advantages of Odoo: the ability to customize the software to meet the unique needs of your business. Fortunately, Odoo provides a great deal of flexibility in which you can customize it without writing any code or developing a module. We will begin by learning how to activate Odoo's developer mode and then back up our database, which is a very important practice when customizing Odoo. After that, we will learn how to add fields to our database and display them on forms and views. Note that customizing Odoo is a very broad topic that would ideally span across multiple chapters; you might consider this an introduction to customization.

The following topics are covered in this chapter:

- Understanding the Odoo architecture
- Entering and exiting developer mode
- Backing up your database
- Restoring data from a backup
- Appending custom fields to models
- Displaying newly added fields in forms and list views

What's new in Odoo 11?

The tools used to customize Odoo have remained relatively the same between Odoo 10 and Odoo 11.

Understanding the Odoo architecture

Before you can begin understanding Odoo, it is important that you have a basic understanding of the framework and underlying architecture that makes up Odoo applications. Each Odoo application has three primary components that make up the final application. Fortunately, you don't have to be an expert developer to understand how the Odoo framework fits together. The three components are **models**, **views**, and **actions**.

Models

In the Odoo framework, models are what hold and manage the data that make up your Odoo application. When you save a sales order in Odoo, the data for the sales order header is stored inside a model appropriately named **sale.order**. Individual data items, such as order date and customer address, are known as **fields**.

Models can also be linked and associated with other models. For example, the **sale.order** model is linked to the **sale.order.line** model by the ID of the sales order. In this chapter, we will be adding a few fields to the **sale.order** model inside Odoo.

Views

Models, by themselves, do not display any information to the end user. Models simply hold and manage the data for the application behind the scenes. Data that is stored from these models is displayed in your applications using views. This allows the **sale.order** model information to display in a variety of different ways. Want to make a very simple custom order screen that summarizes orders for the day? Create a custom view to show the model information in whatever way you wish.

Actions

The third and final component that pulls together the framework is actions. Actions are what trigger the appropriate views to be displayed, or specific actions to take place on a model. For example, when you choose **Quotations** from the **Sale** menu, you are triggering an action that tells the Odoo framework to display the appropriate **sale.order** view. Without actions, the Odoo framework would not know which view to display. Another example of an action would be posting or confirming a sales order. When you click **Confirm**, the Odoo framework calls the appropriate function that then updates the **sale.order** model.

Activating developer mode

To customize Odoo, you must first activate developer mode. Once you enter this mode, Odoo will provide you with a lot more onscreen information as you navigate through the interface. This mode also allows you to make changes to the database and store that information in a file.

To activate developer mode, click on the **Settings** menu. On the far right you will see a panel that contains information about the Odoo installation. At the bottom of the panel, you will see the link to **Activate the developer mode**:

Once you have entered this screen, you can click on **Activate the developer mode** to begin customizing Odoo.

Odoo recognizes that you are in developer mode by adding `?debug=#` to the URL in your web browser. Additionally, Odoo changes the information that is provided when you hover over various fields in the interface. For example, when viewing a sales order record while in developer mode, you can move the cursor over the **Confirmation Date** field to reveal details about how that field is represented internally in Odoo, as shown in the following screenshot:

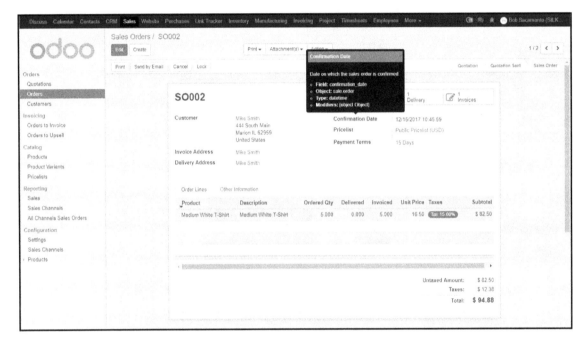

Confirmation Date field

The preceding screenshot demonstrates how Odoo displays information while you are in developer mode. In this example, we can see that the **Confirmation Date** field is named `confirmation_date` and that the field belongs to the **sale.order** object. Additionally, we can see that the field type is **Confirmation Date** and that there are modifiers assigned to the field. This type of information will be of great value as you continue to customize Odoo.

Getting out of developer mode

Once you are in developer mode, there will come a time when you want to exit that mode and continue to work with Odoo as you normally would. To exit developer mode, simply go back to the **Settings** menu and choose the **Deactivate the developer mode** link.

Alternatively, you can simply remove debug=# from the URL string in your browser:

Make sure that you leave the & symbol in place when you remove the debug tag from the URL. If you get any errors or other unusual behavior after removing debug=# from your URL, you can typically use your browser's back button.

If this also fails, you can always restart the browser and log back in to Odoo.

Backing up your database

When you make changes in developer mode, those changes are written into the database associated with the company. One of the major advantages of this approach is that you do not have to write code in Python or create a custom module to implement simple customizations. You don't even have to restart the server. One of the major disadvantages, however, is that there is the potential for making an unwanted change, or one that is difficult to reverse.

Therefore, it is very important and highly recommended that you make backups of your database both before and after you make any customizations while in developer mode.

Do not skip this step!
It is always a good idea to frequently back up your database, but it is absolutely imperative that you back up your database before undertaking any customization.

To back up your database, you must first log out of Odoo. After you have successfully logged out, click on the **Manage Databases** link on the login form. From this screen, you click on the **Backup** link in the top-left corner of the **Database Management** menu:

To back up your database, select the database from the pop-up menu and enter the master password for the Odoo installation (by default, the master password will be admin). Next, click on the **Backup** button.

After you click on the **Backup** button, Odoo will then save your database to your local drive. Depending on the browser you are using and its settings, the prompt you get to save your file will vary. The default filename will end with the .dump extension.

After you save your file, Odoo will download it into the directory you have specified. If this is the first time you have backed up your database, you should also take the time to verify that you can successfully restore the database. While this may seem like an unnecessary exercise, it is important to remember that a backup is only as good as your ability to successfully restore it.

Restoring a database in Odoo

To restore a database in Odoo, click on the **Restore** option in the **Database Management** menu.

To restore your database, you need to provide three pieces of information: the backup file you wish to restore, the master password of Odoo, and a new database name. Clicking on the **Browse...** button in the file selection area will prompt you to select the `.dump` file created when you performed the backup.

After you have specified the file and the other required fields, click on **Restore Database** to begin restoring the database. A small progress bar in the bottom left of the browser will update you on the progress of the restore. Once the restore is complete, log in to the database to make sure everything is working as expected.

Now with a successful backup and restoration, you are ready to begin customizing Odoo. If something goes wrong, you will now have the ability to restore your backup. While customizing Odoo, remember to back up the database frequently.

Adding a custom field to Odoo

One of the most common reasons for customizing Odoo is to collect additional information that is specific to your company. If you are running an insurance company, for example, you may want to specify the policy number on your sales order. If you are working in property management, you might want to store the date on which the lease agreement will expire.

For our working example, we will be adding fields that will help us better manage the data and processes for our silkscreen company. Specifically, we will be adding the following fields to the sales order header:

Field name	Label	Field type	Purpose
x_daterequired	**Date Required**	Date	In the screen printing industry, deadlines drive when production begins and when the product should be delivered to the customer.
x_rush	**Rush Order**	Boolean	Related to **Date Required** is the necessity to flag some sales orders as rush orders. A **Rush Order** can then be prioritized and given expedited treatment.

Custom field names in Odoo are preceded by x_. This is so that field names in future Odoo versions and standard updates will not accidentally conflict with the custom fields you have added.

Viewing the model in Odoo

Odoo allows you to add custom fields to the model if you are in debug mode. Click on **Settings** and then, in the **Database Structure** sub-menu, choose **Models**. You will get a list of all the models that make up your current Odoo installation, as shown in the following screenshot:

Models

Using the standard search tools in Odoo that you have learned about so far, you can now limit the results to just show the **sale.order** model:

sale.order model

You can now click the **sale.order** model to open up the model and display all the fields that make up the **sale.order** model:

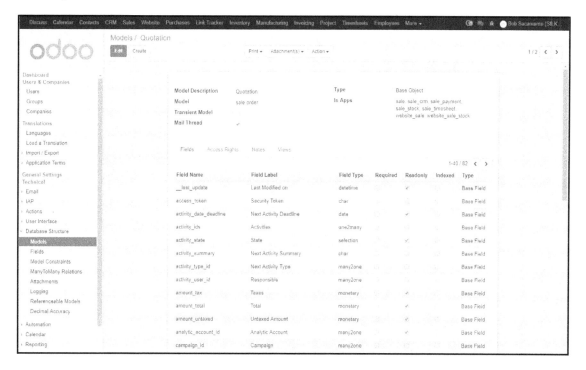

sale.order model

Here, you can examine the name of the field as well as the field type and whether the field is required or not. Some fields are also designated as read-only fields. These fields are often automatically generated or calculated by Odoo.

Examining models in Odoo is a great way to learn more about the structure of the data and how it is organized. This is particularly vital for anyone who wishes to customize Odoo.

Creating a new field in the sale order model

At the top of the form, you can see that the **Model Description** for the **sale.order** model is Quotation. For the purposes of this chapter, we will refer to the model not the model description. Let's go ahead and start adding our custom fields to the **sale.order** model. Please be aware that it can be easy to accidently click **Create** and create an entirely new model. We don't want a new model, but instead we want to add fields to the existing model. Click **Edit** to edit the **sale.order** model, and then scroll to the bottom of the field list and click **Add an Item**:

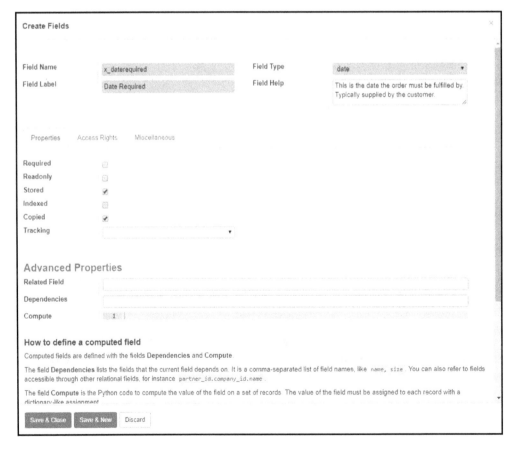

In the preceding example, we have specified our **Date Required** custom field.

The x_ prefix is already specified in the **Field Name**, by default, to encourage the use of good naming conventions. We have filled in the other data required for the field, including setting the **Field Name** to x_daterequired, the **Field Label** to Date Required, and the **Field Type** to **date**.

Click on **Save & New** to finish adding a new field to the **sale.order** model and proceed to enter the remaining x_rush field:

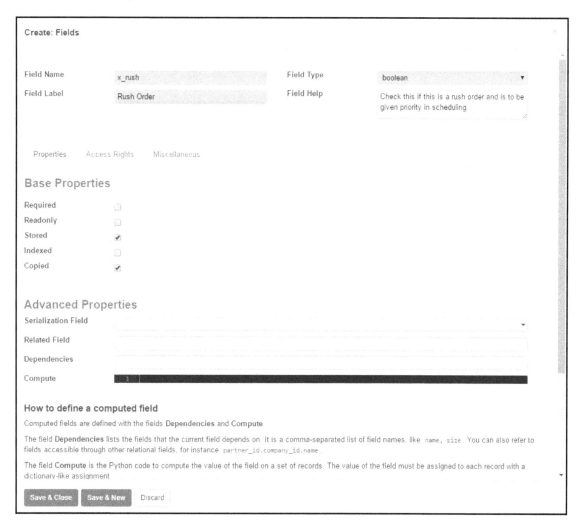

x_rush field

You should notice that this field is very similar to the **date** required field, except that we specified the field type as Boolean. This will tell Odoo's framework to display the field as a checkbox.

Editing the form view

Now that we have added our fields to the model, we want to display them on the form. Fortunately, Odoo provides an editor that makes it easy to add the fields to your view. It would be beneficial to have experience using a text editor with XML here.

The easiest way to edit a view, in this case the sale order form, is to go to the form you wish to edit. Simply pull up any sales order in Odoo and, from the debug menu, choose **Edit FormView**:

Edit FormView

This will bring up the actual XML code that makes up the sale order view. It may look somewhat intimidating to newcomers at first, but the changes we are going to make are very easy. Even better, you can copy and paste an existing field, so you don't have to type all the special characters and understand the syntax.

Now scroll down until you find the line that displays the payment terms on the sales order form. We will add our two custom fields directly below, as shown in the following screenshot:

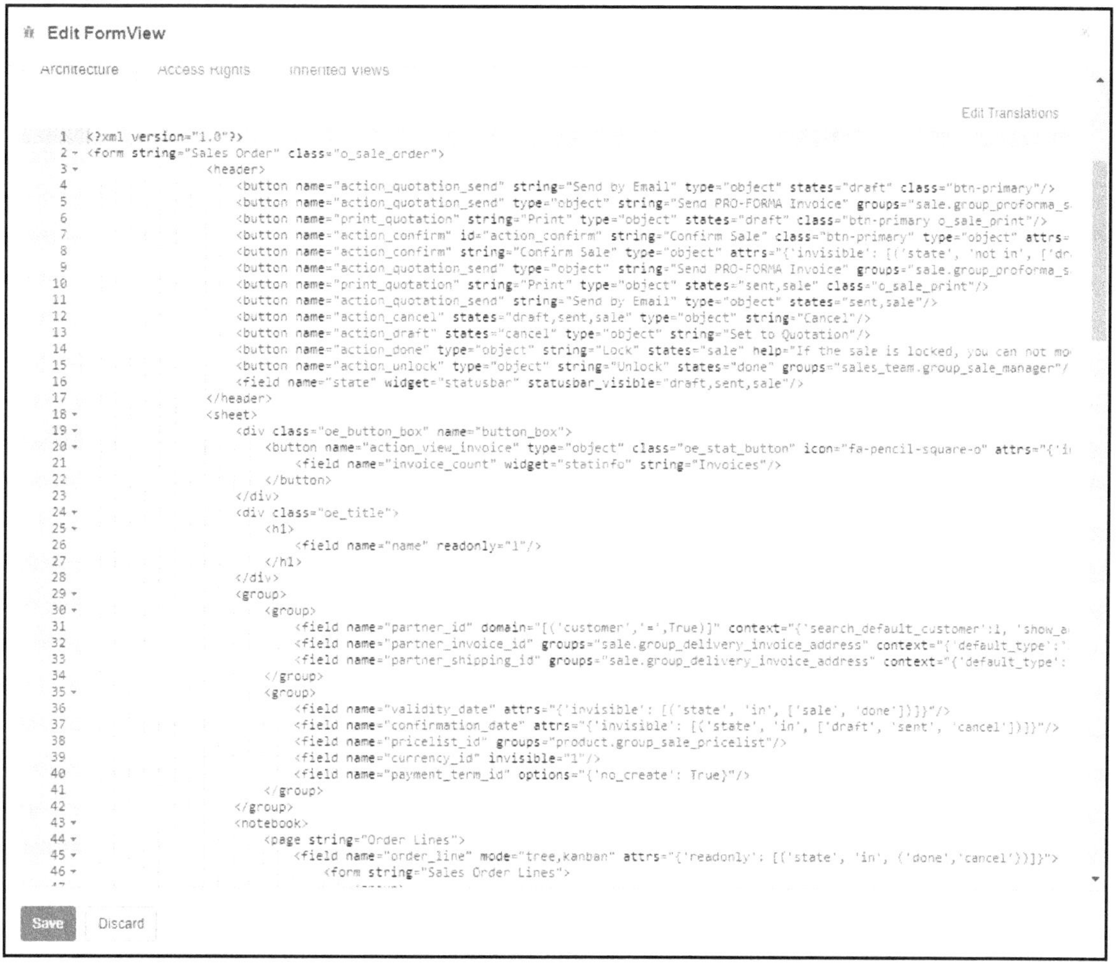

Adding two custom fields

To simplify, you can copy and paste the `payment_term_id` line and then edit it to include the custom field you wish to add. Here, we have added the field for **Date Required** to our view:

```
33          <field name="partner_shipping_id" groups="sale.group_delivery_invoice_address" context="{'default_type':
34        </group>
35 ▾      <group>
36          <field name="validity_date" attrs="{'invisible': [('state', 'in', ['sale', 'done'])]}"/>
37          <field name="confirmation_date" attrs="{'invisible': [('state', 'in', ['draft', 'sent', 'cancel'])]}"/>
38          <field name="pricelist_id" groups="product.group_sale_pricelist"/>
39          <field name="currency_id" invisible="1"/>
40          <field name="payment_term_id" options="{'no_create': True}"/>
41          <field name="x_daterequired"/>
42        </group>
43      </group>
44 ▾    <notebook>
```

Date Required

Notice that we have removed the `options` tag for the purposes of this example. Now you can save the form and refresh it.

As was warned early on in the chapter, changing and modifying Odoo in the database can be dangerous and can break your Odoo installation if you make mistakes.

Please be aware that you may have to hold down the *Shift* key when you refresh your browser to see the change:

As you can see, it is pretty easy to create new fields and then add those fields to views and forms.

Customizing search operations in Odoo

In addition to having the ability to modify the forms and list views in Odoo, you can also customize searching in Odoo to better fit the needs of your organization. For example, when customers place orders, it is common in a business-to-business scenario that you will be provided with a purchase order or another source document that the customer references internally.

By default, Odoo does not include the source document field in your search. You must use the advanced search function each and every time in order to look up a customer's order by the source document they have provided to you. As in much of this book, this example comes from a real-world scenario. When customers call, often they won't have an invoice or sales order number from your company; instead, they may only have their internal source document. Let's see how we can customize Odoo to search the **Source Document** field for a sales order more efficiently.

Specifying additional fields

One of the greatest features of Odoo's developer tools is that you can hover over any field in a form and see important information about that field. For our example, we are going to hover over the **Source Document** field to learn how this field is represented within Odoo's database:

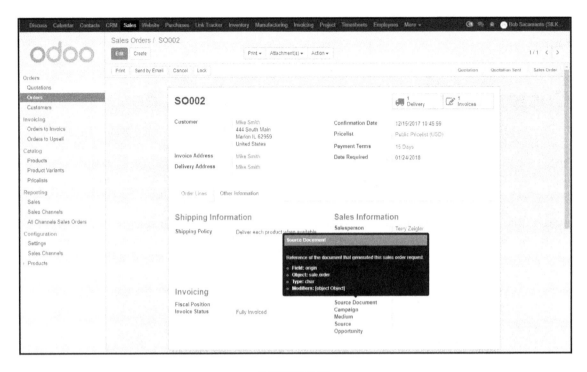

Source Document field

As you can see, the **Field** name for the **Source Document** in the sales order is **origin**. We can also verify that this field belongs to the **sale.order** object and it is of the type **char**.

We will use this information to modify the search view so that we can add the ability to search for a source document in the list view without using an advanced search.

Editing the search view

You edit the search view by navigating to the list for the search you wish to modify. In this case, we will simply click on **Sales Orders** under the main **Sales** menu. Then, under the **Debug View** menu, choose **Edit SearchView**.

The XML for the search view will appear for you to edit, as shown in the following screenshot:

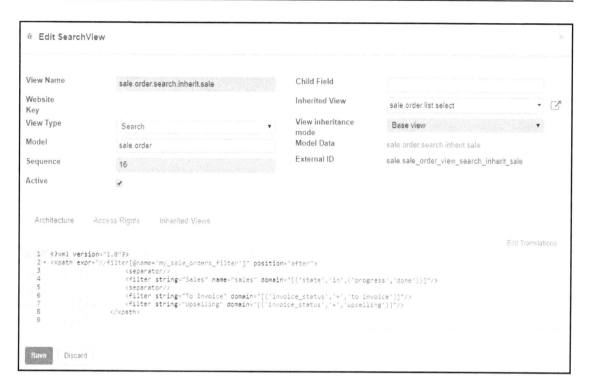

Notice that there is an inherited view specified. This means that the view you are looking at is inherited from **sale.order.list.select**. Click the small icon to the right of the inherited view field to pull up the view it is inherited from.

> A view that is inherited is a view that is based on another view. This is Odoo allows you to extend the existing views and forms with your own content. You inherit the features of the view it is based on.

Take a little time to look at the structure of this form. You will see that many tags start with `<field name="`. Each of these fields define what search fields are available to you in the list's search box.

To search **Source Document**, we only need to add a field tag for the origin field to the list. Here, you can see we have added it under the `product_id` field:

```xml
<?xml version="1.0"?>
<search string="Search Sales Order">
        <field name="name" string="Sales Order" filter_domain="['|',('name','ilike',self),('client_order_ref','ilike',self)]"/>
        <field name="partner_id" operator="child_of"/>
        <field name="user_id"/>
        <field name="section_id" string="Sales Team" groups="base.group_multi_salesteams"/>
        <field name="project_id"/>
        <field name="origin"/>
        <field name="product_id"/>
        <filter string="My" domain="[('user_id','=',uid)]" name="my_sale_orders_filter"/>
        <separator/>
        <filter string="Quotations" name="draft" domain="[('state','in',('draft','sent'))]" help="Sales Order that haven't yet been
confirmed"/>
        <filter string="Sales" name="sales" domain="[('state','in',('manual','progress'))]"/>
        <filter string="To Invoice" domain="[('state','=','manual')]" help="Sales Order ready to be invoiced"/>
        <filter string="Done" domain="[('state','=','done')]" help="Sales Order done"/>
        <separator/>
```

After you have saved the form, refresh the page. If you begin typing in the search box, you will now see that **Source Document** is available in the search list:

When making changes in these forms, all of the previous warnings apply. Make sure that you do not make changes in live systems, and make sure you also have good backups.

Source Document

As you can see, the **Source Document** is added to the search under **Product**, which is the description associated with the `product_id` field in Odoo.

Understanding actions

We've already seen how we can modify views and create custom search criteria, so you should be well on your way to making customizations that are quite useful. At some point, however, when you wish to create a new view or a specific type of filter, you are going to need to understand actions so that you can change the way an Odoo application behaves.

As we learned earlier, we can use actions to trigger views. Let's begin by taking a look at the list of actions that are already in your Odoo installation. While in developer mode, under the **Settings** menu, under **Actions,** choose **Window Actions**. You will be presented with a list, as shown in the following screenshot:

Window Actions

In the previous screenshot, we filtered the list of actions to only those named `sales order`. Let's now create our own custom rush order action that will allow us to create a menu that will pull up only the sales orders that are rush orders. This is a perfect example of simple customization that can save a lot of keystrokes and improve usability, depending on the operation.

One nice thing about customizing in Odoo is that you can often use an existing record as a template and then simply make the custom changes that you require. This dramatically reduces the risk of making a data entry error.

It is recommended when you are first starting out that you consider making one change at a time and testing it out before making additional customizations.

Let's duplicate the first sales orders action in the list that has the **Domain Value** `[('state','not in',('draft','sent','cancel'))]`.

A domain is the technical name for the filter you supply to limit the records.

Click on the edit menu and choose **Duplicate** from the **Action Type** drop-down menu, as shown in the following screenshot:

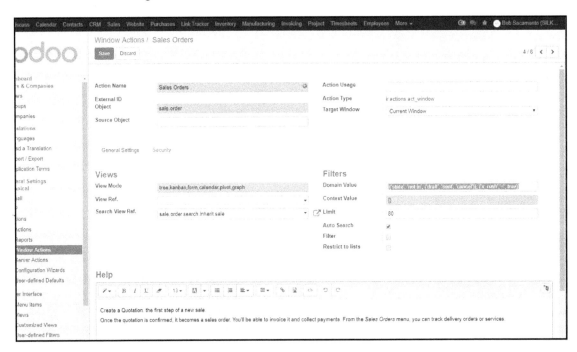

Notice that, after we duplicated the **Action Type**, we changed the action name so that we can recognize that this action will only show orders that have been designated as rush orders.

To actually filter the **sale.order** model by orders that have been marked as a rush order, we need to change the **Domain Value** of our new action. Notice how the **Domain Value** already has a limit that says this cannot be a draft order. We will leave that filter in place and add an additional condition specifying that the order must also be a rush order.

In a large operation, a simple modification like this could reduce a screen that has thousands, or even hundreds of thousands of records, limiting it to a manageable size for that process.

Make sure that you save the changes made to your new action. Now, we can add our new menu.

Creating a new menu

When customizing Odoo, having to create a new menu, that will pull a new view, or an action that will filter that view, is inevitable. This ability to create new menus and tie them to your own custom actions can create a better user experience that is more customized to your specific business requirements.

While in developer mode, go to the **Settings** menu and choose **Menu Items** under **User Interface**:

Menu Items

Like before, you can use the search feature to limit the menu to the sales order's menu item. Just as we duplicated the sales orders action to make it easier to create a custom action, duplicate the sales order menu item as a starting point for your new Rush Sales Order menu, as shown in the following screenshot:

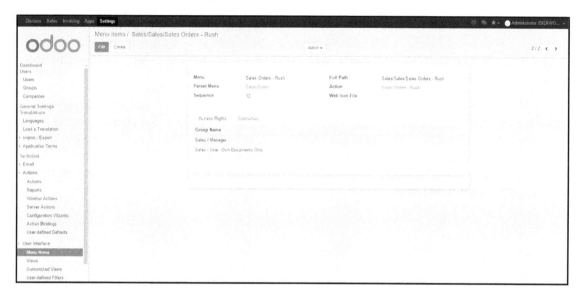

Rush Sales Order menu

Notice how we have changed the name that will appear in the menu and have assigned the **Sales Order - Rush** action to this menu. Odoo now knows that when you select the **Sales Order - Rush** menu item, the **Sales Order - Rush** action will be triggered. Because we modified the **Domain Value** of the action to only include rush orders, we only see the records that match that criteria.

Summary

In this chapter, we started by looking at how to activate Odoo's developer mode. Next, we walked through how to make a backup of the Odoo database and how to restore that database using database management tools in Odoo, while emphasizing the importance of creating backups. Next, we went through the step-by-step process of customizing Odoo, looking at how to add fields to the database, and ultimately to your forms and views. This is by no means a comprehensive guide to Odoo customization; it is merely an introduction to common ways of customizing forms, lists, and searches.

In the next chapter, we will explore how we can use the Odoo report designer to customize reports and export data from Odoo. We will begin by looking at how to customize the company headers and footers that appear on documents. With Odoo, we can use dynamic fields to automatically put values from our database into our reports. Using the new QWeb template language, we will get a great deal of power and flexibility when building reports that integrate well with Odoo.

14
Modifying Documents and Reports

Regardless of how great the built-in reports are in any ERP system, it is inevitable that most companies will need to do some custom modifications to the standard documents and reports. Of course, Odoo is no exception. The goal of this chapter is to provide the reader with a solid introduction to the Odoo reporting framework.

In this chapter, we will cover the following topics:

- How to make simple changes to the headers and footers of your reports
- The basic framework of how Odoo organizes reports and forms
- How to modify and make changes to reports using the Odoo reporting framework and the QWeb template language

Within Odoo, it is possible to make some changes without modifying the documents themselves. For example, you can change the headers and footers that appear on all your reports throughout the company.

A powerful template language called QWeb allows you to integrate data from Odoo into your report. This chapter will walk you through these steps and show you how to modify existing Odoo reports.

 As in other areas of Odoo development, be sure to make frequent backups of your databases. In some of the examples, we will change the database in ways that can make it difficult to recover if something goes wrong.

What's new in Odoo 11?

Report configuration and setup has been improved somewhat in Odoo 11. There are no significant upgrades in terms of capabilities or how you modify or edit reports, but the processes and menu options are different than they were in Odoo 10.

Getting the skills required to modify reports

In my experience, many end users believe that with perhaps an hour or two of training, they will be able to create their own reports. This is not just an Odoo issue—it is a common perception that many end users have when working with an ERP system. Unfortunately, creating or modifying reports is often not easy and should be considered more of a developer task than an end user task. Be prepared to spend a considerable amount of time acquiring the skills required to make significant changes to the documents and reports in Odoo.

Furthermore, reporting has changed dramatically in the past few years. Previously, many companies were dependent on paper reports and Excel sheets to properly communicate information throughout the company. Very often in Odoo, what was previously a physical report can better be managed through filtering and grouping views properly or using the business intelligence features built into Odoo. Be sure to carefully consider your report options from many different angles.

Scope creep refers to projects that continue to grow in complexity beyond the original design. Pay special attention to report requests, as it can be an area in which you can end up with many additional requirements that you did not anticipate.

What is the QWeb template engine?

The **QWeb** template engine can actually be used for many things other than basic reports. The QWeb template is also the main way that all of the website builders and new CMSs generate the HTML to create the page. In reports, QWeb works in exactly the same way as HTML gets generated, but instead directs the output into a PDF file.

The great part about this is that once you learn how to modify reports in QWeb, that same skill will allow you to create dynamic web pages that can tie directly into Odoo.

Company report configuration

When Odoo is first installed, you are presented with a default template that will appear on many of the standard reports. Even if you don't plan to make a lot of major changes to the standard reports in Odoo, it is very likely that you will want to modify the headers and footers and other parts of your report template to be more unique to your company.

To begin editing Odoo headers and footers, it is best if you log in as an Odoo administrator. Furthermore, to access all of the report settings and configurations, you will need to go into **Developer Mode**, as described in `Chapter 13`, *Customizing Odoo for Your Business*. This is accomplished by going to the **Settings** menu and then clicking on the **Activate Developer Mode** link on the right-hand side of the form.

Once you have **Developer Mode** turned on, navigate to the **Settings** menu and click **General Settings**. At the top of the form, you will find the **Business Documents** area:

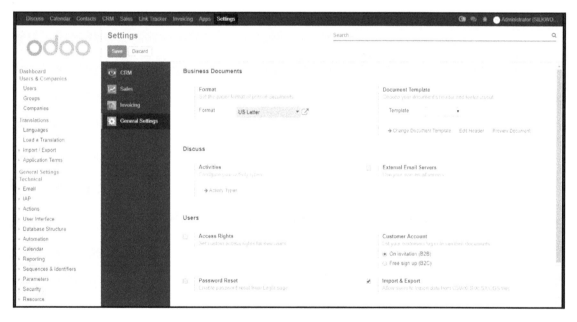

Business Documents area

Before we make any changes at all to our reports, let's go ahead and get a look at one of the default reports.

If you click **Change Document Template**, you will be taken to a form that allows you to choose the default template for your reports. You can see an example of what they look like by clicking **Preview** under one of the document templates at the bottom of the form:

Odoo will then process the report into a PDF and allow you to download it in your browser.

Problems with the Wkhtmltopdf installation

While the majority of Odoo installations go smoothly for primary operations, it is quite common for installations to have problems with a library called Wkhtmltopdf. If you have this problem with your own installation, you will see a message like the following:

Follow the link to `http://www.wkhtmltopdf.org` and look at the resources in the Appendix to learn more about how to install this package so that Odoo can properly display the PDF file.

After the PDF is downloaded, you can view it to see a preview of what your reports will look like. Note that these previews do not use data from your database, but instead use demo data:

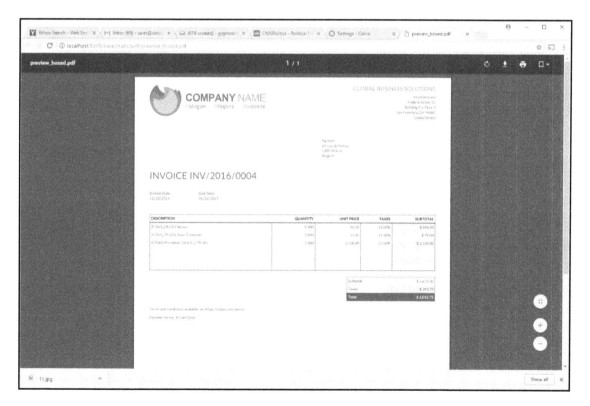

Preview of your report

Specifying the paper format for your reports

Depending on your specific business requirements, it is possible that you will need to have custom paper formats. Fortunately, Odoo allows you to specify a default paper format, as well as indicate which reports should use a given paper format. While you may not need to use this feature, to configure a paper format, simply click the standard edit icon to the right and you will see the available options:

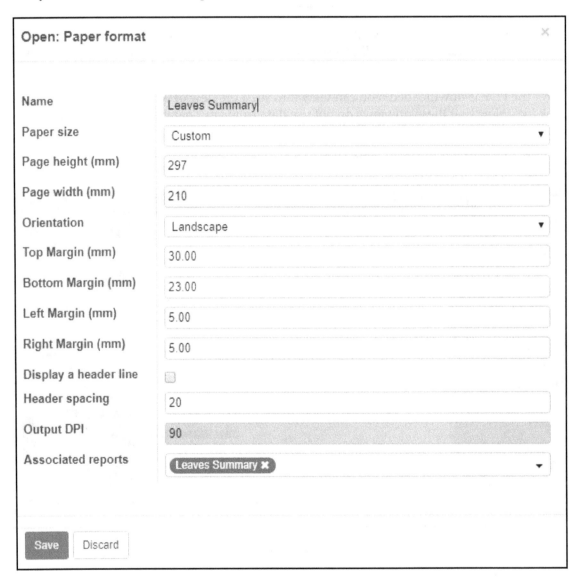

In the preceding example, we can see the custom paper configuration for the **Leaves Summary**. Most importantly, note how the **Associated reports** includes the **Leaves Summary**. This is how Odoo can associate a given report with a specific paper size.

Troubleshooting printers and paper sizes can be tricky. Even if you have your settings correct in this Odoo configuration, you will need to consider the settings in the application you use to print the report, as well as the settings on the printer itself.

Modifying the internal report header using QWeb

From the options we have seen so far, it is clear that while we can create a custom footer, we must do something else in order to change the header for our reports. To make this change, we must edit the actual QWeb source that makes up the header of the report.

Let's look at the QWeb for the company header by returning to the **General Settings** and clicking the link **Edit Header**. The following is a screenshot of the QWeb used for the external report header:

Here, we can see the actual Qweb code that displays the report header in HTML, which is then converted into a PDF report. As was mentioned earlier in the chapter, modifying reports is not something that should typically be attempted by end users. This example is to demonstrate how you can make a small change to a report. By analyzing other reports in Odoo, it is possible to make your own custom reports. Just be prepared for a considerable learning curve if you are new to XML and template languages.

Making our first simple change

You have to start somewhere. When modifying reports, the best approach is to start simple and test each and every change as you make it. Do not expect to go in and make a dozen changes to the header and then run the report without any testing—not until you have a lot of experience.

For our change, note that in the footer of the report, we have the website but not the link to our Facebook page. Depending on your business, you may wish to include alternative social media links on your document. Let's add a bit of Qweb code to append the company's Facebook link to the report.

 Even though the link says **Edit Header**, you edit both the header and footer of your report using this method.

The actual code we will add is very simple, but we can make it easier on ourselves by copying and pasting and then just changing it. If you know HTML, you can use HTML in Qweb code.

The XML code uses an <li> tag to display the information based on the list-inline style. The <i> tag displays the Facebook logo from the *Font Awesome Icon* collection. Finally, we use a <span> tag to display the actual URL from the company model.

When you are done, the edited code should look as follows:

```
21 ▾ ass="footer o_background_footer">
22 ▾ v class="text-center">
23 ▾ <ul class="list-inline">
24       <li t-if="company.phone"><i class="fa fa-phone"/> <span t-field="company.phone"/></li>
25       <li t-if="company.email"><i class="fa fa-at"/> <span t-field="company.email"/></li>
26       <li t-if="company.website"><i class="fa fa-globe"/> <span t-field="company.website"/></li>
27       <li t-if="company.vat"><i class="fa fa-building-o"/><t t-esc="company.country_id.vat_label or 'TIN'"/>: <span t-f:
28       <li t-if="company.social_facebook"><i class="fa fa-facebook-f"/> <span t-field="company.social_facebook"/></li>
29  </ul>
```

Now, you can preview the internal report to see the change:

As you can see, the report now includes the colon separator as well as the phone number for the company. Remember to start with simple changes and examine other reports to learn how to make more complex changes.

Learning how Odoo organizes reports

Unfortunately, the ability to edit the header and footer of the company information does not get you very far. If you spend time with Odoo, it is inevitable that the time will come when you need to make changes to specific Odoo documents. For example, a company may need to customize their quotation or sales order to make it more visually attractive to their customers. Perhaps a company would like to change the appearance of their invoice or the picking ticket they use to pull products from inventory.

However, before you begin to start modifying reports or adding new reports, it is important that you have an overall understanding of how reports are organized within Odoo. First, make sure you have activated **Developer Mode** as you have learned to do in Chapter 13, *Customizing Odoo for Your Business*.

With **Developer Mode** active, you can get access to the reports within Odoo by going to the **Settings** menu, then, in the **Technical** section further down in the menu, you will find the **Reports** option. Clicking it will list the **Reports** in Odoo, as shown in the following screenshot:

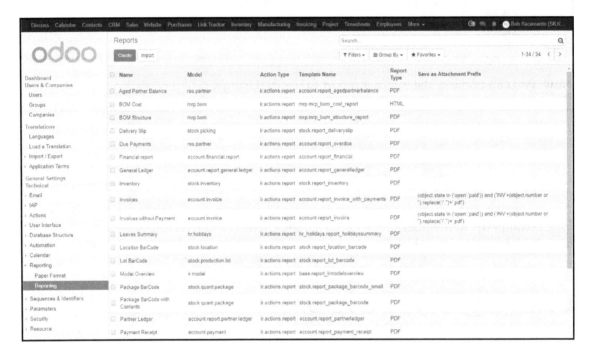

Here, you can see the list of reports in the view with critical information that tells you which model the report is associated with, the type of action used to trigger that report, the template for the report, and the report type.

> The **Save As Attachment** prefix can be used to append a prefix to the beginning of the report name when it is saved.

Understanding the report types

Each of the past few major upgrades to Odoo has brought with it new improvements to the reporting engine. Odoo 10 is no different, and many of the old reports are gone. However, Odoo still provides support for those older types of reports. In the previous screenshot, when you see a report type labelled RML or PDF (depreciated), that is a report that is still using the old reporting mechanism. You can still open up those older reports and make changes to them. However, most of the reports now use Odoo's new Odoo reporting framework, QWeb templates.

Looking at the definition for the Sales order form

As with the other examples in this book, we are going to choose a very common business requirement for this example. Most companies are not going to want to use the default sales order. In fact, after working with hundreds of accounting and ERP systems, I cannot recall any system implementation that involves sales orders where the sales order was not customized at some point.

Using what you have learned in previous chapters, you may wish to bring up a quotation or a sales order and have it ready to print so you can see your changes as they happen. Any changes you make will modify both the quotation and the sales order as they share the same QWeb template.

 Odoo is quite good at allowing you to use more than one tab in your browser for most operations. I often keep one tab open with the document I want to print and then keep another tab open with the report I am editing.

When you are ready to edit the sales order, scroll down the report list, find the **Quotation |
Order**, and click on it. It is also the only report in the default list of Odoo reports that is built
on the **sale.order** model:

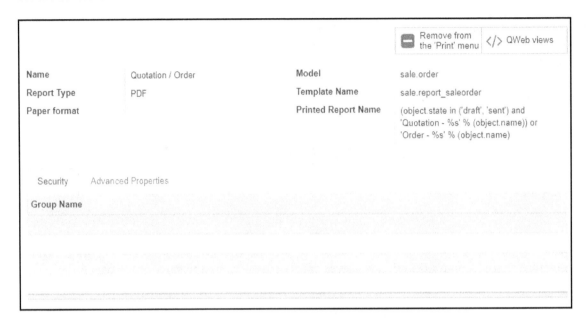

You will notice that there is some basic information at the top of the page and a **Security** tab
at the bottom of the report that is empty. You can use this tab to put additional restrictions
on the report beyond what has already been specified in the **sale.order** model.

The previous screen is primarily the configuration of the report. The views that make up the
actual report itself can be found by clicking **QWeb views**:

This brings up all the **QWeb views** associated with the report. While there are three views listed, the one we are interested in is **report_saleorder_document**. The **report_saleorder** view is basically a container that holds the content of the document view, and you will rarely need to modify this unless you were an experienced Odoo developer.

Click on the **report_saleorder_document** view to open the view:

View Name	report_saleorder_document	Child Field	
Website		Inherited View	
Key	sale.report_saleorder_document	View inheritance mode	Base view
View Type	QWeb	Model Data	report_saleorder_document
Model		External ID	sale.report_saleorder_document
Sequence	16		
Active	✓		

Architecture   Access Rights   Inherited Views

Edit Translations

```xml
<?xml version="1.0"?>
<t t-name="sale.report_saleorder_document">
    <t t-call="web.external_layout">
        <t t-set="doc" t-value="doc.with_context({'lang':doc.partner_id.lang})"/>
        <div class="page">
            <div class="oe_structure"/>
            <div class="row">
                <div class="col-xs-6">
                    <t t-if="doc.partner_shipping_id == doc.partner_invoice_id                    and doc.partner_i
                        <strong t-if="doc.partner_shipping_id == doc.partner_invoice_id">Invoicing and shipping address:</str
                        <strong t-if="doc.partner_shipping_id != doc.partner_invoice_id">Invoicing address:</strong>
                        <div t-field="doc.partner_invoice_id" t-options="{&quot;widget&quot;: &quot;contact&quot;, &quot;fiel
                        <div t-if="doc.partner_shipping_id != doc.partner_invoice_id" class="mt8">
                            <strong>Shipping address:</strong>
                            <div t-field="doc.partner_shipping_id" t-options="{&quot;widget&quot;: &quot;contact&quot;, &quot
                        </div>
                    </t>
                </div>
                <div class="col-xs-5 col-xs-offset-1">
                    <div t-field="doc.partner_id" t-options="{&quot;widget&quot;: &quot;contact&quot;, &quot;fields&quot;: [&
                    <p t-if="doc.partner_id.vat"><t t-esc="doc.company_id.country_id.vat_label or 'TIN'"/>: <span t-field="do
                </div>
            </div>

            <h2>
                <t t-if="not (env.context.get('proforma', False) or is_pro_forma}">
                    <span t-if="doc.state not in ['draft','sent']">Order # </span>
                    <span t-if="doc.state in ['draft','sent']">Quotation # </span>
                </t>
                <t t-if="env.context.get('proforma', False) or is_pro_forma">
                    <span>Pro-Forma Invoice # </span>
                </t>
```

So we are finally here! You have to drill down a little bit to get to them, but after you have done it a few times, it really is pretty easy. Now, we are looking at the actual QWeb report template. Odoo calls these templates views when they are associated with Odoo reports.

If you look through the architecture, you should quickly find elements within it that compare directly to the standard quotation or sales order report.

Here is a sample quotation that was produced using the default QWeb template we are viewing:

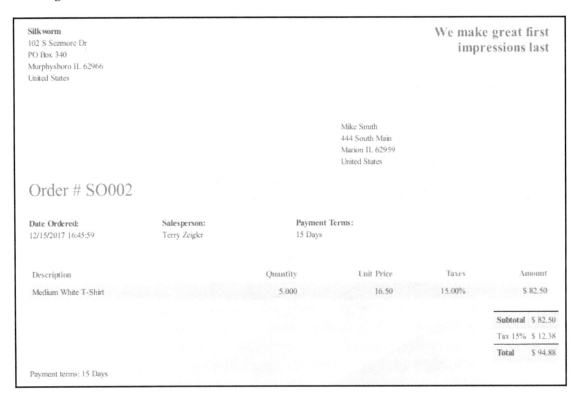

So, as we should always do, let's make a small change and see the result. I cannot emphasize enough how important it is to back up frequently and make small changes when you are first getting started.

So, let's assume that for this change we want to have `Sales Order #:` instead of `Order #` on our report.

This is relatively simple. Click **Edit** as you would on any Odoo form to edit the template. Then, scroll down into the template until you find `Quotation No:`

```
<t t-if="not (env.context.get('proforma', False) or is_pro_forma)">
    <span t-if="doc.state not in ['draft','sent']">Order # </span>
    <span t-if="doc.state in ['draft','sent']">Quotation # </span>
</t>
```

Replace the selected text you see in the preceding screenshot, then replace `Order #` with `Sales Order #`, and then save the document. Be very careful of the changes you make until you understand XML. A less common but worst case scenario is that perhaps the mistake you make will still allow the document to save, but it will be broken.

Because the XML is represented with ordinary text, a little trick you can use is to copy and paste the XML into a text editor to have a quick backup in case you make a mistake or do not get the results you expected.

After you have saved, you should be able to print the document and see your change when you print the order again:

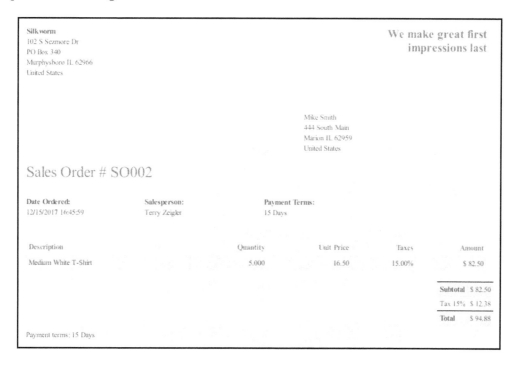

We have made that small change successfully and changed it, but even just knowing how to do this will often allow you to add many things you need to a report.

Creating a new QWeb report in Odoo

As we learned in Chapter 13, *Customizing Odoo for Your Business*, you are often almost never better off creating a blank record, and instead are better served by duplicating an existing record that is close to what you want. For example, we duplicated the Sales Order action and menu to create our custom Sales Order - Rush options.

Let's do the same thing for a new custom Odoo report that you could then tie to an action using the skills you learned in Chapter 13, *Customizing Odoo for Your Business*.

Simply go to the **Settings** menu and pull up the **Report** option to list the available reports. Use the search filter to locate the **Sales Order** form and duplicate it.

Learning more about the power of QWeb templates

Now that we have learned to make that small change, let's look a little closer at how Odoo is able to use the exact same template for both the quotation and the sales order. In fact, you may have already figured out how Odoo does this from looking at the code we modified a little bit.

One of the best things you can do to learn how to modify reports is to look at existing reports within Odoo and see how they accomplish what you wish to accomplish. When trying to solve a problem, see if you can find another report in Odoo that is already doing something similar to what you want.

 It is often a lot easier to copy and paste part of a template you need and then change it rather than trying to get all the < . / ?> syntax straight and just right. It's easier if you are working from a reference point.

Using a t-if to create a dynamic QWeb template report

Much of the power of QWeb allows for you to conditionally show information depending on various fields and information within the document. In this case, Odoo is looking at the status of the order to determine whether the template should have a label for Quote or for Sales Order. Let's take a close look at the syntax so we can understand exactly what it means.

If you don't understand at least some basic XML, now would be a good time to look at some of the available resources we have listed in the Appendix or do a simple Google search on an XML tutorial:

```
<span t-if="o.state not in ['draft','sent']">Sales Order # </span>
<span t-if="o.state in ['draft','sent']">Quotation #:</span>
```

You will notice that each section is wrapped in its own set of `<span>` tags. Then, right after the first span tag starts, we have the `t-if=` condition. Everything between the double quotes is the condition that will determine whether what is included between the span tags will print.

In this specific case, o represents the order. We use the period, or dot, notation to specify which field we want to check. In this case, it is the **State** field. Even if you are not a programmer, if you read it out and ignore the confusing syntax and punctuation, it should start to make sense. The only difference between each of these `t-if` statements is the word `not`, which follows `o.state`. When the state of the order is not in draft or sent, then it is an order. When the state of the order is in draft or sent, then we have a quote.

If XML and programming is very new to you, some of this could be a bit confusing, but if you take some time to look at existing reports and use some of the resources in the appendix to learn more, you will be customizing Odoo reports in no time.

Summary

In this chapter, we started by walking through how to change the templates on company reports through Odoo to modify the header of your report. After that, we learned about Odoo's reporting system and how reports are organized within Odoo. Finally, we learned how to use the powerful QWeb template language to make changes to reports.

In the next chapter, we will explore how to build our own custom applications in Odoo.

Discovering Custom Odoo Modules 15

While Odoo has a lot of built-in and community modules, it is inevitable that there will be quite a few businesses that will have requirements that will be difficult to achieve with the modules that are currently available. The Odoo framework offers developers the ability to extend Odoo to accomplish business objectives and (hopefully) make Odoo fit in better with the workflow of the company. However, before you attempt to write custom Odoo modules, it is important that you completely understand the functionality of Odoo and the various modules that are available in the community.

In this chapter, we will cover the following topics:

- Learning the basic structure of an Odoo module
- Using a module to add additional fields to your Odoo system
- Extending the views in your Odoo instance to include new fields
- Making changes to the available states in an Odoo workflow

Through careful configuration, many business objectives can be achieved without writing custom modules. Before you go down the path of writing custom Odoo modules, it is important that you make absolutely sure that the business requirements are clear and you have thoroughly explored all the options available inside Odoo. There are many settings that provide additional functionality to the Odoo system. You don't want to spend days, weeks, or even months building an Odoo module to then find out that much of that functionality was already available.

The goal of this chapter is to introduce you to custom module development in Odoo. Even if you are a beginner and don't know much about programming, you should be able to follow along and build a module in Odoo. If you don't know Python or XML, you will likely find some aspects of this chapter a little more challenging. Fortunately, there are many resources in the Odoo community that can help you along your path to Odoo development.

Exploring the Odoo application and module directory

In addition to the built-in Odoo modules and the various settings that can change the way Odoo functions, there is also a growing collection of custom Odoo modules written by the community. When you find a business requirement for which you believe you may need to do some custom module development, take the time to go to the Odoo application repository and search for modules that could perhaps fit the purpose. Even if the module is not exactly what you are looking for, there can often be a lot of valuable code in those modules that can help you with your own module development.

 You can find the Odoo application and module repository at
https://www.odoo.com/apps.

Even more importantly, these applications are invaluable for studying how to build and customize applications in Odoo. When you get stuck trying to solve a development problem, the Odoo source code and the available applications that you can find in the Odoo application repository are often all that you need to find the solution.

In Odoo development, we can sometimes refer to custom applications and modules interchangeably. For the most part, modules are customizations that extend Odoo applications with additional functionality. Odoo applications would typically add an entire new set of features that would be more substantial than a module. There is, however, no real difference between them in how you approach development. Both are created in the same way.

Building our first Odoo module

One of the best features of the Odoo framework is that we can extend Odoo and write our own modules without having to modify any of the Odoo source code. Instead, the changes we make are all contained in their own directory and their own files.

The primary advantage of this is that when Odoo modifies its source code with patches or bug fixes, we do not have to worry about our changes getting overwritten. Also, while we may still need to modify our code if Odoo makes a dramatic change to its source code, there is a reasonable chance that the changes required will be minimal.

WARNING

Like in other areas of Odoo development, you should make frequent backups of your databases. Some of the examples we will show make changes to the database that can be difficult to undo.

Each module in Odoo has some basic requirements for it to be properly recognized by the Odoo framework and installed. Once we successfully install our module, then the framework will extend Odoo with the appropriate functionality.

Preparing your basic development environment

Before you can begin creating an application, you must get yourself situated on the server on which you wish to do your development. This includes having an installation of Odoo that you can use just for development. You should not be doing any development on a production server. For this example, we are going to assume that you have followed installing Odoo on an Ubuntu server, as was outlined in Chapter 1, *Setting Up Odoo 11*.

Finding your Odoo configuration file and installing it

During your installation of Odoo, a configuration file was created that contains the necessary parameters for starting your Odoo server.

In the Ubuntu desktop, you can use the key combination *Ctrl* + *Shift* + *T* to bring up a Terminal window.

If you have performed a manual installation, then this file is in the Debian directory. We will now look at the Odoo configuration file so we can find the directory for our Odoo installation and modify the addons_path to contain our new directory:

```
🗙 🗕 🗖   ubuntu@ubuntu: ~/odoo/debian
  GNU nano 2.5.3              File: odoo.conf

[options]
; This is the password that allows database operations:
; admin_passwd = admin
db_host = False
db_port = False
db_user = odoo
db_password = False
;addons_path = /usr/lib/python3/dist-packages/odoo/addons




                        [ Read 8 lines ]
^G Get Help    ^O Write Out ^W Where Is  ^K Cut Text  ^J Justify   ^C Cur Pos
^X Exit        ^R Read File ^\ Replace   ^U Uncut Text^T To Spell  ^  Go To Line
```

You can use the following command to edit the configuration file:
`sudo nano /etc/odoo/odoo.conf`.

You will notice that the very last line in our configuration file contains the addons_path to the location of the source of the Odoo applications.

Nano is a relatively simple text editor. A few of the more important commands you will need to use include the following:

- *Ctrl+O* to write out any changes you may make. You will be prompted for a file name.
- *Ctrl+X* to exit Nano.
- *Ctrl+C* to cancel an action.

After exiting Nano, you can verify the location of the Odoo applications by using the following commands in the Terminal:

```
cd /usr/lib/python3/dist-packages/odoo/addons
```

If you use the `ls` command, you will then see the directories containing the source code for the Odoo applications.

Specifying a custom directory to hold our Odoo modules

We will begin by creating a directory to hold our Odoo module. We have two options for where we can create the directory to hold our module. For our first option, we could create our directory in the `addons` folder where all the rest of the add-ons for Odoo are stored. This method is easy and allows Odoo to see our module simply by restarting the Odoo server.

A more preferred method, and the one we will use for this example, is to create a separate folder to hold our add-ons. This method has the advantage that we keep our modules separate from the standard Odoo modules.

Create a new directory to hold our modules by typing the following command in the Terminal:

```
sudo mkdir /home/mymodules
```

For Odoo to find this directory, we need to modify the Odoo configuration file that we looked at previously:

```
sudo nano /etc/odoo/odoo.conf
```

Here we can see a screen-shot of the configuration file:

```
ubuntu@ubuntu: ~/odoo/debian
  GNU nano 2.5.3              File: odoo.conf

[options]
; This is the password that allows database operations:
; admin_passwd = admin
db_host = False
db_port = False
db_user = odoo
db_password = False
addons_path = /usr/lib/python3/dist-packages/odoo/addons, home/mymodules




                         [ Read 8 lines ]
^G Get Help   ^O Write Out ^W Where Is  ^K Cut Text  ^J Justify   ^C Cur Pos
^X Exit       ^R Read File ^\ Replace   ^U Uncut Text^T To Spell  ^  Go To Line
```

We have edited the `odoo.conf` file to contain the `mymodules` directory within our `home` directory to store our custom Odoo modules.

Now we need to create a directory to hold the actual module itself:

```
sudo mkdir /home/mymodules/silkworm
```

When you are getting started, it is important that you understand how to create these required files and how they work together. Depending on the build of Odoo that you have installed, you can use scaffolding to more quickly create an Odoo application. While templating can save time, how it is used has undergone a lot of alteration, and the syntax for using it changes frequently. It is therefore recommended that you always keep yourself aware of techniques for creating an Odoo application without relying on scaffolding.

Contents of your module directory

Within our module directory, `silkworm`, we will create two files that are required in every Odoo module.

To navigate to our module directory, use the following command:

cd /home/mymodules/silkworm

These two files must always be named the following:

- `__init__.py`
- `__manifest__.py`

Although it is difficult to tell, in both cases there are two underscores together at the beginning and then another two underscores just before the file extension. You must name these files exactly this way to have a valid Odoo module.

These are Python files, and they can be edited with any text editor. We will begin by defining these two required files.

Creating and editing the files

Depending on your operating system of choice, there are a variety of editors you could use to create and edit the files for your module. In Windows, you could use something as simple as Notepad. In Ubuntu, there are also several choices, including Nano, Vi, or Vim.

 Most developers will use a more full-featured editor such as Microsoft Developer Studio on the Windows platform or PyCharm on Ubuntu.

The __init__.py file

The purpose of the `__init__.py` file is to specify the Python files you wish to include in your module. At a minimum, you will usually have one Python file, but you could have more or fewer depending on the complexity of the module you are developing. If you had a Python file with your code, and that file was named `codexample.py`, you would have to import `codexample` inside the `__init__.py` file. You will notice that you don't have to include the `.py` extension inside the `__init__.py` file.

To create the __init__.py file in Ubuntu, make sure you are in the module directory and use the following command:

```
sudo nano __init__.py
```

This will bring up the blank text editor.

For our example, the __init__.py file will contain one line that specifies the name of the file in which we will be placing the Python code for our module:

```
import silkworm
```

The __manifest__.py file

The __manifest__.py file is essentially a manifest for your Odoo module. It describes the necessary attributes of your module to the Odoo framework. Sometimes, this file is also called the module descriptor file.

To create the __manifest__.py file in Ubuntu, make sure you are in the module directory and use the following command:

```
sudo nano __manifest__.py
```

The structure in the file is what is called a **dictionary** in Python:

```
{
    'name': 'Screen Printing',
    'version': '1.0',
    'description': """
This module adds functionality for
    screen printing companies
""",
    'author': 'Greg Moss',
    'depends': ['base','sale'],
    'data': ['silkworm_view.xml'],
    'demo': [],
    'installable': True,
    'auto_install': False,
}
```

This is how the __manifest_.py file appears when edited in Nano.

The __manifest__.py file contains a single Python dictionary. Even if you don't know Python, the syntax is rather simple if you have had even a little experience in programming. When you install a module in Odoo, this file describes the details the framework needs to properly configure your module.

- name: The name entry is what will appear in the modules listing inside Odoo.

- version: This allows you to specify a version number for your module. This will be valuable as you extend the functionality of your module, as you will need to keep track of the various releases.

- description: This description will appear when you prepare to install the module in Odoo. It should clearly describe the purpose of the module to someone who may be entirely unfamiliar with it. You should take the time to fill out this entry. Even this little bit of documentation can help someone who is trying to utilize the module in the future.

 In this example, note the triple double-quotes before and after the description value. Python uses this syntax to allow you to continue a string on multiple lines.

- author: Providing the name of the author of your module is also important, as it could help future users track down the main person who can provide assistance.

- depends: The preceding elements were pretty self-explanatory, and are mostly for documentation purposes. This entry, however, tells the framework what other modules your module will build upon. At minimum, you will need to include base as one of your module dependencies. In our example, we will be extending the sales order system, so we have also included sale as one of the module dependencies.

- data: The data item specifies the XML view files you wish to include in your module. We will cover view files in depth later in this chapter. If you plan to change something in Odoo's forms or user interface, it will most likely involve creating a view file. Other types of data files can be specified here, such as files containing initial data or access rights, but for our example we have named only the silkworm_view.xml file.

- `demo`: Odoo provides a rather convenient method of including demonstration data with your module. When you create your database, you have the option to include demonstration data with that Odoo instance. We have left this blank for our example, but if we wished to make demonstration data available when the module is installed, we could fill in this entry.

- `installable`: This is an entry that you may use to temporarily disable a module for installation. Most often it will be `True` because you want the ability to install the module in an Odoo instance.

- `auto_install`: When this entry is set to `True`, Odoo will automatically install this module when it finds that all the dependency modules are installed. If you have no dependencies, this means that it will be automatically installed when you create a new database. Given Odoo's modular application approach, you typically would not want to have the `auto_install` flag set to `True` for most module development.

Extending an Odoo model in silkworm.py

Next, we create another file named `silkworm.py`. We will begin by creating a module that performs the same customizations we performed through **Developer Mode** in `Chapter 13`, *Customizing Odoo for Your Business*.

Why would we want to put our customization into a module rather than just using Developer Mode?

First off, changes made through Developer Mode are isolated within that instance of Odoo. If you decide you wish to create a new database, you will have to make all the developer changes by hand, again. More importantly, when you make the changes in a module, you have much more control over the final results.

 Developer Mode is very powerful for quickly looking at views, analyzing fields on forms, and understanding more about the Odoo framework. However, it is typically far better to make any actual changes by creating a module rather than modifying the views or models in Developer Mode. So unless you are using Odoo Online it's better to avoid changes in **Developer Mode**.

Using a module to add custom fields to a model

In Chapter 10, *Creating Advanced Searches and Dashboards*, we added **Date Required** and **Rush Order** to our sales order model. Now let's see how we can do exactly the same thing in our module.

In our __init__.py file, we only had one line, the import silkworm command.

To add the **Date Required** and **Rush Order** fields to our sales order, we can place the following in the silkworm.py file:

```
from .import models, fields

class silkworm_sale_order(models.Model):
    _inherit = 'sale.order'

    daterequired = fields.Date('Date Required')
    rush = fields.Boolean('Rush Order')
```

Please note that these are not custom fields created in Developer Mode proceeded by an x_. In Python, the from command allows you to specify which libraries you wish to utilize in your custom classes. For our simple example, we are only pulling in models and fields.

Inheriting from the sales application in Odoo

In our class statement, we specify the silkworm_sale_order class, and it has the models.Model parameter. Remember that when learning the Odoo framework, it will take a bit of time to get familiar with the syntax. Right now, you don't have to necessarily understand why you are specifying models.Model; just understand that it is required with most classes:

```
_inherit= 'sale.order'
```

For those new to object-oriented programming in general, the _inherit statement essentially makes the functionality of the Odoo sales application available to your class so you can extend it with your own fields and methods.

Next, we can extend the Odoo sales application with our two custom fields:

```
daterequired = fields.Date('Date Required', required=True)
rush = fields.Boolean('Rush Order')
```

You will note that in the syntax we also specify the data types and provide the labels we want to display in the views inside Odoo. Note that we have also set `required=True` for the `daterequired` field so that the user will be forced to provide this data when they create a sales order record if that field is on the view.

Python conventions

Unlike many programming languages, Python takes white space very seriously. In fact you must exactly indent your code or the Python compiler will generate an error. For example, the `_inherit` attribute is indented exactly four spaces over from the `class` command.

Adding the fields to our sales order view

Now that we have specified the fields we want added to our sales order model, we must create our view file that will display the fields in the sales order header. We have specified the name of this file inside `__manifest__.py` within the `data` entry. For our example, the file name is `silkworm_view.xml`.

Using your editor of choice, create the `silkworm_view.xml` file. In this file, enter the following code:

```xml
<?xml version="1.0" encoding="utf-8"?>

<Odoo>
    <data>
        <record id="sale_view_order_form" model="ir.ui.view">
            <field name="model">sale.order</field>
            <field name="inherit_id" ref="sale.view_order_form"/>
            <field name="arch" type="xml">
              <field name="payment_term_id" position="after">
                <field name="daterequired"/>
                <field name="rush"/>
              </field>
            </field>
        </record>
    </data>
</Odoo>
```

Now, let's walk through this code and describe what it does. Odoo specifies views using the XML syntax. The first line in the file is the standard element you will find at the top of many XML files, specifying the version and type of encoding used.

The next thing to bear in mind is that Odoo view files contain beginning and ending Odoo tags. Inside those tags there are matching opening and closing `data` tags. To modify or add views in your custom Odoo module, you add `record` tags.

Each record must have an `id`. In this case, we also have a `model` tag that is specified as `ir.ui.view`:

```
<record id="sale_view_order_form" model="ir.ui.view">
```

This is a framework convention, and you will learn about other models that are available as you continue to study Odoo development.

Next, we must specify the base `model` with which this view interacts. For our example, this is `sale.order`. This relates directly to the fact that we have added the fields to the `sale.order` model in our Python file:

```
<field name="model">sale.order</field>
```

If instead you were adding additional fields to the purchase order header, you would specify `purchase.order`.

Use **Developer Mode** in Odoo to mouse over fields and determine which models they relate to. To find the view names you need to use, go into **Manage Views** in Developer Mode. This can save you a great deal of time when developing in Odoo.

Next, let's look at the line that contains `inherit_id`:

```
<field name="inherit_id" ref="sale.view_order_form"/>
```

In much the same way that we had to inherit from `sale.model` when we created our `silkworm_sale_order` class, we must inherit from the `sale.view_order_form` view so that we can add the additional fields.

How did we know that we had to inherit from `sale.view_order_form`? One big trick in finding the value you require is to use edit form view while in Developer Mode.

For this example, while on a sales order in Odoo, choose **Edit FormView** from the developer menu. You will then get taken to the form that shows you exactly the **External ID** you need to add fields to the form:

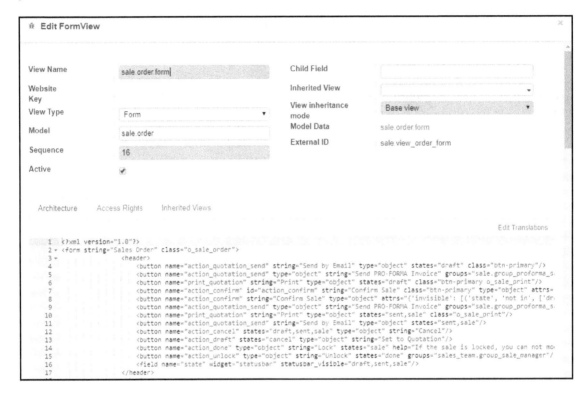

The **Edit FormView** screen shown here shows the **View Name** that has been assigned to the view we are currently looking at. Now we know that the **External ID** we need to use is **sale.view_order_form**.

The External ID is a unique identifier for the view you are working on. This is how the Odoo framework knows which view you are referring to.

When you are adding fields to a form, it is important for Odoo to have the information it requires to determine exactly where the fields should go. In this example, we are telling the Odoo framework we want to first find the field named `payment_term_id`. Next, we use `position="after"` to specify that we want the fields to appear after `payment_term_id`.

In addition to `after`, the position attribute can be specified as `position="before"` to place a field before that element or `position="replace"` to replace an element. So if instead of `after` you used `replace`, the `payment_term_id` field would be replaced by new fields that we add down below.

Once again, we can use Developer Mode to visually find the field name we require. In the following screenshot, we have moved the mouse over the customer reference field to reveal the details about that field:

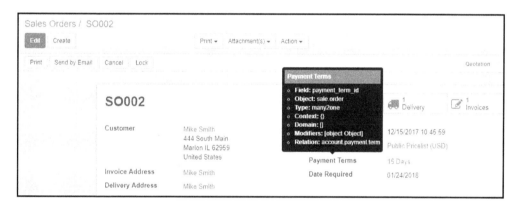

Now that we know where to add our fields, we can specify custom fields to display:

```
<field name="daterequired"/>
<field name="rush"/>
```

Getting ready to install our module

Right now, our module is very simple and just adds two fields to our sales order form. We should still quickly review the files you should have in your module directory:

- `__init__.py`
- `__Odoo__.py`
- `silkworm.py`
- `silkworm_view.py`

When you run Odoo in Ubuntu, it is good practice to run the service under a special account that has limited permissions. This is set up automatically when you use the Debian install. Therefore, we need to change the permissions on our module directory so that Odoo can properly access the files. Use the following command to set the permissions:

```
sudo chown odoo:odoo /home/mymodules -R
```

To install the module, you must also restart the Odoo server. If you don't restart your server, then Odoo will not see your module. Enter the following command:

```
sudo /etc/init.d/odoo stop
```

Then enter the following command:

```
sudo /etc/init.d/odoo start
```

In the top menu, click on **Settings** and choose **Update Modules List** from the menus on the left. You will see the following screenshot:

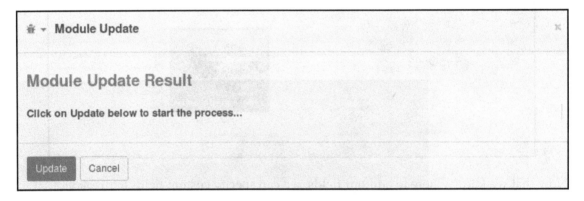

On the **Module Update** screen, click on the **Update** button. Once you have clicked **Update**, Odoo will refresh the available list of add-ons.

Next, we will install the module. Click on **Apps** from the menu on the left.

Remove the **Apps** filter from the search box (yes, this entire process is somewhat counter-intuitive). Once you take off the **Apps** filter, you can search for silk to locate your module for installation:

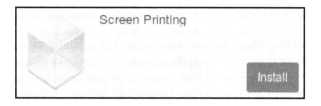

Click the **Install** button to begin the installation process.

After a few seconds, the screen will refresh. You can now pull up a sales order and see the fields added to your form:

This screenshot of a sales order shows the custom fields added in our module.

When developing, it is sometimes inevitable that a module may not install correctly, or that, after installing, you will have an error that will prevent you from logging into Odoo. If you find yourself unable to resolve the error, one workaround to get Odoo back up and running again is to rename the module directory. This prevents Odoo from locating the module to install.

Troubleshooting your module installation

You won't be the first Odoo developer who created a module from scratch to not have it show up in the list of apps. There are a few things you can check if you don't see your application in the list.

First of all, it is always good to know how to check the logfile for errors in your Odoo installation. This is particularly important while you are developing an Odoo module. If you followed the standard Ubuntu Debian install, you can open the logfile and view it with the following command:

```
sudo nano /var/log/odoo/odoo-server.log
```

To demonstrate how this can be useful, we have modified the `silkworm_view.xml` file to contain a small error. When we attempt to install the module, we get an error that we can then view in the `odoo-server.log`:

```
● ● ●   adminuser@ubuntu: /home/mymodules/silkworm
GNU nano 2.5.3                    File: /var/log/odoo/odoo-server.log

    doc = etree.parse(xmlfile)
  File "src/lxml/lxml.etree.pyx", line 3427, in lxml.etree.parse (src/lxml/lxml.etree.c:85131)
  File "src/lxml/parser.pxi", line 1803, in lxml.etree._parseDocument (src/lxml/lxml.etree.c:124287)
  File "src/lxml/parser.pxi", line 1823, in lxml.etree._parseFilelikeDocument (src/lxml/lxml.etree.c:124599)
  File "src/lxml/parser.pxi", line 1718, in lxml.etree._parseDocFromFilelike (src/lxml/lxml.etree.c:123258)
  File "src/lxml/parser.pxi", line 1139, in lxml.etree._BaseParser._parseDocFromFilelike (src/lxml/lxml.etr$
  File "src/lxml/parser.pxi", line 573, in lxml.etree._ParserContext._handleParseResultDoc (src/lxml/lxml.e$
  File "src/lxml/parser.pxi", line 683, in lxml.etree._handleParseResult (src/lxml/lxml.etree.c:112276)
  File "src/lxml/parser.pxi", line 613, in lxml.etree._raiseParseError (src/lxml/lxml.etree.c:111124)
XMLSyntaxError: expected '>', line 13, column 10
2017-01-12 22:37:26,851 20943 ERROR SILKWORM-DEV odoo.http: Exception during JSON request handling.
Traceback (most recent call last):
  File "/usr/lib/python2.7/dist-packages/odoo/http.py", line 638, in _handle_exception
    return super(JsonRequest, self)._handle_exception(exception)
  File "/usr/lib/python2.7/dist-packages/odoo/http.py", line 675, in dispatch
    result = self._call_function(**self.params)
  File "/usr/lib/python2.7/dist-packages/odoo/http.py", line 331, in _call_function
    return checked_call(self.db, *args, **kwargs)
  File "/usr/lib/python2.7/dist-packages/odoo/service/model.py", line 119, in wrapper
    return f(dbname, *args, **kwargs)
  File "/usr/lib/python2.7/dist-packages/odoo/http.py", line 324, in checked_call

^G Get Help    ^O Write Out    ^W Where Is    ^K Cut Text    ^J Justify    ^C Cur Pos     ^Y Prev Page
^X Exit        ^R Read File    ^\ Replace     ^U Uncut Text  ^T To Spell   ^  Go To Line  ^V Next Page
```

When we look at the error log, we can see the **XMLSyntaxError** that was introduced by the error we put into the `silkworm_view.xml` file. The error log is your first stop in attempting to solve these problems.

Now that you know how to identify problems in an installation, here are some typical things to check for that could be preventing your module from installing properly:

- Verify that the permissions are set correctly on your files. You can use `ls -l` to list the files with their permissions.
- Make sure that the addon path for your module directory is in the configuration file. You can verify that it is set by examining the log file. It is in one of the first lines in the log file after restarting the server.
- Stop and restart the Odoo server.
- Check whether `your __manifest__.py` file is missing, is named incorrectly, or has a typo.
- Verify that you have no indentation problems within your Python files
- Sometimes it can help to *Shift*+refresh your browser when installing a new application.
- Always start simple. When in doubt, test out your models first, then add in the view files once you have verified that the models have been modified as you expected.

Using a module to add a filter to a search view

One very nice feature of Odoo is the flexible and easy-to-use search functionality that is provided on every list view. With a module, you can add additional filter options that make it easier for users to find the information they are looking for. In our real-world example, we have placed an importance on rush orders. Therefore, it would be desirable to have a filter option on our sales order view that will limit our listing so it only displays rush orders.

Here is how the final search filter view will appear after we implement the module changes:

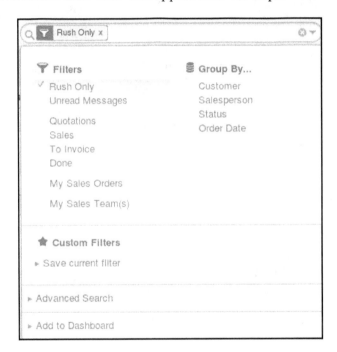

When **Rush Only** is checked, the sales order list view will limit the orders to those orders that are specified as rush orders. Users can now quickly locate rush orders without creating custom filters. This is an example of how a small change can have significant, real-world benefits to usability. Best of all, with Odoo you are making these changes without modifying any of the base Odoo source code.

Adding the code to create the rush order filter

The code segment will naturally be added to the `silkworm_view.xml` file. It will have the same record structure as our other modification. Adding this code segment and updating the module will implement the change we want:

```xml
<record id="sale_view_sales_order_filter" model="ir.ui.view">
    <field name="name">sale.order.search</field>
    <field name="model">sale.order</field>
    <field name="inherit_id" ref="sale.view_sales_order_filter"/>
    <field name="arch" type="xml">
      <field name="name" position="after">
        <filter name="rush" string="Rush Only"
         domain="[('rush','=',True)]"/>
      </field>
    </field>
</record>
```

Let's look at some of the more important elements of this code segment. It follows a similar structure to the modification that added fields to our form. What is most important when looking at the code in any module is to identify the `inherit_id` field's `ref` value. This is what ties your view modifications to the view in the base module.

In this case, our `inherit_id` is `sale.view_sales_order_filter`.

> Use Developer Mode to look up the view name from inside Odoo. Navigate to the view you want to work with and, in the developer menu, you can choose the manage view to see the **External ID** of the view. You can also use Developer Mode to quickly look at the syntax of views and use them to help you determine how your filters should be structured.

Creating the filter

The filter is specified by one line of XML code:

```xml
<filter name="rush" string="Rush Only"
 domain="[('rush','=',True)]"/>
```

In this code, we specify the name of our filter and the string we wish to display in the search view. The filter is applied with the domain parameter. We specify the field from our sales order model and that it must equal true in order for this filter to be valid.

The technical name for this syntax in Python is a **tuple**. It is possible to include multiple filters in the domain. For example, we can also specify that we only want sales orders that are confirmed by specifying an additional condition in our filter:

```
<filter name="rush" string="Rush Only"
  domain="[('rush','=',True),('state','=','progress')]"/>
```

Odoo considers a confirmed sales order to be in a state named progress. With this change, our **Rush Only** filter will also limit the sales orders to those that are confirmed.

Using Odoo to create websites and web services

In previous examples, we have been extending the Odoo framework to include additional fields in models and functionality in our views. Odoo also provides a powerful framework for creating your own websites and web services that can integrate easily with Odoo applications.

Let's see how we can create a simple web service that displays rush orders on a page.

We begin by creating a controller that is tied to a URL. When we navigate to this URL in our browser, the controller will do whatever processing we require.

Create the controller file using the following command in your Terminal window:

```
sudo nano controller.py
```

Add in the following code to create a simple output so we can test our controller and make sure it is functioning properly. Place this code in the controller.py file:

```
from odoo import http

class Web_RushOrders(http.Controller):
    @http.route('/orders/rush/', auth='public')
    def index(self, **kw):
        return "Rush Orders"
```

You must now edit the __init__.py file to include the new controller file:

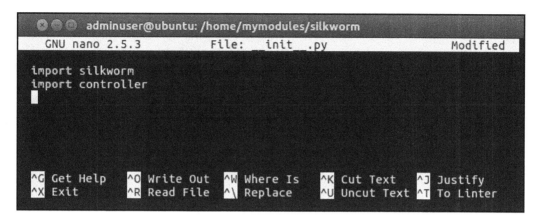

You can edit the __init__.py file by using the following command:
sudo nano __init__.py.

This allows the controller.py file we have created to get picked up by the Odoo framework.

Now start and stop the Odoo server and navigate to http://localhost:8069/orders/rush.

You will then see the custom web page displayed as follows:

Now that we have tested our controller and have a very simple page, let's see how we can hook into the Odoo sales application and display our rush orders.

Creating an XML template

For testing purposes, it was fine to output some text to our web page to verify that our controller is working. When you are designing a full website, however, it can be very tedious, and it is considered bad practice to mix your Python code and logic with your HTML code that you will use to display your website. Templates allow us to more easily separate the programming logic of our applications from the information we display.

Create a file to hold the template we will use to display our rush orders:

```
sudo nano template.xml
```

Enter the following code into the editor:

```
<odoo>
   <data>
      <template id="index">
         <title>Rush Orders</title>
         <table>
            <t t-foreach="rushorders" t-as="rushorder">
               <tr>
               <td><t t-esc="rushorder.name"/></td>
               <td><t t-esc="rushorder.daterequired"/></td>
               </tr>
            </t>
         </table>
      </template>
   </data>
</odoo>
```

You will see that we are using XML in much the same way as in earlier examples. The HTML code used is simple, and we have only included the name (sales order #) and the daterequired field.

Most significantly, you will see that we are using a foreach loop that will go through the orders and display the name in one column and then the daterequired in another column.

Now we need to update our controller to pass along sales order data to the template.

Open up the controller.py file and change the contents to the following:

```
from odoo import http

class Webrushorders(http.Controller):

    @http.route('/orders/rush/', auth='public')
```

```
def index(self, **kw):
    Orders = http.request.env['sale.order']
    return http.request.render('silkworm.index', {'rushorders':
Orders.search([('rush','=',True)])})
```

Everything stayed the same until we got inside the `index` method. First, we define `Orders` to give us access to the **sale.order** model.

In our final line, we use the `http.request.render` method to access the template and pass along our orders. The `Orders.search` method is passed the filter that limits the order to those in which the **rush** flag is **True**.

When we save our `controller.py` file, we stop and restart the server and then update the module. We can see the results in the web browser:

Make sure you flag a few orders in your system as **rush** or you will get an empty page.

Integrating with the Odoo API

Often, when developing custom applications, you are going to need to create solutions that involve interoperability with other systems and platforms. For example, perhaps you need to integrate with a third-party CRM application to create records inside of Odoo. The API is also quite useful for data migration.

Connecting to the API

Accessing the API is relatively easy. We begin with the code that imports the required libraries and creates a connection to the Odoo server:

```
import xmlrpclib
url = http://localhost:8069
```

```
db = SILK-DEV
username = 'admin'
password = 'admin'
info =
 xmlrpclib.ServerProxy('https://localhost:8089/start').start()
url, db, username, password =
    info['host'], info['database'], info['user'], info['password']
```

Filtering and returning records through the API

We can use the same domain filters we used to limit rush orders to use the API to return a list of sale order IDs that match:

```
models.execute_kw(db, uid, password,
    'sale.order', 'search',
    [["[('x_rush','=',True),('state','=','progress')]]])
```

Using the search_read method

While the preceding code only returns the IDs of the records, the new Odoo API allows you to both search and read the actual fields from the model with one single API call. Here, we return some fields from the sales order header:

```
models.execute_kw(db, uid, password,
    'sale.order', 'search_read',
    [[['x_rush, '=', True], ['state', '=', 'done']]],
    {'fields': ['name', 'country_id', 'comment'], 'limit': 5})
```

Creating custom themes in Odoo

Odoo offers a powerful integrated Web Builder application you can use to publish your own business website. You can purchase themes from Odoo's app store but it is also highly desirable in some instances to build your own custom themes. This is a very advanced topic but below are some of the basic steps to follow in building your own custom theme.

Basic architecture of Odoo themes

Odoo themes are more complicated than a simple set of HTML pages or a simple dynamic page that uses JavaScript. Odoo's theme framework is built around blocks in which you can use drag and drop to assemble both your page structure and your page content. Before you start trying to create your own themes make sure you are thoroughly comfortable with the basics of creating pages in Odoo's Website Builder.

If you are serious about developing themes, then you will need to understand the main technologies that make up the framework. These include Bootstrap, jQuery, jQuery UI, and underscore.js. Also, like other Odoo development tasks, you will gain a lot of insight by examining the existing themes that are included with a basic Odoo installation.

Creating an Odoo theme using scaffolding

To create an Odoo theme you basically use the same structure as any other Odoo module. You will need a main folder to hold your theme files. This folder should be named theme_ followed by the name of your theme.
Fortunately, you can use scaffolding to create a template for your module so you don't have to create all the files from scratch. To create our custom theme use the following command in a Terminal window. Make sure you are in the directory that contains odoo-bin and that you use the correct name for your custom add-on directory.

```
./odoo-bin scaffold -t theme "Silkworm Theme" custommodules
```

The scaffolding includes references to empty files inside the __manifest__.py file. Go in and clear out these references so your file looks like the following:

```
{
    # Theme information
    'name': "Silkworm Theme",
    'description': """ A custom theme example
""",
    'category': 'Theme/Creative',
    'version': '1.0',
    'depends': ['website'],

    # templates
    'data': [
    ],

    # Your information
    'author': "Your Name",
```

```
    'website': "",
 }
```

Specifically, we have removed references to the `options.xml` and `snipets.xml` files.

You can now restart the Odoo server and refresh the app list. The Silkworm Theme will now appear ready to install. You can now **Install** the theme and make sure there are no errors with the basic template:

Let's see how a `layout.xml` file is used to add new elements to the Odoo header.

Modifying the default Odoo theme header

When you install the basic Odoo theme you will have a default Odoo header that has a navigation menu with the company logo. We can create an XML file that will extend the theme. Begin by creating a file named `Layout.xml` and placing it inside the `views` folder.

```
<odoo>
  <data>
    <template id="custom_header" inherit_id="website.layout"
    name="custom Header">
      <xpath expr="//div[@id='wrapwrap']/header" position="attributes">
        <attribute name="id">custom_message</attribute>
      </xpath>
      <xpath expr="//div[@id='wrapwrap']/header/div" position="after">
        <div class="container">
          <div class="alert alert-info mt16" role="alert">
            <strong>Welcome to Silkworm! </strong>
          </div>
        </div>
      </xpath>
```

```
        </template>
      </data>
    </odoo>
```

You will need to modify your __manifest__.py file data element to reference this new file.

```
'data': ['views/layouts.xml'],
```

To see your changes, you will need to restart the server and **Upgrade** the theme:

After you have upgraded the theme you can navigate to any page on the website and see the change:

Creating a custom page layout

In the previous example we learned how to modify the website template header to then modify the look of every page on the website. Next we will see how we can create a page that has a specific layout.

Let's say we want to create a unique page for art approval. We know that we want this to have a specific layout and look different than the rest of the site so we can create a specific layout page for it. In this example we will just list a few recommendations for customers when approving the art. You can however extend this with any layout you choose.
We begin by creating a file `Pages.xml` and paste in the following code:

```xml
<odoo>

  <record id="services_page" model="website.page">
    <field name="name">Art Approval</field>
    <field name="website_published">True</field>
    <field name="url">/approval</field>
    <field name="type">qweb</field>
    <field name="key">theme_tutorial.artapproval_page</field>
    <field name="arch" type="xml">
      <t t-name="theme_tutorial.artapproval_page_template">
        <t t-call="website.layout">
          <div id="wrap">
            <div class="container">
              <h1>Art Approval Checklist</h1>
              <ul>
                <li>Check the spelling of all proofs</li>
                <li>Verify your color selections</li>
                <li>Provide detailed feedback on any changes</li>
              </ul>

              <!--- Area for Snippets === -->
              <div class="oe_structure" />
            </div>
          </div>
        </t>
      </t>
    </field>
  </record>

</odoo>
```

Let's talk a bit about some of the specific elements. The `record` tag uniquely identifies our page. The `model` attribute is how Odoo knows that this entire record should be handled as a website page. The name element, name to our page and flag it as being published. The `url` field specifies where the page resides in the site. You will use this to navigate to the page. The type will always be qweb as that is the template language Odoo uses for the pages. We then have a key that is used internally by Odoo.

Looking at the actual content of the page you can see that we use a `t` element to specify our theme name and the call to `website.layout`. All of this then drills down to where we finally have the `div` with our container class. It is within here that we can specify the exact layout and default content for our page. In this case we have put some simple instructions as an example.

Finally, we have a `div` at the bottom with the class `oe_structure`. This is where we can now drag and drop blocks in Web Builder to manage the content in the page.

Add the reference to `pages.xml` in your `__mainfest__.py` file and upgrade the theme. If you are successful the result should look like this:

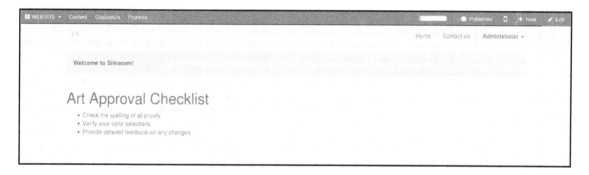

This should give you a pretty good start at understanding theme development in Odoo. There is much more to learn for building snippets and your own blocks.

Summary

In this chapter, we learned about the basic Odoo structure for modules. Files must be named in exactly the way the Odoo framework expects, and you must follow this structure for your module to properly load into Odoo. We explored how to extend Odoo with additional fields and display them on forms. Next, we extended our custom module with a workflow example. This allowed us to see how we can peek into existing Odoo modules to assist us with developing our own module.

16
Comparing Community and Enterprise Edition

Beginning with Odoo 9 and continuing through to Odoo 11, Odoo SA started offering a licensed version of Odoo known as the **Odoo Enterprise edition**. This edition offers several enhancements over the free Community edition of Odoo, including an entirely redesigned user interface. In addition to actual enhancements to the software itself, the Enterprise edition also includes version upgrades and bug fix guarantees that require Odoo SA to respond and attempt to fix any known bugs you may come across in core Odoo applications.

In this chapter, we will cover the following topics:

- The primary differences between Odoo Community and Odoo Enterprise
- Improved accounting reports and external integration for the Enterprise edition
- Sales management enhancements for VoIP integration and subscriptions
- Enterprise shipping connectors
- Manufacturing applications: PLM, Maintenance, and Quality

The primary goal of this chapter is to help provide information that will help you decide which version of Odoo is right for you.

There are many features and options in Odoo Enterprise that we will not have the opportunity to cover within just one chapter in this book. It is recommended if you are considering Odoo that you look at your specific requirements and research how Odoo Enterprise may be of benefit.

Getting an overview of the Community and Enterprise editions

While there are a lot of significant, and some not so significant, differences between Odoo Community and Odoo Enterprise, Odoo SA does provide a quick reference sheet that summarizes at a glance the differences between the two versions. You can find this quick reference at `https://www.odoo.com/page/editions`:

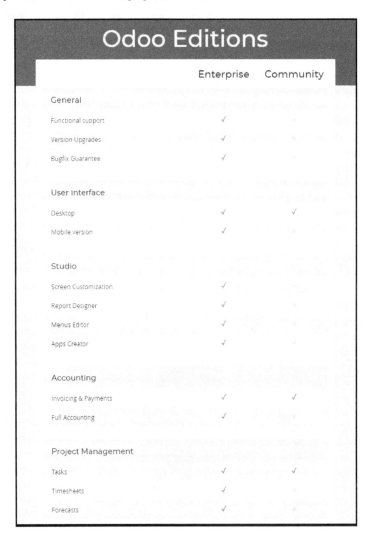

While the checklist does give you a high-level view of what the differences between the various versions of Odoo are, unfortunately there is no explanation or additional details as to what each of these features provides. To learn more, we have to take a look at the Odoo Community and Enterprise editions side by side.

Using the Odoo runbot to compare Odoo versions

One thing to consider when comparing the Odoo Community edition to the Odoo Enterprise edition is that Odoo Enterprise requires that you pay license fees. At first, you may think that makes it difficult to try Odoo Enterprise for yourself; fortunately, there is a handy service called the Odoo runbot that will not only help you compare Community and Enterprise, but can also help you test out any version of Odoo.

You can access the Odoo runbot by going to `runbot.odoo.com/runbot`, as shown in the following screenshot:

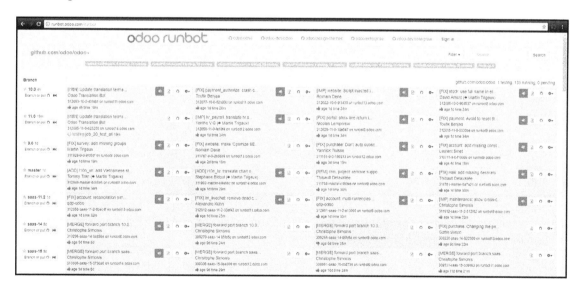

When you first come to the Odoo runbot, you are presented with a list of Odoo Community builds. You will notice that there are branches for 9.0, 10.0, 11.0, and the master branch, which is the current build that will eventually become Odoo 12. If you keep scrolling down, you will find many alternative builds that are for specific configurations or testing. For the purposes of this book, we will be focusing on the 11.0 branch.

Launching Odoo Community edition from Odoo runbot

Using the Odoo runbot, you can launch any of the Odoo instances by clicking on the small icon on the far left, shown as follows:

After you have clicked the button, a new window will open that allows you to choose between two databases.

One of the databases is just the base Odoo installation, while the other contains all of the Odoo applications. For our purposes, we are going to use the database that has all the applications already installed.

The password for all runbot installations is `admin`, as shown in the following screenshot:

After you have selected the database and entered the password, you log in to the runbot instance just like you would any version of Odoo.

Remember, this is the Community edition of Odoo 11. While we will spend more time discussing Odoo Enterprise and the features that make it unique, it is still valuable to have the Community edition open to make it easier to see the differences between the two.

Now, let's go back to the Odoo runbot page and open the Enterprise edition of Odoo in a separate window.

Launching Odoo 11 Enterprise from Odoo runbot

Now that you have Odoo 11 Community up and running in a window, let's go ahead and start Odoo 11 Enterprise in a separate window.

First, begin by opening a new browser window or a new tab in the same browser. Then, simply navigate to the Odoo runbot just like we did earlier in the chapter. This time, however, instead of launching the Community branch, use the link at the very top labeled `odoo/enterprise`.

After you have clicked the link, the runbot page will refresh and show the branches for the Enterprise version of Odoo.

Now, you can click on the connect button and log in to the Odoo Enterprise edition in the same way you did with the Community version.

You should now have both Odoo Community and Odoo 11 Enterprise running in separate windows on your computer, making it easy to switch back and forth and compare features. Best of all, you didn't have to provide an email address, install any software, or pay any license fees.

 WARNING
Unlike a standard Odoo installation, runbot installations are only temporary and anything you put into them can be wiped at any time. The runbot is best for situations like this, when you just need to check some specific Odoo functionality.

Finally, take the time to arrange the windows in a way that works best for your current workspace and monitor configuration. For example, if you have two monitors, you could put the Community edition on one monitor and the Enterprise edition on the other monitor.

Examining the Odoo Enterprise interface

Without a doubt, the most noticeable difference between Odoo Community and Odoo Enterprise is the interface. In fact, the entire set of application menus is gone and has been replaced with a page of icons that allow you to launch any of the installed applications, as shown in the following screenshot:

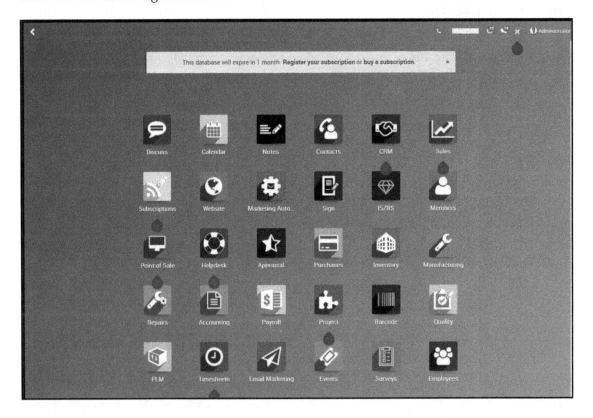

As we are only using this Odoo 11 Enterprise installation to check out the features, you can ignore the database expiration notice at the top. It's also worth noting that the exact applications that you see available may be slightly different or in different locations than the previous example. Remember that other people are accessing these same instances; you can't be certain that settings will be exactly the same as a default installation.

Examining Odoo 11 Enterprise Accounting

While the interface enhancements are easily the most obvious differences between Odoo Community and Odoo Enterprise, the reports in the **Accounting** application are perhaps the most valuable functional improvements over their Community version equivalents.

Let's look at the dynamic Enterprise reports by clicking on the **Accounting** icon to launch the **Accounting** application as follows:

Once the **Accounting** application opens, notice that the menu that would have typically been on the side in Odoo Community is now along the top. This design allows for a lot more usable screen real estate for your applications:

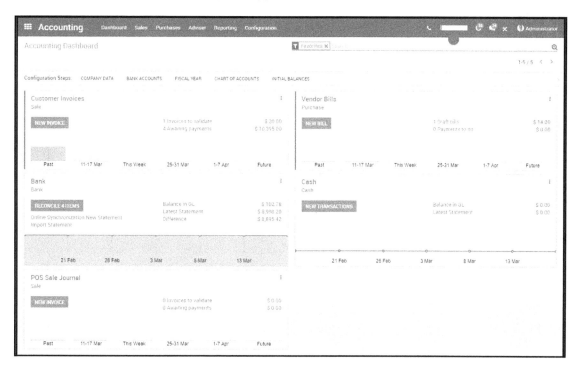

Aside from the **Accounting** menu appearing across the top and the buttons looking slightly different, there is not much difference between Odoo Community's **Accounting Dashboard** and **Odoo Enterprise** on this screen. It should be noted that you must have full accounting features turned on, as described in Chapter 6, *Configuring Accounting and Finance Options*, to have access to the dashboard in **Odoo Community**. One of the primary differences we will look at in this chapter is the Accounting reports that come with Odoo Enterprise.

Looking at Odoo 11's dynamic Accounting reports

In **Odoo Community**, **Accounting** reports are launched with a wizard that allows you to specify the filters before a PDF document is created that you can open in any PDF viewer. Odoo Enterprise does away with that clunky approach completely and allows you to bring up a report immediately within Odoo without having to create a PDF file.

Let's look at the **Odoo Enterprise Profit and Loss** statement by choosing **Profit and Loss** from the **Reports** menu, as shown in the following screenshot:

If you take the time to switch over to **Odoo Community** and attempt to produce the same profit and loss report, you can quickly appreciate the improvements in **Odoo Enterprise**. Even better, the reports are dynamic. There are also a variety of options at the top to change the filters used on the report and to perform comparisons between different periods:

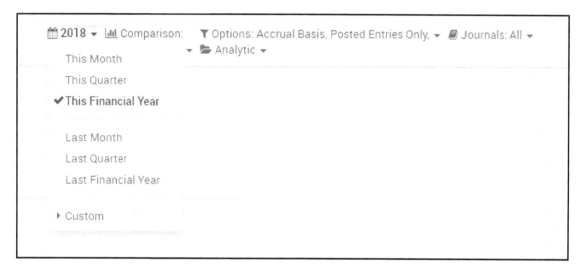

Another nice feature is that the reports have drill-down capabilities. For example, you can open the **Operating Income** tab and click on the **Product Sales** account to bring up a menu that will take you to the general ledger for the account, or even allow you to add a note to the item on the report, as shown in the following screenshot:

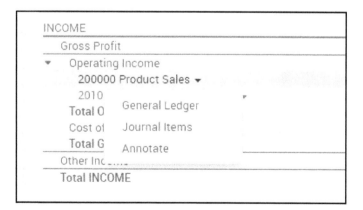

Even though the reports show up immediately, it does not mean that you give up the option to have them in PDF format. At the top-left side of the reports, you have buttons that allow you to export the report to a PDF or an Excel file.

Using the bank integration features of the Enterprise edition

While dynamic reports may be the flashiest part of the Enterprise **Accounting** application, the Enterprise version offers more robust import options as well. To get a better idea of what options are available in the Enterprise edition, you can go to the **Settings** menu and then choose **General Settings** in the Community edition. Now, in Odoo 11 we have an improved interface for navigating the various application settings. Simply click on an application and you will see a small **Enterprise** tag next to the options that are only available in the Enterprise edition of Odoo. In the following example, we have selected the **Manufacturing** application and are able to see the various options that require the **Enterprise** edition:

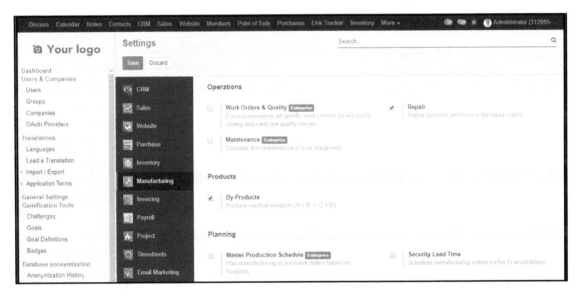

It is far beyond the scope of this chapter to go through each of these options, but you will notice that the one at the very top is an option for **Work Orders & Quality**. We will look at these Enterprise applications later in the chapter. Further down the screen, under **Planning,** you will see that there is an option for a **Master Production Schedule**. Fortunately, from what you have already learned, you can use the runbot to easily see what these features look like in the Enterprise edition.

Depending on your own requirements you may find certain Enterprise options very important for integrating Odoo into your business.

Sales-related enhancements

As **Sales** is a very popular Odoo application, it is not surprising that the Enterprise edition of Odoo contains several applications that are not in the Community edition but are designed to provide additional features. While not as significant as the dynamic reports or enhanced interface, Enterprise's options for **Sales** can be quite useful, depending on your business requirements.

Automating calls with VOIP integration

If you have a sales team that must make or take frequent calls, the built-in VOIP integration in Odoo Enterprise can be a real time-saver. Instead of your sales team having to look up incoming calls within Odoo manually, Odoo's VOIP integration will automatically locate the contact within Odoo when the call comes in.

Unlike other Enterprise options, if you are installing VOIP in an Enterprise installation yourself, you will need to add the **Odoo VOIP** application, as follows:

Using the VOIP module to play calls is easy. You can bring up the dialing panel by clicking on the small phone icon in the top center of the screen. You can also click on any phone number field in Odoo to bring up the dialing panel. All the relevant details for the calls you need to place will be listed, along with several other buttons that let you handle how you manage the call:

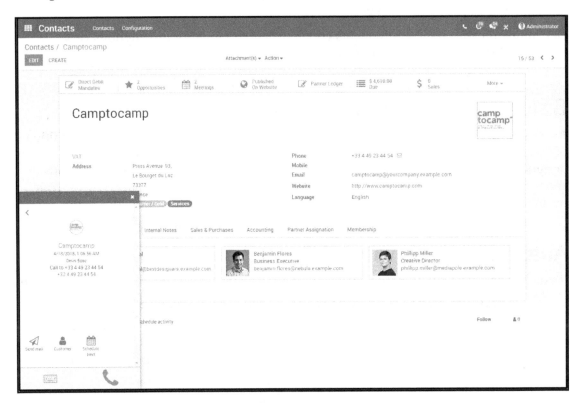

To configure and set up the VOIP application, some technical expertise is required so that you can properly integrate it with your phone system.

Understanding the Subscriptions application

Like the VOIP module, the **Subscriptions** application is also installed separately. When you open the **Subscriptions** application, you are presented with a rather full-featured KPI dashboard that lets you track your subscriptions, as shown in the following screenshot:

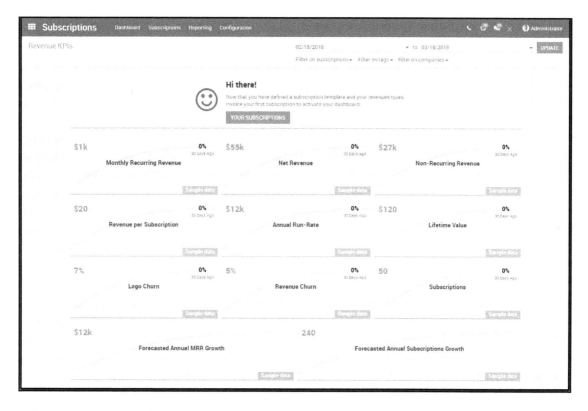

Subscriptions are configured as templates that allow you to easily see critical information such as the number of subscribers. Click **YOUR SUBCRIPTIONS** to see the current templates that are set up in the system. The following screen appears after clicking:

As you can see, the **Subscriptions** template displays its important information in a list format by default. Clicking on a **Subscriptions** template will display the details of the subscription; as you can see there are many options available:

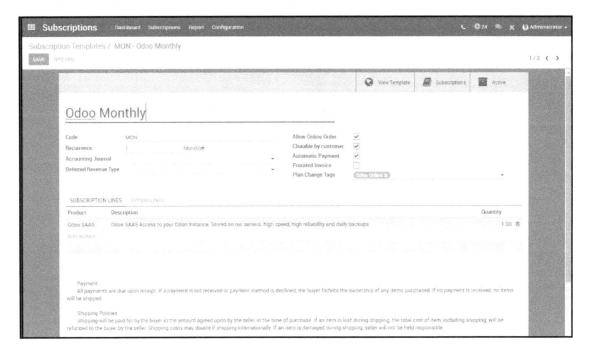

Like many of the applications in Odoo, it is important to take the time to gain experience with configuring subscriptions and testing different scenarios to find out what works for you. If you are running a business that has subscription-based sales, the **Subscriptions** application is a reason to strongly consider Odoo Enterprise.

Understanding the available shipping connectors in Enterprise

As many companies are involved with shipping products, the availability of shipping connectors in Odoo Enterprise may be of major consideration for some companies. These Enterprise shipping connectors hook into the Odoo inventory and e-commerce service, allowing you to automatically create the required transactions inside the selected shipping system.

If you only need Odoo Enterprise for shipping connectors or another feature or two, check the Odoo App store. There are many third party Odoo applications that work with Odoo Community and offer similar functionality to Odoo Enterprise.

To configure your Odoo shipping connectors, go into the **Inventory** application, then to the **Configuration** menu, and click **Settings**:

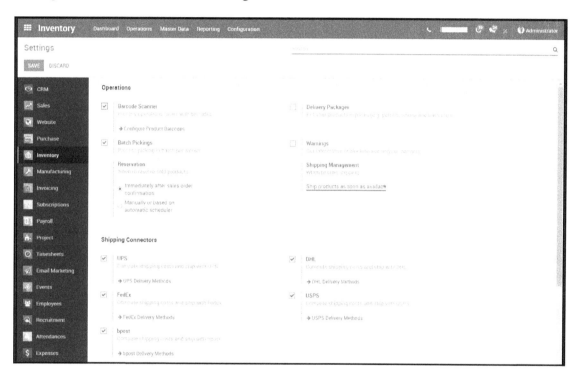

After you have checked which shipping connectors you would like available, you can use the **Delivery Methods** option under the **Configuration** menu to see all the connectors and configure them as required, as shown in the following screenshot:

As you can see from the list, Odoo Enterprise offers quite a few connectors. As with the VOIP integration, you will need some technical expertise and all the configuration information from your shipping system to be able to properly configure the connector.

Understanding the available manufacturing applications in Odoo

Perhaps of all the applications, the Enterprise edition offers some of the strongest incentives to consider it should these applications fit your business requirements. These applications include **Product Lifecycle Management (PLM)**, Maintenance, and Quality.

Product Lifecycle Management

When you are working in a production environment, it is likely—if not inevitable—that there will be changes to the build process of various items. Perhaps you get a new vendor for a part, or a small design change requires you to add or remove parts from a bill of material. Managing these changes can be very time-consuming. This is where the Product Lifecycle Management application comes into play. You can access it with the **PLM** icon from the main Enterprise menu:

Clicking on the PLM application icon will take you to the PLM Dashboard, which in this demo version is lacking any real data. Click on the **Engineering Changes** button to bring up the Kanban view that displays the stages that are currently defined for the product life cycle, shown as follows:

Here, we can see that the stages **New**, **In Progress**, and **Validated** are all expanded. The **Effective** tab is checked when the cycle is complete.

Let's see what an **Engineering Change Order** looks like in the PLM application by clicking the **Create** button:

We have filled in a little bit of information on the form so you can see an example of how it may be used. You will notice that we also have a short summary that will describe the change that must be managed.

The **Type** defaults to **New Product Information**. The PLM application is designed to work for a new product that you wish to manage the cycle of—or you can create a change order for an existing product.

One nice thing about the PLM application is, in addition to managing changes on your bill of materials, it also lets you manage changes on routing, or on both the BoM and routing. This gives you a great deal of flexibility when managing changes in the production process.

To complete our change order, we must know what **Product** the order is for and its associated **Bill of Materials**. Each of these fields you can add on the fly, making it easy to configure a new product and the associated change order right from this screen.

Finally, the PLM application provides an effective date so you can decide exactly when you want the change order to go into effect. This makes it easy to manage complex changes that are coming up in future product builds. One example would be a model year changeover that requires your Bill of Materials to change on a specific date, which could take many weeks of configuration.

Handling maintenance requests

Another common requirement in manufacturing operations is the handling of maintenance requests. A maintenance request can involve a machine that is malfunctioning, or even a work environment that needs attention to become more productive. The Odoo Maintenance application integrates the handling of maintenance requests directly into the manufacturing process. Click the Maintenance icon on the main Enterprise menu to bring up the Maintenance dashboard as follows:

You will then be taken to the **Maintenance** dashboard:

You will see that the Odoo **Maintenance** application divides maintenance requests by teams. In the previous example, we have three teams configured to handle the requests. Under the **Internal Maintenance** team, we can click the button that says **3 TO DO** and pull up the requests, as follows:

Here, we can see that one of the requests is **New** and the other two requests are **In Progress**. Click on the **Battery drains fast** maintenance request to view the details:

As you can see, there are a lot of details within this request that help us identify exactly what needs to be done to address the problem. In our example, we know who the request was **Created By**, what **Equipment** was involved, and the **Request Date**, among other important items.

In addition, Odoo will automatically fill in the **Manufacturing Order** or the **Work Order** if a maintenance request is made during one of those processes. When you are ready, you can set a scheduled date for the repair, as well as a priority level to help you manage what items your maintenance team should be focused on.

You can also quickly look at your equipment to see which items have outstanding maintenance requests. Click on the **Equipments** menu to see your equipment in the Kanban view, as shown in the following screenshot:

Using this view, you can quickly see what equipment needs the attention of your maintenance team.

Managing production quality in Odoo

As your team is manufacturing items, it is inevitable that situations in which you need to address the quality of the product will arise. This could be because you received raw materials that were not adequate, because there is a problem in the process, or it could be something that needs more investigation to determine why a product is not meeting your quality expectations. Regardless of the reason why, Odoo's Quality application can help you better manage quality in your manufacturing operations.

Click the **Quality** icon from the main Enterprise menu to view the **Quality dashboard**, as follows:

Like the Maintenance application, the Quality application breaks quality alerts down into different teams. In the dashboard, you can see there is currently one quality team defined, the **Main Quality Team**:

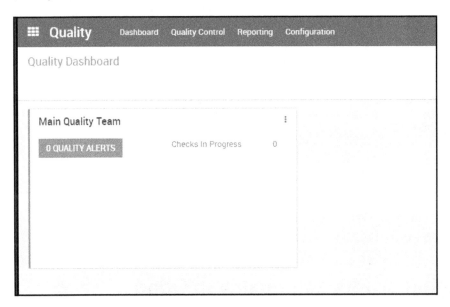

While we don't have any active quality alerts, let's go ahead and click on the button so we can see the stages that have been set up by default to manage our quality alerts:

As you can see, PLM, Maintenance, and Quality are all designed in a similar way. As always, we can click **Create** to enter a Quality Alert, as shown in the following screenshot:

Here, you can describe the product and any variants, as well as which lot the product was in, in case that the quality issue is to do with a specific lot. Items that you specify in **Corrective Actions** are automatically presented when someone begins a manufacturing order. This makes it easy to quickly alert someone in manufacturing when there is a quality issue, and provides them with clear instructions on what they need to do to verify, or if necessary fix, the product quality.

Using Odoo Studio

Odoo Studio is an Odoo Enterprise-only application that allows you to customize Odoo and even create your own custom application without creating a Python module, as discussed in `Chapter 15`, *Discovering Custom Odoo Modules*. There are some pros and cons to using Odoo Studio.

The advantages of Odoo Studio are as follows:

- You can make simple changes to Odoo applications without writing Python code
- Screen designers make it easy for you to change the UI without using verbose XML code
- You can draft prototype applications in a fraction of the time it would take to create a full Odoo application
- You can get close to full-blown Odoo applications using server actions
- You can import and export Odoo Studio, giving you some ability to reuse your work between Odoo Enterprise installations
- Modifying the views in Odoo Studio and the capabilities that are available is pretty much the same as if you were developing an Odoo application

The disadvantages of Odoo Studio are as follows:

- Nothing you do in Odoo Studio can be used in the Community edition of Odoo
- Despite many enhancements to Odoo 11, there are major limitations compared to writing custom Odoo applications
- Because of the way you develop with Odoo Studio, it can often be very difficult to manage processes within production installations

Modifying the Sales application with Odoo Studio

You can install Odoo Studio as you would any other application. Remember, however, that you must have Odoo Enterprise to use Odoo Studio. Once again, we can use the runbot to try out some of Odoo Studio's features if we want to.

As Odoo Studio is already installed on the runbot, we can simply go to the application we wish to modify to get started. Click on the **Sales** menu and open a **Quotation**.

Now, to edit the **Quotation** you can click on the **Odoo Studio** Edit button in the top-right corner of the interface. It looks like a crossed wrench and pencil, shown as follows:

Once you turn on **Odoo Studio**, the interface will change to show you the tools that you can use to modify the form. It's very clear when you are in **Odoo Studio** and editing your application. You can easily switch out of **Odoo Studio** by just clicking the icon again:

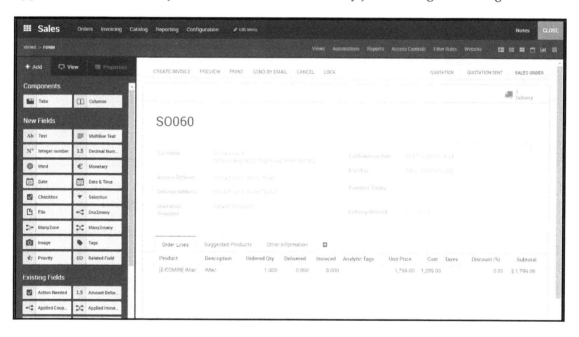

Let's add a **Rush Order Checkbox** to our form. Simply click and drag the **Checkbox** from the right and place it on the form where you wish it to display. At that point, you can edit the properties for the checkbox so that it will display as you wish, as shown in the following screenshot:

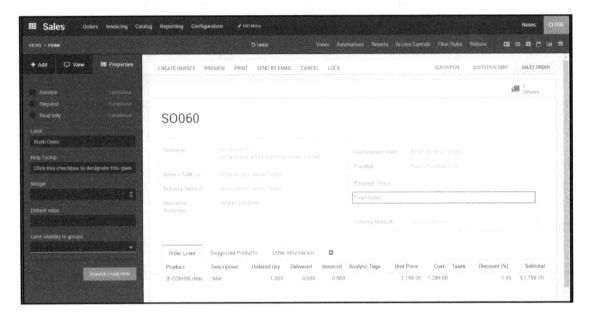

Take the time to experiment with the options available under **Properties**. When you click the **Close** button, the form will refresh and you will see your changes applied.

This chapter provided a brief introduction to Odoo; it would be easy to dedicate a whole chapter to Odoo Studio, or perhaps even an entire book. There are a lot of options available in Odoo Studio and you can expect to take some time learning how it all fits together.

Summary

In this chapter, we learned about some of the more important features that are part of Odoo Enterprise. We learned a bit about the new interface and how Odoo Enterprise restructures the menus to better use screen real estate. We took a look at the powerful dynamic accounting reports, as well as bank account integration. Then, we examined the Sales application and studied how Odoo Enterprise offers VOIP integration, as well as a Subscriptions application. We examined Odoo Enterprise's shipping connectors and how they can be used to connect with external shipping systems. Finally, we took a look at Odoo's new manufacturing applications that are only available in the Enterprise edition.

In this book, we have covered a wide range of topics in an attempt to give you a solid foundation. We started with trying out the online version of Odoo and how to perform an install of Odoo on Window or Ubuntu. As we moved through the book, you learned about the major applications that make up the Odoo business platform, as well as some real-world examples of how they may be used. Later in the book, you learned how to administer and customize Odoo, as well as how to use Odoo as a CMS for your website. Finally, we finished the book by exploring the basics of customizing Odoo and even how to build your own Odoo application.

Like any ERP system, becoming an expert in Odoo will require many hundreds of hours of research, experimentation, and hard work.

Another Book You May Enjoy

If you enjoyed this book, you may be interested in another book by Packt:

Odoo 11 Development Cookbook - Second Edition
Alexandre Fayolle, Holger Brunn

ISBN: 978-1-78847-181-7

- Install and manage Odoo environments and instances
- Use Models to define your application's data structures
- Add business logic to your applications
- Add automated tests and learn how to debug Odoo apps
- Learn about the access security model and internationalization features
- Customize websites built with Odoo, by writing your own templates and providing new snippets for use in the website builder
- Extend the web client with new widgets and make RPC calls to the server

Leave a review - let other readers know what you think

Please share your thoughts on this book with others by leaving a review on the site that you bought it from. If you purchased the book from Amazon, please leave us an honest review on this book's Amazon page. This is vital so that other potential readers can see and use your unbiased opinion to make purchasing decisions, we can understand what our customers think about our products, and our authors can see your feedback on the title that they have worked with Packt to create. It will only take a few minutes of your time, but is valuable to other potential customers, our authors, and Packt. Thank you!

Index